Principles of Public Secondary Education

PRINCIPLES OF PUBLIC SECONDARY EDUCATION

Harold C. Hand

Professor of Education, University of Illinois

HARCOURT, BRACE AND COMPANY   NEW YORK

EDITOR'S FOREWORD

Like the little boy who found that a book he was asked to read "tells me more about penguins than I care to know," we who are concerned with education have perhaps been told more about the current crisis in education than we care to know. But it may be that we have been inundated with details, with superficial "solutions" to imperfectly understood problems, when we know instinctively that the trouble lies very deep indeed. For the crisis is one in *public education*. And public education, as an American institution, is based on principles too rarely stated, too rarely understood, too rarely even recognized.

This book is an attempt to derive these principles from facts that we all accept, to state them clearly, and to show what they imply for the solution of the pressing educational problems confronting everyone, but especially teachers, today. The attempt is successful.

Harold C. Hand has long been known for his work with teachers, prospective teachers, high school students, and professional organizations in the continual struggle for the improvement of public secondary education. This book is a necessary building block for the kind of American education of which he is a part.

Willard B. Spalding

PREFACE

This is the plan of this book—a result of many years of teaching and thought.

The book begins by reminding the reader of the chief kinds of professional problems which teachers in the public secondary schools unavoidably encounter.

It then makes clear that there are no easy solutions to any of these problems; that the teacher's only safe guide is a body of principles of action validly grounded in fundamental truths about education. Essentially, one must repair to these fundamental truths if one is to be secure in his assessment of the welter of controversies which whirl about the public secondary school—controversies which relate to who should be served by the school (some or all youths?); what it should teach for college entrance and for life and living (calculus, principles of healthful living, recreational skills, Shakespeare, or what?); how this should be taught (by methods traditional or modern?); by whom it should be controlled (by laymen or by professional educators?).

The next chapter presents these fundamental truths. As phrased here, they are but eight in number.

In the next chapter these *truths* are applied to the situation in the United States to give us basic *principles* of public secondary education which are valid in this country. At the level of generalization employed in this part of the book, there are nine of these basic principles. The first sets forth the all-inclusive task of the American public secondary school; each of the remaining eight states some necessary condition which must be fulfilled if this all-inclusive task is to be performed as fully and as capably as possible. Taken together these eight principles state the conditions necessary and sufficient to fulfill the all-inclusive task set forth in the first. These eight principles variously stipulate what the orientation of the public secondary school must be, what it must teach, how this must be taught, whom it must serve, and by whom it must be controlled, if the all-inclusive task which the American public secondary school is obligated to perform is to be accomplished as completely and as effectively as possible.

In each instance, the basic principles enunciated in the fourth chapter are applied, throughout the following chapters, to the professional problem in question in a search for valid clues to the proper resolution of that problem.

The concluding chapter invites the reader to look back over the history of secondary education in this country for purposes of tracing out the past fortunes, and of assessing the future prospects, of each of the basic principles set forth in this book.

Now that we have given a thumbnail sketch of what this book contains, it may be of interest to note how the manuscript was developed. The approach epitomized above was first embodied in a fairly lengthy syllabus which was then employed for four successive semesters in the author's classes at the University of Illinois. In class discussions it was possible to observe what the students' reactions to the various facets of this approach were—to note what seemed to be understandable and to make sense to them, and to detect what seemed to be in need of improvement. Also, anonymous criticisms were solicited from the students each semester. From the insights thus gained, revisions in the syllabus materials were made each semester. During these two years the first drafts of most of the chapters in this book were completed; at the beginning of the third year these first drafts supplanted the pertinent parts of the syllabus and were employed as text materials. By the beginning of the last of the seven years during which this book was in preparation, this supplanting of the syllabus had been completed. Before they were committed to print, all the chapters in this book were first used as text materials by two or more classes, revised in the light of student criticism, employed again with two or more other classes—in many cases with as many as eight—and again revised.

In preparation for the final work of revision, criticisms of some or all parts of the materials were solicited from colleagues whose judgments would be respected by any knowledgeable person in the field of secondary education: Dean Charles W. Sanford, Dean

Willard B. Spalding, Professor Kenneth B. Henderson, Professor Camilla M. Low, and Professor B. Othanel Smith. It is a pleasure to acknowledge their valuable help; the manuscript was greatly strengthened at many points in consequence of their constructive criticisms. I am also grateful for the help in respect to the concluding chapter in the book given by another distinguished colleague, Professor Archibald W. Anderson, a nationally-known scholar in the field of the history of education. Special mention should also be made of the assistance received from Dr. Charles R. Hicklin; as part of his final examination for the doctorate, he applied the criteria afforded by his extensive study of logic and semantics to a thorough-going dissection of the manuscript of the fourth chapter of this volume. When relayed to me by his faculty adviser, Dr. Hicklin's paper proved to be of great value in the work of revising the manuscript.

I am no less indebted, though for a different reason, to Mrs. Julia P. Snyder and Evelyn Lois Farrell. Their expertness in typing, their skill in manipulating small mountains of duplicated materials, and their cheerful willingness to adjust their routines to my many vagaries eased my task to no small degree.

Most of all, however, I am indebted to the several hundred University students who, in a very real sense, helped me to write this book. Thanks to their assistance, more than a few ambiguous or illogical statements, inconsistencies, and cloudy concepts were detected in the early drafts of the manuscript. The book also suffers less from unnecessary wordiness and from the lack of helpful examples than would have been the case had it not been employed repeatedly in manuscript form with the several successive groups of young men and women who have been my students over the past few years. I regret that it is not feasible to record their names here, for the debt I owe them is both very real and very great.

Harold C. Hand

UNIVERSITY OF ILLINOIS
JANUARY, 1958

CONTENTS

part I

PROFESSIONAL PROBLEMS:

THEY MUST BE FACED

chapter 1

SOME PROFESSIONAL PROBLEMS

OF SECONDARY SCHOOL TEACHERS

A successful teacher in our secondary schools must have more than a good general education and a scholarly knowledge of his teaching specialty. He must also be able to deal competently with the professional problems which arise in the course of his work. The purpose of this chapter is to discuss the more important of these professional problems. And the purpose of the whole book is to offer as much help as possible to those who want to learn more about how to deal with these problems successfully.

Deciding what to teach

At first this may seem a simple problem, but it is not. What the teacher teaches should (1) help the pupil as much as possible, and (2) be as valuable as possible to the community which supports the school. In our rapidly changing world these problems can never be settled permanently. A competent teacher will bring to them a continuously renewed insight. A teacher who evades or misconstrues the problem of what to teach can maintain neither satisfactory enrollments nor good discipline in his classes; nor can he help his pupils to grow in intellect or in attitudes.

Some college students who are preparing to teach do not understand this, and as a result do not see the need for making themselves competent to decide what to teach. They think instead that they will be able to rely on the textbooks they plan to use in their classroom instruction. Successful teachers know that a teacher cannot use a textbook wisely unless he first understands what he is going to teach and how he is going to teach it. A good textbook is necessary, but no substitute for a thorough organization of the subject in the teacher's mind. No textbook or combination of textbooks can circumvent the difficulties which plague a teacher who has not satisfactorily determined what he should teach. These difficulties include, among others, the apathy of students, resulting in problems of discipline in the classroom, and the apathy or even the disapproval of the students' parents.

Teaching effectively

How to teach effectively is by no means the simple problem that some people believe it to be. We have encountered some college students—but no successful teachers—who think one needs no more than a firm grasp of his subject and the ability to imitate the teaching methods employed by a favorite professor. Follow-up studies which have been made of these young teachers during their first year on the job, however, show that they change their minds very quickly. A scholarly grasp of one's subject is, of course, necessary, but these follow-up studies show that the teaching methods which they observed at the university are ineffective in dealing with many, if not most, high school pupils. Most beginning teachers say that what they need more than anything else is guidance in the methods of effective secondary school teaching.

Improving the holding power of the school

The American public school is committed to the principle of equal educational opportunity. Every public secondary school should attract and retain to the point of graduation all the educable youths of its community whose education is not otherwise provided for.

Most school superintendents, principals, and experienced teachers are keenly aware of this obligation of the public secondary school. So are most members of boards of education, parents, and other adults in the community. Indeed, it is not too much to say that most Americans believe that a good high school education is the birthright of every child. Parents may be expected to object to any teacher who operates in ways which deny this birthright to any child. Here the teacher will be judged much more by what he does, or fails to do, than by what he says. Parents and administrators will expect him to do everything within reason to make the education he offers so valuable that all educable boys and girls of secondary school age will want to continue to attend high school.

To make the high school program of real value to all youths and to enable all youths to attend and feel that they really belong is not easy. The problem is a complex one. The program of the school must be made to take account of the full range of individual differences in aptitude and interests. Standards must be made such that every youth will be taxed to the limits of his capabilities, but no youth will be required to perform at a level of which he is innately incapable. How to do these two things is certain to perplex anyone who has not given careful thought to the problem.

Nor is this all. The financial costs of attending high school are so high at the present time that some young people can scarcely afford to attend at all. Many others cannot find the money required to do the things the wealthier pupils do, and hence do not feel that they really "belong." Many attitudes of the pupils who do attend— and those of some teachers as well—must be changed before the high school can be made a place where all youths will feel accepted and comfortable. Here, clearly, is a major professional problem which confronts every public secondary school teacher.

Maintaining good school-community relations

No teacher is likely to be happy in his work unless the relations between the school and the community are good. If they are not, there is certain to be either public apathy to, public misunderstanding of, or active public antagonism to some, if not many, of the things the school is doing. This frequently lowers a teacher's morale and makes it difficult for him to teach well.

As all successful school superintendents and principals know, few things are more necessary to the competent operation of a school than good school-community relations. What the teachers do or fail to do chiefly determines whether the relations between the school and the community will be good, indifferent, or bad. Consequently, superintendents and principals prize the teacher who improves this relationship. And they cannot be blamed for hoping that the teacher who fails in this important respect will seek some other kind of employment.

Maintaining good discipline

All teachers are confronted with the problem of maintaining discipline, and those who are successful have learned how to deal with this problem effectively. Successful teachers recognize, however, that difficulties in respect to discipline almost invariably arise out of more basic problems which confront every teacher. These basic problems cause the difficulty of which poor discipline may be merely symptomatic. There is no easy way to make a serious discipline problem disappear. Until its underlying causes are perceived and remedied, the discipline problem will remain, even though it may be partly hidden or suppressed. These more basic problems demand our primary attention.

Supervising extra-class activities

School superintendents and principals are eager to find teachers who are willing and able to sponsor pupil activities outside their classes. This is not the simple matter that it may appear to be. How does a teacher answer these questions: How can the spending of public funds to support extra-class activities be justified? What are pupils supposed to learn through extra-class activities? How can a teacher make certain that pupils derive as much benefit as possible from these activities? What kind and degree of control are desirable in a school club? Should participation in extra-class activities be regulated by some kind of point system? How may the development of pupils in extra-class activities best be evaluated, recorded, and reported? All these questions, and many others, are pertinent to the teacher's role in supervising extra-class activities.

Assisting in the guidance of youth

Many high schools now insist that classroom teachers offer guidance (as we shall define it later) as well as instruction to the young people in their charge. To be sure, such schools usually have specialized guidance workers or counselors on their staffs, but these counselors provide directly only a small part of the guidance needed by the pupils and often deal only with the more difficult cases. Much of the work of guidance falls to the classroom instructors, who must cooperate closely with the guidance specialists in developing guidance programs and who must learn to integrate guidance procedures with the more traditional elements of classroom teaching. More and more high schools are adopting this concept of integrated guidance and instruction, which is supported not only by common sense but by the results of research.

Teachers who are conversant with good guidance practices are better qualified to serve in the modern high school than those who are not. How to provide effective guidance is one of the most recent problems (but by no means the simplest) of the professional teacher.

Appraising and reporting pupil achievement

From time to time teachers must make a report to parents on the progress of their children. Prospective teachers often think that this aspect of the teaching job offers no particular difficulty; each pupil, they feel, should simply get what he or she deserves—Susan her A, John his B, Dorothy her C, Jim his D, and Harry, alas, his F. That is all there is to it.

But what does Susan's A signify? Does it mean that in terms of achievement she has surpassed all the pupils who were given lower marks? Or that, given her capacity to learn, her achievement is all that can reasonably be expected of her? Or does it represent a compromise of some kind between these two methods of reckoning? Obviously, here are three different ways to compute Susan's grade.

And what about that unfortunate F for Harry? Was he given this mark because he failed to achieve what could reasonably be expected of him? Or because his achievement was less than that of the Jims, Dorothys, and Susans in his class? Suppose the latter is true. Suppose that Harry worked as hard as the others, and did as well as he could. Is it fair to brand him a failure if he is compelled to attend school when his teacher is unable to teach him effectively enough to allow him to learn what he is expected to learn?

Experienced teachers know that these problems are far from being hypothetical. They arise regularly in every school. They cannot be evaded, nor can they be solved easily.

Cooperating in curriculum development

Deciding what should be taught and how to teach it are functions of curriculum development. Earlier paragraphs may have given the impression that the teacher determines these things by himself, but only rarely is this the case. To be of maximum benefit, whatever is taught must be made a fruitful part of the pupil's whole sequence of learning experiences. Something has gone before and something else will follow. If what is taught at any given time is to be as meaningful and beneficial as possible to the pupil, the entire sequence must be carefully planned. This, of course, involves other teachers.

Curriculum planning also involves the board of education, the school superintendent, the principal, parents, other laymen in the community, and even the pupils themselves.

The members of the board of education are responsible to the people of the community for the work of the school. They determine or at least approve the general policies which govern the operation of the school, and they delegate to the superintendent or principal the responsibility for seeing that these policies are carried out. Policies may, of course, originate with the teachers. The impetus behind policy decisions often comes from the teaching staff, and in general in good schools the suggestions of the teachers significantly influence the decisions of the board members and the administrative officers of the school. But the board members must approve all policies, regardless of their origin, before they are put into action. For this reason, these officials are necessarily involved in the work of curriculum development. Generally they are happy to find teachers who want to improve the curriculum—at least in our better schools.

Parents and other laymen in the community should also have a voice in curriculum development; after all, it is the children, the community's future citizens, who will benefit or suffer from whatever is taught. Since the strength of the community is greatly affected by the education given its youths, all citizens, not only the parents, have a stake in what is taught in the schools. How the school teaches what it teaches—that is, what techniques are employed in instruction—is the proper province of teachers and other professional educators, and should not be determined by laymen. But the objectives of the school—what kinds of things the pupils are to learn —certainly are the concern of the community at large, because the pupils' education helps determine what kind of citizens they will become. Hence all really sound programs of curriculum development require the participation of parents and other laymen as well as teachers and the officials of the school administration.

Finally, the pupils themselves should participate. More than any other group they have a stake in what is to be taught. They should not be permitted to dictate the content of their instruction, but the interests they express should certainly be considered.

As we have already pointed out, the question of what should be taught can never be answered with finality. The curriculum must be changed continually if it is to help promote the advancement of our civilization. Superintendents and principals of good schools know this, and they value the teacher who realizes that he should contribute willingly and systematically to the month-by-month and year-by-year development of the curriculum.

Helping to administer the school

In the typical high school a number of administrative functions are detailed to teachers which they must be willing and able to perform if the school is to operate effectively. Teachers are required to help, for example, in registering pupils, in keeping records, and in estimating the school budget. In a well-administered school, teachers help the principal or superintendent in many other ways as well. Thus it is necessary for teachers to possess at least an elementary knowledge of the theory and practice of internal school administration.

Conclusion

Before this book was published, the manuscript was used experimentally in a number of university classes. We asked the students in these classes to test the application of what we have said in the preceding paragraphs of this chapter by constructing a "test" of their own. We suggested that they set down in one column the professional problems of teachers which we have discussed. Then we asked them to add two other columns, one headed "my best high school teacher," the other "my worst high school teacher." In rating each teacher for his competence to deal with each of these professional problems, we suggested that the students employ these code numbers: 1, very competent; 2, competent; 3, average; 4, incompetent; 5, very incompetent. With few exceptions, the "best" teachers were rated "very competent" or "competent" in dealing with all of the ten problems. The most frequent exception had to do with the appraising and reporting of pupils' achievements. Several of the students felt that even their best teachers were not competent in this respect. Generally, the "worst" teachers were rated low on most counts. No "worst" teacher was said to have handled competently as many as half of the ten professional problems. The present readers of this book may find it instructive to analyze their own "best" and "worst" high school teachers in a similar way.

The problems to which we have called attention in this chapter confront all teachers in public secondary schools. Teachers should prepare themselves to deal competently with them. The purpose of this book is to help its readers acquire more of this competence.

BASIC PRINCIPLES:

THE ONLY RELIABLE GUIDE

THE ROLE OF PRINCIPLES

AND FUNDAMENTAL TRUTHS

IN EDUCATION

In Chapter 1 we noted a number of important professional problems commonly encountered by teachers in public secondary schools. How can one best prepare himself to deal with these problems successfully?

Ours is a rapidly changing world, in which no two communities, no two schools, no two pupils, no two parents, and no two teachers are alike. Consequently no pat solution will permanently resolve any of the problems discussed in Chapter 1. Each situation requires a solution specially adapted to it. To be most effective, teachers and parents must rely on a body of basic educational principles which will guide them in their efforts to discover the particular course of action suitable to any given set of circumstances.

Teachers should, of course, know what these basic principles are. And to understand them, to be confident of their validity, teachers must know the fundamental truths from which these principles of education derive. In order to illustrate this relationship between "truth" and "principle," as we are using the terms here, let us look at a few simple examples.

In the northern hemisphere, the movement of air around a low-pressure area, or storm center, is counterclockwise. This is a fact, or fundamental truth. What principle of action derives from it for pilots who want to attain the greatest possible ground speed with their airplanes?

"To achieve the greatest possible ground speed when traveling in the vicinity of a storm center north of the equator, airplanes must be flown to the right rather than to the left of the low-pressure area." The reason is obvious: the ground speed of an airplane is its air speed plus or minus the velocity of the prevailing winds. An airplane flown to the right of a storm center will be helped by a tail wind, while an airplane flown to the left will be hindered by a head wind.

Now let us borrow two examples from home economics. Mrs. Jones, let us say, is about to buy a floor covering for a room in which she wishes to create the illusion of spaciousness. If she knows that a plain surface appears larger than a figured surface of the same dimensions—a species of fundamental truth—then she will know what principle to follow in selecting her rug or carpeting: "To create the maximum illusion of spaciousness in a room, its floor covering must be plain rather than figured."

Next let us suppose that Mrs. Brown has a room in her house whose ceiling, she thinks, is too high. She cannot afford to have a carpenter lower the ceiling or put in a false one, but her budget will permit her to have the present ceiling repainted. What color should she choose in order to create the illusion she wants? A dark-colored mass appears closer to the viewer than a light-colored mass of the same size and in the same location. What is the full statement of the principle of action based upon this fundamental truth which should guide Mrs. Brown?

The validity of any principle of action may, of course, rest upon more than one fundamental truth; as a matter of fact, most such principles probably do. Let us turn now to an example in which at least three fundamental truths are involved. We know (1) that condensation of moisture occurs when warm air is cooled to the dew point, (2) that cotton will absorb moisture, and (3) that cotton fibers are damaged when this occurs rapidly. Let us suppose that one must store a cotton-filled mattress in the attic during the summer. What is the principle that must guide one's action if all possible damage to the mattress from moisture is to be avoided? "To keep to the minimum any damage to cotton products stored in an attic, one must find a way to keep hot summer air from being trapped in the attic when the roof of the house cools."

Again, cold-water pipes are often insulated in order to keep them from "sweating." The principle here is: "To keep a cold-water pipe from 'sweating,' it must be insulated from the warmer air around it." This principle is derived from the fact, or fundamental truth, that condensation occurs when warm air is cooled.

Another example of a principle of action can be drawn from the region of personal experience: "To appear tall, one must select clothing in which the dominant lines run vertically instead of horizontally." What is the fundamental truth from which this principle derives its validity?

These examples demonstrate the meaning which we attach to the terms "principle" and "fundamental truth": As we use the terms a *principle is a statement of what must be done if a stated result is to be achieved; a fundamental truth is the fact which makes the principle valid.* Principles tell us what to do; if our principles are grounded in fundamental truths, our actions will be the right actions.

There is no single way to apply a principle. The airplane pilot must fly his aircraft to the right of a low-pressure area in order to make the greatest possible ground speed when he is near a storm center, but the altitude at which he will encounter the strongest tail wind will vary according to a number of other factors. And the particular shade of dark paint which Mrs. Brown chooses will be determined by considerations of taste, but some shade of dark color she must use if the illusion of nearness is to be created. In other words, it is precisely because we cannot contrive inflexible rules of action to meet all the contingent factors which may or may not be operative in any given situation that we must rely upon principles to guide us in formulating our plan, our rule of action, for each situation with which we are confronted. Let us consider three additional examples, again from fields other than teaching.

First, a skilled aircraft mechanic services the landing gears of three airplanes, each of which differs from the others. Two airplanes have tricycle landing gears, but the wheels of one are retractable while those of the other remain extended during flight. The third has a conventional landing gear which is not retractable. Thus each of these airplanes is in some respects unique. The aircraft mechanic knows the fundamental truths which pertain to structural designs, hydraulics, the strengths of various materials, and the like, and he uses the principles which are derived from these truths to guide him in servicing various kinds of aircraft with which he is faced.

The fact that he does indeed service each aircraft efficiently shows that he knows the alternative ways in which the same principles may be applied to unique situations.

Second, in the course of a few months a certain dentist equips half a dozen of his older patients with dentures. Each patient has a different oral cavity; no two patients have the same tolerance for the preliminary work which must be done; each presents unique problems. Yet the dentist serves each patient well. He draws in each case upon the same basic principles, derived from the same fundamental truths of physiology, etc., but he applies them individually to the unique problems of each patient.

Third, a certain physician competently diagnoses and prescribes on the basis of the principles which are derived from the body of fundamental truths which compose his science. As his patients differ, so does the treatment he prescribes for them, even if several of them suffer from the same disease. The physician, even more than the rest of us, realizes that the same principle applied to two complex situations may well yield two different rules of action.

Like the competent aircraft mechanic, dentist, and physician, a capable teacher not only knows the fundamental truths pertinent to his profession, but also commands a body of basic principles derived from these truths, and is skilled in recognizing and utilizing the alternative ways in which these principles can be applied to the unique situations he encounters.

In the course of his daily work, the competent aircraft mechanic, dentist, physician, or teacher solves hundreds of minor problems very rapidly and seemingly without any effort. He is able to do this because the fundamental truths and the principles of action derived from them have been so thoroughly *overlearned* that they are ingrained in his nervous system—implanted so deeply that he uses them without actually calling them to the level of consciousness. Because he has had so much experience in using these truths and principles, because he has applied them so often to recurrent minor problems which, although each is unique, are nevertheless similar, he is able to carry through his process of thought habitually, effortlessly, and almost instantaneously.

But let this aircraft mechanic, dentist, physician, or teacher encounter a problem outside the normal range of his experience, and his decision will be far from effortless or instantaneous. It will be made laboriously, for the thought process must now be consciously and formally conducted. In most cases he will know what principles to apply, and his study will be to determine which application of these principles will produce the best results. But in some cases he may not even know which principles are applicable to his problem, and he will be driven back to the level of fundamental truth, where he will consult, as it were, the permanent facts that will help him to discover or rediscover the principles of action which he needs.

"Thinking with principles"—the virtually spontaneous and habitual application of basic principles to common problems—is a process which everyone practices continually. Each person uses a great many important principles regularly in his daily activities. These principles have long since been overlearned, so that he often uses them without realizing that he is applying principles at all.

To help his students understand these phenomena, the author has asked them to list a score or more of the sensible things which they did almost every day without stopping to decide whether or not they should do them or to wonder why they were doing them. Then he asked them to explain why they did these things. Their answers, in nearly every instance, revealed the operation of a basic principle sanctioned by one or more fundamental truths.

Several students said that they were habitually careful when using sharp knives or razor blades. Others mentioned that they brushed their teeth regularly. Some pointed out that they chose a green necktie or scarf when they wore a brown suit. One replied that she always sprinkled clothes before ironing them. Another said that he put gasoline in his father's tractor only when the motor was cold. And so on. The students had no difficulty in thinking of a great many sensible acts which they performed regularly without taking apparent thought. When they stopped to examine the real reasons for their actions, they generally found that they had used overlearned principles of action based on similarly overlearned fundamental truths.

It is just such an overlearning of the fundamental truths and principles pertaining to education that one must acquire if he is to fulfill his sense of mission by making himself an effective public school teacher. We shall present these truths and principles in the two chapters which follow.

chapter 3

TRUTHS FROM WHICH

VALID PRINCIPLES OF EDUCATION DERIVE

Certain fundamental truths relate to education everywhere. By *education* we mean the process by which *learning* is facilitated. By *learning* we mean any persistent change in either overt or covert behavior. And by *everywhere* we mean in all the parts of the world in which human life is found.

These truths are indeed fundamental. They give rise to imperatives for education everywhere. They must be acted upon if human life is to continue and if individual or societal well-being is to be achieved.

To formulate principles of secondary education designed to achieve these ends, then, one must know what these fundamental truths are.

We shall state first the most fundamental of these truths. We shall give only a small part of the evidence which confirms this fundamental truth—but enough to show that its connotation is universal. We shall also keep to this minimum the evidence which confirms the other truths which seem to require substantiation. Some of these require no proof, for their validity is self-evident. These last we shall simply elaborate somewhat in order that their significance may be emphasized.

Man must learn in order to survive

Consider the human infant—any human infant, regardless of the country in which he is born. A newborn baby is helpless. He cannot procure food; left to himself, he will starve. He cannot clothe or shelter himself; left alone, he will die of exposure to the elements. He cannot dispose, in socially approved or hygienic ways, of his body wastes. He cannot transport himself. He cannot communicate, though he can relieve his rudimentary sensations by expressing them. Left entirely to his own devices, he would be destroyed by fire, wind, flood, or marauding beasts, or he would die from starvation, exposure to the elements, or disease.

The behavior of which the human infant is capable at birth enables him to do very few things. He can breathe, open and shut his eyes, move his arms and legs haphazardly, suck, swallow, digest food, eliminate body wastes, coo and cry—and very little else. He is completely dependent for survival upon what other human beings— who were once as helpless as he—do for him.

Obviously, these other human beings have changed their behavior in many important ways since they themselves were helpless infants. They can procure food, clothing, and shelter for themselves and their dependents. They can protect themselves and their offspring against accidents, disease, and other hazards. They can communicate both meaningfully and extensively. They can perform all manner of complex physical actions. Since their infancy, they have changed their behavior in these and many other ways which are necessary to the continuance of the race. And it is important to note that all these changes in their behavior are persistent.

How did these lasting changes in behavior—changes which we call persistent—come about? Not, as people used to believe, through the automatic unfolding of instinctive or inherited behavior patterns. They came about through learning. Unlike the lower animals, human infants do not come equipped with behavior patterns that are more or less fixed at birth. After the moment of birth they must learn virtually every new pattern of behavior which they practice. Without learning, the child cannot sit up, creep, walk, run, climb, swim or acquire any other physical skill. He must learn in order to communicate—to speak, to write. He must learn in order to feed and clothe himself. He must learn in order to protect himself against the elements, accidents, disease. And, if the race is to continue, he must later not only reproduce his kind but learn to rear his offspring.

So far we have spoken only of overt or observable behavior, nearly all of which is learned. The same thing is true of covert behavior.

The newborn infant is a kind of cultural blank check. He appears to value nothing but the rudimentary comforts of his body—warmth, the refreshments of sleep and food, and a certain freedom of movement. All the values which he will later assign to other things, he will have learned to value, often slowly and perhaps even painfully. As an infant, he hates or loves no one. All that he will later love or hate, he will have learned to love or hate. He has no sense of right or wrong. Later, he will have formed a moral sense by learning hundreds of distinctions between right and wrong actions. He is neither bold nor timid, brave nor cowardly. All that his personality will later reveal of these qualities, he will have learned. He cannot reason. The reasoning power that he will later manifest will be acquired by learning. He has no cultural preferences; that is, there is nothing in his infant character or heritage which inclines him toward any particular language, mode of dress, political creed, religious belief, or the like. All that he will later prefer, he will have learned to prefer. Only what he learns as he grows older will determine what is to be entered on the cultural blank check which a human being represents at birth.

Fortunately, man is equipped at birth with a marvelously complex nervous system which enables him to learn an immense variety and number of overt and covert patterns of behavior. But he must make actual this potential if the human race is to survive. Truly, man must learn in order to survive. This is the most fundamental of the truths about education.

Man must learn in order to improve his lot

The fact that man must learn in order to improve his lot could be illustrated in countless ways. We have chosen five illustrations from contemporary American life to illuminate this truth. Among the many critical dangers which confront our people are injury and death on the highway, exposure to racial or religious intolerance, want in the midst of potential abundance, national impoverishment from the depletion of natural resources, and embroilment in war. Nothing in man's original nature automatically makes him behave in ways which will create highway safety, better relations among persons of different races or religious beliefs, increased purchasing power, good conservation programs, or international good will. Each of these improvements in our natural or social environment can be effected only if we learn to behave persistently in new ways. Learning is the key to all man's efforts to enhance the living conditions of men anywhere.

Hence, no less than to survive, man must learn in order to improve his lot.

Man can survive and improve his lot only within the context of society

Most of the things which the young must learn in order to survive and improve their lot can be acquired only from their elders. This education of the young by their elders must be continued at least through infancy; in modern societies it lasts much longer. But while this education is going on, the elders must also keep themselves alive. To make possible the rearing of their young and the improvement of their own living conditions, men must procure food, clothing, and shelter; they must safeguard themselves against accidents, disease, and external enemies.

To attain these common goals, men have found it necessary to band together into communal enterprises, into societies. These societies have ranged from loose tribal groups to the consummately complex nations we know today, but they have all shared certain characteristics. They have been groups of individuals united by a common interest and combined, however loosely, into a recognizable organization.[1] Only within society can man survive and improve his lot.

Education is always intended to ensure the survival of society

A direct consequence of the preceding fundamental truth is that the survival of society is prerequisite both to the continuance of human life and to the development of man's effort to improve his living conditions. It is no wonder that men everywhere are determined to ensure the survival of the societies in which they live.

No society can survive and continue to safeguard and satisfy its members unless those members carry on certain basic social processes.

[1] This is the definition of society in the *Encyclopedia of the Social Sciences*, ed. by Edwin B. H. Seligman and Alvin Johnson, The Macmillan Co., New York, 1932.

Yet men cannot perform these processes until they have learned to do so. Consequently, education—the means by which learning is expedited—is everywhere intended to make men competent to perform these basic social processes in the ways of which their society approves.

Stated in terms of what it is that men must do in order to survive and advance, these basic social processes can be set forth in the following eight statements. Men must learn to

—Think and communicate.
—Provide themselves with a body of commonly held values, beliefs, and aspirations, i.e., with "social cement."
—Earn their livelihoods.
—Provide for their physical security, i.e., manage their natural resources, strengthen their bodies, and safeguard themselves against accidents, disease, and external enemies.
—Provide for their aesthetic and spiritual needs.
—Provide for their leisure time.
—Regulate human conduct through social organization based on authority.
—Rear and educate their children.

Societal survival requires that the last of these processes, which is in a sense the most important, be so conducted that children (and all other aliens to the culture) will in turn carry on all of these basic social processes in ways which are approved by their society. The members of any society can transmit what they value in their cultural heritage to their successors—the youth and the assimilable aliens —only if they can devise an educational system which will implant in the minds of the learners the values, beliefs, appreciations, aspirations, skills, and bodies of knowledge which relate to these basic social processes. The competence with which this educational function is performed in any society is a basic determinant of the degree to which the men of that society will be able to improve the conditions of their lives from one generation to another.

Education always relates to a particular society

Although the same basic social processes are carried on in all societies, we know that each society, either from choice or necessity, performs these social processes in a somewhat different way.

All men must think and communicate, but the languages and the postulates which they employ in thinking differ from society to society. How deeply each society cherishes its own tongue is attested by the failure of any international language (Esperanto or basic English, for example) to take root in any country. Whoever we may be, it is only our own language that we are willing to see universalized.

Men in all societies shape their ways of life according to their own schemes of values, beliefs, and aspirations. These ways of life, which command man's deepest loyalties, differ markedly from society to society. Men give their lives in battle to preserve their way of life.

Similarly with each of the other basic social processes. Consider the different ways in which men throughout the world feed, clothe, and shelter themselves, manage their natural resources, safeguard themselves against the hazards of social disorder and enemy attack, gratify their spiritual and aesthetic needs, and so on. Aesthetic tastes, for instance, vary so fundamentally that men from one culture may be unable to understand or appreciate the greatest works of art which have been produced by another culture. The customs of dress, diet, and architecture of people who may live within close proximity of one another are often quite different. Seldom has there been a time when cultural differences did not engage men in serious conflict, provoking anxieties and hostilities which often enough have changed the course of human events. Men are forced by their environment and history into cultural preferences and loyalties which exert a strong hold upon their minds. And in each society the socially approved way of rearing and educating the young tends to assure the survival of that society's culture.

Thus, though all men strive toward similar goals of social permanence and cohesiveness, they manifest markedly different patterns of behavior and belief in working toward these ends. The basic social processes can be pursued in remarkably different ways.

Most men believe that in the main the culture pattern of their own society represents the good, the true, the beautiful, and the just. They not only cherish their way of doing things, but insist that the rising generation and all other newcomers share their viewpoint. Among other things, they demand that all aliens to their culture, those who arrive by birth and those who arrive by immigration, speak their language, adopt their values, share their aspirations, honor their traditions, and be loyal to their institutions.

This process by which aliens are assimilated has three important characteristics. First, it is a prerequisite to societal survival. Second, it can be accomplished only through education. Third, it is a tremendous and never-ending task.

In 1951 approximately 4,000,000 aliens to our culture arrived in the United States. About 5 per cent of them came with some knowledge of our way of life, and many of these could even speak our language. These were the immigrants from other lands. But the remaining 95 per cent knew absolutely nothing about our language, values, aspirations, institutions, or history; they were utterly ignorant of our way of life. These, of course, were the 3,750,000 children who were born here during that year. Such a titanic wave, falling year after year upon our society, would swamp us, one might think; yet we have not foundered. Our educational agencies, all of them together, have dealt successfully with this huge influx of ignorance by shaping these new minds to our ways of thinking and feeling. It is a feat in every way as spectacular as the more commonly applauded exploits of modern technology.

The school is only one of many educational agencies

Learning is manifested by a persistent change in overt or covert behavior. He who has learned either knows, appreciates, values, believes, or does something which formerly he did not know, appreciate, value, believe, or do. Any agency which enables one to change one's persistent behavior is, therefore, an educational agency.

Historians tell us that in very primitive societies the institution which we know as the school did not exist. Yet we know that infants born into those societies acquired many persistent changes in their behavior; in short, they learned. We also know that the experiences of daily living which these children shared with their elders provided most of their education.

In much the same way children today, even in our highly sophisticated societies, receive a large part of their education from agencies other than the school. These agencies bring about persistent changes in a child's behavior—they teach him to know, to appreciate, to value, to believe, or to do new things. He learned much even before he entered school. He could talk, walk, run, climb, and play games. He could feed and dress himself and attend to many other personal needs. He had learned to avoid many dangers. He could make friends. He had acquired hundreds of likes and dislikes, some idea of right and wrong, and a body of firm beliefs about the nature of the material world, other people, and his own personality. These and many other things had been learned without the help of formal schooling.

Who helped to make all these persistent changes in his behavior? His parents, other members of his family, his playmates, and probably his Sunday school teacher. He had probably listened to the radio and gone to the movies. He had persuaded someone to read the newspaper comic strips to him. Before he ever set foot in a school, many people had helped him to learn a good deal.

During his school days, his teachers helped him learn many important things, make many significant changes in his behavior. Nevertheless, he continued to learn as much or more outside of school, or at any rate outside of the school's formal academic program. He watched television and listened to the radio. He went to scores of movies—hundreds, probably. Perhaps he attended concerts, the theater, the opera. He read. He may have gone to camp, or joined such organizations as the Boy Scouts, the YMCA, the CYO, or the 4-H Club. He dealt with businessmen as a customer and perhaps as an employee. He made many contacts with authority—agencies of the various governmental units within whose jurisdiction he fell— if not in his own right, then vicariously through his parents. He spent a good deal of time with friends of his own age, with whom he exchanged information. His family, of course, continued to influence him, and so in all likelihood did his church.

In other words, he was influenced repeatedly by the principal educational agencies of our modern world: the home, the church, other character-building organizations, the media of mass communication, the business community, the government, the peer group— all these in addition to the school.

His experiences were by no means unusual; quite the contrary. The school is only one—though a very important one—of the many educational agencies in modern societies.

**To serve society best,
the school must give a top-level priority
to those necessary educational tasks which it can perform
more competently than can any other agency**

Obviously, if individual and societal well-being are most fully to be attained, each of the basic social processes must be carried on with all the competence which, in toto, the educational agencies in question can engender. This can be accomplished only if in toto, the educational agencies do not needlessly neglect any of these processes. But such neglect is certain to occur if any agency gives a low instead of a top priority to any necessary educational task which it is capable of performing more adequately than can any other agency. If it is to serve society best, then, the school must give top priority to *all* the basic social processes with which it is potentially most competent to deal.

Furthermore, if any educational agency assigns a top-level instead of a lower level priority to undertakings which other agencies could perform more effectively, it is likely to divert some of its needed resources from the necessary educational tasks which it is potentially most competent to discharge. To be certain that it is serving society best, the school must give top-level priorities to *only* those basic social processes with which it is most competent to deal.

What the top-priority tasks of the school turn out to be when this fundamental truth is applied will probably differ somewhat from one society to another and from one generation to another within the same society. The capacities of the other educational agencies vary significantly from society to society and from generation to generation within the same society. For example, in a society which cherishes an official state religion the educational role of the church will be significantly different from what it is in a society which officially separates church and state. The burden of religious education on the public schools in these two countries would be considerably different.

Or consider another illustration: Denmark has developed a vigorous public health program in which all citizens are required by law to participate. There an agency other than the school is the most competent to teach people how to live healthfully. Another country has virtually nothing of this sort, and its members live in incredibly unhygienic conditions. There the school may be the only educational agency which is potentially competent in respect to the basic social process in question.

In Chapter 4 we shall make clear what the top-level priorities of the American public secondary school turn out to be when the fundamental truth presented in this section is applied in our own country. But to assert what the top-level priorities of the schools in *other* countries should be, one would need to know not only what the capacities of all the educational agencies in each country are, but what values the citizens of each country seek most eagerly. In the present state of our knowledge, these things are unknown for many of the countries in the world.

Thus far we have considered how the chief responsibilities of the school should be determined. Now let us see how its secondary tasks should be determined.

Three considerations are pertinent here. First, what is the relative importance of these other tasks: how much does the performance of each promise to enhance individual and societal well-being? Second, to what extent might these tasks be performed adequately by other educational agencies? Third, to what extent will the performance of these tasks interfere with the areas of instruction which it is most important that the school teach?

For much the same reasons, when these three criteria are applied, the tasks which it is less important for the school to perform will vary from one society to another. Moreover, in complex societies these variations will occur in different regions and even in different communities within the same region. And the importance of the tasks can change with the passage of time, so that some of the chief educational undertakings of the school in one period may be reduced to secondary importance at some later time. In Chapter 4 we shall note what the less important as well as the top-level priority tasks of the public secondary school in this country should be.

To educate most effectively, the school must apply what is known about the learning process

The business of the school, we have said, is to facilitate learning. Unless those who are in charge of the school understand the learning process and the conditions which facilitate learning, and unless they apply this knowledge to their conduct of the school, the school cannot possibly function with maximum effectiveness.

For example, suppose a school attempts to teach the nonsectarian moral values held by the society which the school serves. Now ideas of right and wrong are, in the main, learned by a process known as internalization, whereby the student observes the teacher's ideas of right and wrong and appropriates them. Most students will do this only if three conditions are met. First, they must admire the teacher and want very much to be like him. Second, the teacher must typify in what he says and does the ideas of right and wrong which are to be internalized. Third, the teacher's behavior must be consistent in these respects; he must persistently manifest these ideas of right and wrong. Of course, the teacher need not be a professional schoolteacher. He may be an admired parent, a brother or a sister, a businessman, a baseball player, a movie star, or a fictional character. For some youths Steve Canyon and Joe Palooka are very effective teachers in this respect.

A student may learn facts and skills from a teacher whom he dislikes. Evidence from research shows that he will usually learn more from teachers he admires, but nevertheless he need not want to be like his teachers in order to learn from them. But the ideas of right and wrong held by a disliked teacher will not be transmitted to his students as readily as those of an admired teacher. If a school does not apply this bit of knowledge about learning—that is, if it is indifferent to whether or not its teachers are admired by its students—obviously it cannot teach moral values as well as it could if it did.

From their study of educational psychology, students discover that modern educational knowledge provides helpful answers to such important questions as the following: How are students best taught to generalize, to think critically, to be creative, to evaluate, to memorize, or to acquire physical skills? How is transfer of training best secured? How is learning affected by competition, conflict, distribution of practice, failure, frustration, grouping, goal setting, incentives, insight, knowledge of progress, level of aspiration, meaningfulness, organization of instruction, promotion policy, punishment, rest and relaxation, retention in grade, reward, sequence, size of instructional unit, social approval, social climate, tension reduction, and whole versus part approach?

The answers to these and other questions shed much light on the learning process. Used well, they will facilitate learning. Therefore, the school must apply them if it is to function as effectively as possible.

Summary

We have discussed briefly eight fundamental truths relevant to education. We hope our discussion has helped the reader to consider thoughtfully the deep needs which education fills in the lives of men. No teacher, and no one who aspires to become a teacher, can afford to overlook these roots of educational theory. Each of them must be taken into account in order to formulate valid principles of secondary education for our own country.

1. Man must learn in order to survive.

2. Man must learn in order to improve his lot.

3. Man can survive and improve his lot only within the context of society.

4. Education is always intended to ensure the survival of society.

5. Education always relates to a particular society.

6. The school is only one of many educational agencies.

7. To serve society best, the school must give a top-level priority to those necessary educational tasks which it can perform more competently than can any other agency.

8. To educate most effectively, the school must apply what is known about the learning process.

chapter 4

BASIC PRINCIPLES

OF AMERICAN PUBLIC

SECONDARY EDUCATION

The truths set forth in the preceding chapter lie at the foundation of education everywhere. They must be honored if valid principles of education are to be established for this or any other nation.

In this chapter we shall employ these fundamental truths to derive basic principles which tell how the American public secondary school (the high school) should be conceived. These principles set forth what the basic task of the public high school is, how this institution should be oriented, what it should teach, whom it should serve, and how its teachers should teach if its basic task is to be accomplished. In addition, the concluding principle tells how the public secondary school must be controlled if it is to be a *public* institution in the finest sense.

Three characteristics of the public secondary school

But before we formulate these basic principles we shall note three important facts about the American public secondary school. One of these is that in this country we use the terms "elementary," "secondary," and "higher" (or "adult") to designate respectively the education of preadolescent children, adolescents, and adults. But there is very little general agreement on when adolescence merges into adulthood. In most of our communities, formal secondary education terminates at the conclusion of grade twelve, the last year of high school. In a large and increasing number of communities, junior colleges (grades thirteen and fourteen most commonly) have been established. Some authorities regard the junior college as an upward extension of secondary education, others as a part of higher or adult education. In this book, however, the term "secondary" will signify the education of youth from the seventh through the twelfth grade in school. The public secondary school, then, is the publicly supported and publicly controlled institution for the education of youths in these grades.

Second, the American public secondary school represents the middle rungs of a single educational ladder. Americans have good reason to be proud of their *single* system of public schools—a social invention which originated in our country. In many other parts of the world, the school systems are still dual: one system, usually inferior and abbreviated, is maintained for the masses of young people, while another, superior and more extensive, serves the upper classes. This duality tends to keep the common people in the inferior status to which they have been relegated in such societies and to safeguard the position of the favored classes. In this country the dominant idea, though it has occasionally been violated, has supported a single system of public schools open to all, a single educational ladder whose lower rungs are represented by the public elementary school, the middle rungs by the public secondary school, and the top rungs by publicly supported institutions for adult education. Obviously, the concept of a single educational ladder accords well with our ideal of an open-class society, a society in which one may rise above (or fall below) the socioeconomic status of his family to whichever socioeconomic level his capabilities and industry may warrant.

There is an important corollary to this fact. If the public secondary school occupies a middle position in our single system of public education and if we are to have the best possible educational program, the work of the secondary school must be related to the work of the elementary school below and, for a large and steadily increasing number of its students, to the work of the college above. The educational ladder must be so constructed that each student who has negotiated the rungs which represent the elementary school will find that the first of the middle rungs is within his grasp yet far enough removed from the rung on which he stands to make its attainment a worthwhile accomplishment for him; otherwise, his progress up the ladder will be impeded by a hazardous gap or stalled by a weakening of incentive. Similarly, the middle rungs, which represent the secondary school, must continue far enough upward to enable those who can do college work to achieve a secure foothold on the lower rungs of the top part of the ladder, the part which symbolizes our institutions of higher learning. In other words, the program of the secondary school must be well integrated with the programs of the elementary school and the college if our single educational system is to make its maximum contribution to the general welfare.

The third fact to which we call attention is simply a particularization of the sixth fundamental truth presented in Chapter 3. The public secondary school is only one of the many agencies by which American youths are educated. The principal nonschool agencies which have an important influence on the education of youths are the home, the church, other organizations devoted to the welfare of young people, the media of mass communication, the business community, the government, and the peer group. The work of the secondary school should be intelligently integrated with what our youths learn, or may learn, at the hands of these other agencies. If the school duplicates the work that is being carried on successfully by other agencies, the results will be a needless dissipation of the school's resources, an unjustifiable neglect of the other educational services which only the school can typically provide, and a wasteful competition among intracommunity agencies.

With these three facts in mind—that the American public secondary school is a school for adolescents, that it occupies the middle position in the public school structure, and that it is only one among many agencies by which our youths are educated—let us turn now to a discussion of the basic principles of public secondary education in our country—principles which, as has already been noted, will tell us what the school's basic task is, what its orientation must be, what it must teach, how this must be taught, whom it must serve and by whom it must be controlled if its basic task is best to be accomplished under public auspices. The first basic principle sets forth the all-inclusive task of the public secondary school, and each of the others states a necessary condition which the secondary school must satisfy if its all-inclusive task is to be accomplished as effectively as possible. All of the basic principles are interrelated, but we will deal with them one by one.

What is the basic task of the public secondary school?

To answer this primary question we must use several of the fundamental truths considered in the last chapter.

In Chapter 3 *society* was defined as a group of individuals who share a common interest and who are united in some identifiable form of organization. It is explicit in the Preamble to our Constitution that to "promote the general welfare" is one of the chief common interests of our society. Indeed, this interest seems to include all others, for this quite certainly was the end which the Founding Fathers had in mind when they declared that the purpose of the people of the United States was to "establish justice," "provide for the common defense," and "secure the blessings of liberty to ourselves and our posterity." By definition, therefore, any agency which is intended to ensure the survival of American society must be committed to the promotion of the general welfare of the American people.

Furthermore, education always relates to a particular society (see Chapter 3); it is always intended to ensure societal survival; certain basic social processes must be carried on in order to ensure societal survival; the ability to carry on these basic social processes is not innate; the purpose of education everywhere is to make men capable of carrying on these processes. We have seen that these necessary processes are to think and communicate; to bind the commonwealth together with a body of commonly held values, beliefs, and aspirations; to earn a living; to provide for physical security, to fill recreational, spiritual, and aesthetic needs; to regulate human conduct through social organization and control; and to rear children in such a way that they in turn will carry on all of these basic social processes in ways of which their society approves.

We have also seen that the American public secondary school is an agency for the education of adolescents, but that it is only one among many such agencies. It is also important to note, for our purposes here, that of all the agencies by which our adolescent youths are educated, the only one which is publicly controlled and hence accountable to the total public is the public secondary school.

From these facts four things follow. First, the public secondary school is obligated to promote the general welfare of the American people—to help make the community "a better place in which to live and in which to make a living," as Professor Briggs, in his Inglis Lecture, remarked so succinctly.[1] Second, the public secondary school can discharge this obligation only if it teaches the American people to carry on the basic social processes upon which the strength of the United States and the well-being of each citizen depend. Third, since it is a school for adolescents, the American public secondary school is properly concerned only with what must thus be learned during adolescence; much that is necessary will have been learned by the completion of the elementary school years, and much must await the maturity of post-high school years. Fourth, since it is but one among many educational agencies which serve youth, but the only one which is accountable to the total social interest, the American public secondary school is obligated, not to perform all these necessary educational tasks alone, but so to shape its program that society will benefit to the fullest extent from the learnings which all of the educational agencies of the community collectively afford. Clearly, then, we may accept as valid the principle that follows:

PRINCIPLE I. | *The American public secondary school is obligated to promote the general welfare: it must assist in teaching youths whatever they need to learn during adolescence in order to carry on those basic social processes on which the strength of the United States and the well-being of each citizen depend.*

How should the public secondary school be oriented?

We have just seen what the basic task of the public secondary school is—to assist in ensuring societal strength and individual well-being. This refers to the future, for students are being prepared to live tomorrow, not yesterday.

If this were a static world or one in which change is imponderably slow, an exclusive orientation to the past would be desirable. The future would differ little from what had gone before, and an exclu-

[1] Thomas H. Briggs, *The Great Investment,* Harvard University Press, Cambridge, 1930.

sive study of the past would be an excellent preparation for the life of today and tomorrow. But we live in quite a different kind of world.

A century ago we were predominantly a rural people; today most of us live in cities or towns. Then our food, clothing, and shelter came to us directly through the energy of men and beasts on the farm or from handicrafts and simple manufacture. Today our farms are highly mechanized; complex machines have replaced handicrafts and crude factories. Then there were relatively few occupations, and virtually none save the learned professions required even a high school education. Today we have more than 20,000 occupations, and employers of virtually all but unskilled labor seek, demand, or are required by law to recruit persons with high school, college, or graduate school training. Then most young people learned their occupational skills through apprenticeship, and they began to work at an early age—although apprenticeship was rigorously controlled in many places, child labor laws were only beginning to find acceptance. Today business and industry in half our states are forbidden by law to employ workers under the age of sixteen; and the Fair Labor Standards Act of 1938 prohibits the interstate or international shipment of goods produced in establishments which employ people under sixteen years of age. Many industries today will not employ workers who are less than eighteen years old unless they are high school graduates. In contrast to former customs, young people now are subjected to widespread social and economic pressure to continue in school at least until they have graduated from high school.

One hundred years ago most American families were economically self-sufficient to a degree which for most of us is almost incomprehensible. Today we are part of an international and intranational network of economic interdependencies.

Formerly, communication and transportation were slow and uncertain. Today we may communicate with people in any major city on earth in a few seconds; we can fly to any part of the world in less than forty hours—and who knows how much this time may be reduced in a few years?

Two or three generations ago we had no telephones, no radios, no television sets, and our newspapers were small and primarily local. What a difference the years have made! Now telephones, radios, and television sets are commonplace and our newspapers are composed chiefly of material gathered by a few giant news-gathering agencies.

These and thousands of other changes have transformed American life since 1850. Any school which concentrated wholly on the past would be grossly inadequate to our present needs. We can see this even more vividly when we try to visualize the enormity of the changes which are probably ahead, changes so momentous that they will make those of the past seem minor by comparison. The age of jet propulsion, automation, and nuclear energy, which we are entering now, will make greater demands than ever upon our intelligence, sensibility, and training.

The secondary school of today can best serve its students only if it faces the future. But to help its students face this future, it must enable them to draw from the past as much as possible that is of value to them in their cultural heritage.

The job is huge, let there be no mistake about that. One can see this clearly when one looks at culture through the eyes of the cultural anthropologist. To him, a culture is all the things, abstract and concrete, which man has created—his ideas, his beliefs, his ideals, his skills, the aesthetic objects he has created, the thought patterns he has evolved, the customs he has shaped, the laws he has made, and the institutions of which he has been the architect. From this ever-increasing mass of creations, a knowledge of all that can contribute to the improvement of our lives—and even the ill-formed or evil elements of our cultural heritage can contribute to our understanding—must be passed on to each new generation if humanity is to progress.

This is a huge and difficult undertaking. It is a never-ending task to record, organize, and reproduce our composite cultural heritage. But the transmission of that heritage to our youth is even more difficult. Obviously, the success of those who mediate this knowledge can be no greater than their command of it; therefore, the education of teachers themselves should never end. No less apparent, to acquire their legacy from the past, students must make themselves competent in the idiom in which this knowledge is communicated.

Of all the educational agencies which serve our youths, the secondary school is the most competent to deal with many of the important elements of our cultural heritage. The home, the church, and the other agencies we have discussed bring young people many important aspects of their cultural heritage. But the vast areas of knowledge which derive from the explicit thoughts and actions of the past, as opposed to the beliefs and practices which reach us in a more generalized form, are largely the specific province of the school, for no other agency can transmit them as well.

Since culture is the accretion of all man's creative acts, each school subject which touches in any way upon what man has done is perforce a reservoir of the culture. One of the functions of these subjects is to pass on the best that is known about the aspects of human living to which each subject relates. To transmit all that is valuable in our cultural heritage is to pass on the best that is known in agriculture as well as art, in child rearing as well as in classical music, in mechanics as well as in mathematics, in leisure-time play as well as in literature, in education as well as in ethics. This does not mean that all elements of the cultural heritage are equally important or that the public school should emphasize equally all the elements of our cultural heritage with which it is properly concerned. But it does mean that the teachers of all high school subjects have some part in transmitting the cultural heritage to the rising generation and that each teacher must stress this aspect of his work if youths and society are to be served well.

What we have pointed out in the preceding paragraphs is summarized in the following principle:

PRINCIPLE 2. | *To promote the general welfare most fully, the public secondary school must build on the past but orient itself to the future.*

What should the public secondary school teach?

There are three educational tasks to which the public secondary school must assign its highest priority if societal and individual well-being are best to be assured. Also, there is an additional undertaking of considerable magnitude which the capable performance of these three primary tasks makes necessary. In this section we shall show why each of these tasks either merits a top-level priority or is necessary to the accomplishment of the school's first responsibilities. In so doing, we shall derive four additional principles.

In Chapter 3 we saw that the basic social processes which must be carried on in order to ensure societal and individual well-being depend upon the ability of the American people to think and communicate; to bind themselves together with a body of commonly held values, beliefs, and aspirations; to earn their livelihoods, to provide for their physical security; to provide for their aesthetic and spiritual needs; to provide for their leisure time; to regulate human conduct through social organization; and to rear their children in such a way that they in turn will be able to carry on these basic social processes in ways approved by our society. And we also observed that none of these processes can be carried on unless people have learned how to do so.

Consequently, we arrive at an exceedingly important question: Which of the basic social processes should the school emphasize in order best to integrate its program with the activities of the other educational agencies in the community? In other words, where do the public secondary school's chief responsibilities lie if the community is to achieve a maximally beneficial program among all the educational agencies which serve its young people?

The answers to this question are complex and important. They can best be discussed under a number of headings.

Teaching youths to think and communicate

Because man is endowed with the capacity to learn how to reason abstractly and communicate his ideas, he is able to improve the conditions of his existence. But the fact that he is born with this capacity for learning to think and communicate does not mean that he is born with the abilities themselves. On the contrary, as we observed in Chapter 3, he can acquire this ability only through learning.

Only rare persons of extraordinary genius can acquire in the normal course of out-of-school life what they must learn in order to think and communicate effectively in the modern world. True, the home and family, the business community, the church and similar organizations, the activities of work and play, and the media of mass communication can and often do help in teaching youth to think and communicate. But these nonschool agencies cannot deal with the problem systematically, nor are they intended to do so. Without the secondary school, the work of teaching youths to think and communicate cannot be performed adequately in any modern society.

To learn to think, speak, read, write, and listen well, one needs many understandings, attitudes, appreciations, and skills which can be acquired only through well-planned and adequately motivated sequences of learning experiences. These learnings can be acquired only under the supervision of persons who, in the aggregate, have a scholarly grasp of the several pertinent bodies of organized knowledge, a secure command of the learning process, a knowledge of and access to the necessary instructional materials, and sufficient time to teach well. Of all the youth-serving educational agencies, only the secondary school typically satisfies these specifications.

Teaching youths to think and communicate is of the utmost importance, for individual and societal well-being are contingent upon their learning to do so. Since the secondary school is more competent than any other agency to help youths acquire this necessary learning, this task must be made a top-priority undertaking of the American public secondary school.

But something more should be said about this business of teaching pupils to think. As recently as fifty or sixty years ago it was almost universally believed that by studying particular school subjects a student could acquire the generalized ability to think. It is a belief with a long history. In the sixth century the curriculum which was beginning to be established in medieval schools comprised seven subjects, all of which were directly related to the everyday needs of the monastic orders. These divisions of learning came to be known as the seven liberal arts. Three of them, grammar, rhetoric, and logic, were called the trivium. The other four, arithmetic, geometry, music, and astronomy, were called the quadrivium.[2] Centuries later, after the work of John Locke (1632-1704) had popularized the theory of faculty psychology, many people came to believe that a study of the seven liberal arts yielded the generalized ability to think.

As time passed the belief persisted that the study of particular subjects could develop the generalized ability to think, but people began to disagree about which subjects possessed this power. By the middle of the last century the modern foreign languages had been admitted to the charmed circle, but many educators who had been steeped in the tradition of the trivium and quadrivium were still inclined to deny the claims of such subjects as history, economics, political science, sociology, chemistry, physics, botany, physiology, and zoology. Only a classical education could really teach one to think, these people said; the upstart physical, social, and life sciences could not. Hence, the argument ran, they could not be counted among the "disciplines."

By the end of the first decade of this century, psychologists had

---

[2] For a discussion of these divisions see Paul Monroe, *A Textbook in the History of Education*, The Macmillan Co., New York, 1930, p. 268.

exploded the theory that the mind is made up of faculties (such as memory and reason) and had demonstrated that what is learned in one subject does not automatically transfer to other areas of thought. Students who had learned to reason logically in mathematics, for example, often were unable to reason well when confronted with problems in economics or political science. No single combination of subjects has yet been found which will so "discipline the mind" that by studying the subjects as they are traditionally taught one will acquire the ability to reason well in all of life's varied circumstances.

This does not mean that a study of English, foreign languages, history, the social sciences, mathematics, and science is not necessary if one is to think and communicate in these fields of knowledge as effectively as the modern world requires; it simply means that what is learned in one subject or in a given combination of subjects will not automatically make one a competent thinker in other fields.

What the psychologists discovered a good many years ago is, as a matter of fact, what common sense should have told us: what a person learns are the insights and skills afforded by the acts which he performs. If he generalizes these insights, he will then have formed concepts. Concepts are generalized insights and the stuff of which principles are made.

If a student plays football, what he learns first are the insights and skills which pertain to playing football; if he then generalizes these insights aptly and sufficiently he learns the principles which govern the playing of football. Some of these insights may be generalized subconsciously through the student's natural tendency to order his experience, in which case they will not be verbalized; but most are probably verbalized (at least subvocally) while they are being learned. Later, they may become habits and be applied with little or no reflection, hence with little or no use of language.

If a student deals mentally with if-then relationships in mathematics or any other subject, what he learns first are insights which pertain to deductive reasoning; if he generalizes these insights aptly and sufficiently he learns one or more principles of deductive reasoning. In this case, however, language is always the medium of learning and the vehicle of expression.

How well a student plays football or reasons deductively will depend upon two things: first, on how well he commands the whole range of principles and skills which he must master; second, on how well he applies the principles which are pertinent to the situations which confront him in playing football or in thinking his way through from premise to conclusion.

The good football coach teaches his players the skills and principles of charging, blocking, ball handling, tackling, punting, and so on, but he does not stop there. He also gives his players as much guided practice as possible in assessing (deciding which principles to apply) and solving (applying the principles which are pertinent) the kinds of problems which he expects them to face in the Siwash game the following Saturday: he scrimmages his team against the Siwash plays and defensive formations which have been reported to him by his scouts.

What the good football coach does for his players is roughly analogous to what the teacher must do for his high school pupils if they are to function effectively in out-of-school life, i.e., if they are to transfer their learning. If we want our students to think and act intelligently when they are faced with agricultural problems, for instance, we must give them guided practice in applying the pertinent principles and skills to the kinds of agricultural problems we expect them to face. Similarly, if we want our young people to think and act intelligently about political problems, we must not only teach them the pertinent principles and skills but give them practice in applying these principles and skills to a representative variety of political problems. If we want our students to apply the principles of science to problems in their everyday lives, we must give them practice in so doing as they learn the principles. If we want our youths to manage a home wisely and to rear children intelligently, we must teach them to understand and apply pertinent principles and skills. The same techniques of guided practice should be applied to every subject that is taught. If we want our youths to perceive and use the practical wisdom afforded by a study of history, foreign languages, art, music, and so on—in other words, if we want them to derive from their academic training the ability to understand and conduct themselves effectively in the world in which they live—then we must give them experience in applying the principles and skills which we teach them.

What we have said about the teaching of particular skills and principles does not, however, imply that there is no such thing as the generalized ability to think or that this ability cannot be developed by high school students. If young people are taught skillfully, they can learn from direct guided experience that the effective thinker does certain things regardless of the subject of his thoughts.[3] One of the top-level priority tasks of the school should be to help young people learn these principles and skills of effective thinking, to fix these as deeply as possible in their minds and to habituate them to the use of these principles and skills in as great a variety as possible of life's recurring situations. To habitually think well, students must have the kind of particularized instruction and guided practice sketched in the preceding paragraph.

All the subjects of the secondary school curriculum should contribute significantly to the work of teaching pupils to think. Every teacher of every subject in the curriculum should feel himself obligated to make this a top-level concern.

Every teacher should also stress the importance of the communication skills. It requires special expertness to teach the principles and skills of speaking, reading, writing, and listening. It is reasonable to expect this expertness of teachers of English and speech, but not of all teachers. But all teachers must stress the importance of these principles and skills in their work if they are to put their own subject matter across, or if their colleagues in English and speech are to have the reinforcement necessary to the effective teaching of the language arts.

What we have said in the preceding paragraphs of this section is epitomized in the following principle:

PRINCIPLE 3. | *If societal strength and individual well-being are best to be assured, one of the top-level priorities of the public secondary school must be to teach youths to think and communicate.*

Teaching youths to understand, appreciate, and practice the principles of American democracy

We observed in Chapter 3 that one of the things a people must do in order to ensure the survival of their society and to enhance their individual well-being is to provide themselves with a body of commonly held values, beliefs, and aspirations, that is to say, with the ingredients of a common feeling which will act as a "social cement." In the United States this social cement derives from a system of

---

[3] Kenneth B. Henderson, B. Othanel Smith, et al., *Guide to Clear Thinking*, Illinois Curriculum Program, Office of Superintendent of Public Instruction, Springfield, Ill., 1954.

values, beliefs, and aspirations which lies at the heart of our way of life, our American democracy. These are our ideals—ideal modes of conduct which originate in the beliefs held by nearly all of us. Like all ideals, ours are seldom fully realized in action, but this in no way invalidates their worth to us as our guiding objectives.

Our democratic ideals may be inferred from the historical documents which we consider great, the institutions which we support, the court decisions which we honor, the laws by which we govern ourselves, the customs to which we subscribe, and the qualities which we celebrate in our heroes and admire in our fellow citizens. Many scholars have studied this mass of evidence in an attempt to define the American democratic feeling and the beliefs on which it rests. We have consulted the works of a number of these scholars [4] in making the following compilation:

1. We hold that all human beings are of supreme and equal moral worth, that human life and well-being are to be valued above all material things, and that the worth of all persons should be equally respected at all times. Hence we assert:

[4] James Truslow Adams, *The Epic of America*, Little, Brown & Co., Boston, 1931.

Charles A. Beard, *A Charter for the Social Sciences*, Charles Scribner's Sons, New York, 1932.

Charles A. Beard and Mary Beard, *The Rise of American Civilization*, The Macmillan Co., New York, 1933.

James Bryce, *The American Commonwealth*, rev. ed., The Macmillan Co., New York, 1941.

George S. Counts, *Education and American Civilization*, Bureau of Publications, Teachers College, New York, 1952.

Ralph H. Gabriel, *The Course of American Democratic Thought*, The Ronald Press Company, New York, 1940.

Harold J. Laski, "Democracy," from *Encyclopedia of the Social Sciences*, Vol. 5, The Macmillan Co., New York, 1932.

Daniel L. Marsh, *The American Canon*, Abingdon Press, Nashville, 1939.

Alexander Meiklejohn, *What Does America Mean?* W. W. Norton & Company, New York, 1935.

Charles E. Merriam, *Civic Education in the United States*, Charles Scribner's Sons, New York, 1934.

Gunnar Myrdal, *An American Dilemma*, Harper & Brothers, New York, 1944.

Edgar Eugene Robinson, *Social Education*, Stanford Education Conference, 1939.

T. V. Smith, *The Promise of American Politics*, U. of Chicago Press, Chicago, 1936.

Alexis de Tocqueville, *Democracy in America*, H. S. Commager, ed., Henry Reeve, tr., Oxford U. Press, New York, 1947.

—That all evaluations of all policies and of all institutional arrangements should be made principally in terms of what each does to promote human welfare, and that the well-being of each person should count equally in all such evaluations.

—That the good life, however conceived, should be made equally available to all persons through equality of educational opportunity, equality at the ballot box, and equality before the law.

2. We believe that human beings should be the architects of their own destiny, that they have the capacity to govern themselves wisely, that the distribution of this capacity does not follow the contours of caste, class, family, religious denomination, or property ownership lines. Hence we repudiate all doctrines of rule by hereditary or divine right and reject totalitarianism, dictatorship, and tyranny. We assert:

—That the people are sovereign and that government derives its just powers from the consent of the governed; that human beings are the masters rather than the instruments of the state.

—That government *for* the people can be assured only if there is government *by* the people.

3. We have faith in human intelligence. We believe that by thinking man can build a better world. Consequently, we assert that man can best improve his lot only if there is an unrestricted play of free intelligence upon all problems. Evidences here are:

—The guarantees given in our Constitution to freedom of thought, belief, speech, assembly, and press; freedoms which are not to be curtailed by any person, majority, or (except in time of extreme emergency) even by the government itself.

—Our determination to maintain these freedoms as the necessary condition for creating new insights, new attitudes, new knowledge, or other new modes of behavior; and the realization that whoever to any degree denies any of these freedoms to that degree stifles intelligence.

—The high value we place on accuracy and integrity because we believe that false knowledge enslaves the minds of men, leads them into error, and so injures humanity.

4. We believe in the rule of law, in a written constitution which brings government and public officials as well as all other persons under the rule of law, in law which is made by representatives of our own choosing, in law which prevents the exercise of arbitrary power by persons clothed with the authority of the state, in law which upholds the rights and enforces the obligations of men in their ordinary pursuits and associations. Our ideal is self-government, that is, self-imposed law and order.

5. We believe in the principle of majority rule with the complete protection of the rights of minorities; we believe that the will of the majority should prevail, that anyone who believes that decisions of the majority are inimical to any democratic principle is morally obligated to attempt to change these decisions through persuasion based on reason, that all minorities which seek to change the will of the majority through persuasion based on reason should be fully protected by law in the right to do so. However, except for the action necessary to introduce a test case in the courts, we believe that all minorities are obligated to abide by the will of the majority even while they work to change it.

6. Within our own country, we are determined that there shall be freedom for peaceful social change, and we insist upon the peaceful settlement under law of all internal disputes. We believe that ballots, not bullets, are the proper instruments for resolving internal differences of policy, and that men should abide by the decisions of the courts in respect to those disputes which they are unable to resolve at the conference table.

7. We assert the individual's unrestricted right to freedom in all respects as long as it is not injurious to the common good; we declare that every person has the right to worship in his own way, think his own thoughts, speak his mind on any matter not liable to create a clear and present danger to others, dress in any fashion not corruptive of public morals, seek employment in any lawful occupation of his own choosing, search in whatever social class he will for a marriage partner, and live in any state of the Union in peace.

In acutely truncated form, these are the ideal modes of conduct to which the American people aspire. For the American public secondary school, they constitute both a mandate and a charter of freedom. Because the source of the school's sanction is the American people and because the comprehensive goal of education is to induct newcomers into the parent culture, the public secondary school is obligated to educate its young people in the service of these American ideals. Conversely, no public school in this country can legitimately educate in the service of contrary ideals, for to do so would be to subvert our society.

Because the behavior of some Americans falls short of the ideal modes of conduct which we have suggested above, critics say that these are not the ideals to which Americans really subscribe. But the test of an ideal is not whether its adherents live up to it, though naturally one would expect their behavior to point in the direction of the ideal; the test is whether most people recognize the ideal and aspire toward it. One can confidently assume that an ideal is firmly fixed in the culture of a society if most of the people of that society show by their behavior that they do recognize the ideal and aspire toward it. As Professor Engler has pointed out, "There has always been an antidemocratic tradition in America . . . violence, bigotry, and jingo as well as contempt for reason and the capacities of the average man [are] its essential if varying components." [5] But he immediately adds that these antidemocratic components have not been as dominant a part of our culture as "the values of reason, humanism, and democratic procedures." Trends in social behavior afford another test of an ideal; it is certainly operative if its adherents show by their behavior that they are approaching it. A third test might be called the "conscience test." The people certainly hold a given ideal if progress toward it gives them a feeling of virtue, and deviation from it gives them a feeling of guilt.

When these three tests are applied to the behavior of the American people, there can be little doubt of the validity of the ideals we have just outlined. These ideals are self-imposed standards of excellence against which most of us measure our individual and our societal accomplishments. As we have already observed, they constitute both a mandate to and a charter of freedom for our public secondary schools.

All the other educational agencies provide our youths with a rich variety of experience which teaches the democratic way of life. Homes, governmental bodies, churches, and recreational agencies conducted in a democratic way surround our youth with an environ-

[5] Robert Engler, "Collectivism—Domestic Variety," *New Republic*, Vol. 13, No. 10, Mar. 5, 1956, p. 13.

ment which is highly educative in this respect. Important elements of the democratic way of life are also learned from the media of mass communication and the business community. Although these nonschool educational agencies sometimes inflict undemocratic experiences upon our youth—a shortcoming of which the school is also guilty at times—the milieu which they furnish is on the whole democratic. All the other educational agencies of our society are, in effect, partners with the school in the business of teaching the democratic way of life.

But there is one essential aspect of this fundamental educational task which only the school can perform well. This is teaching youth to understand and to appreciate American democracy. In a world in which democracy is engaged in a struggle for survival against totalitarianism, freedom can endure only if those who now enjoy its benefits are capable of defending the democratic way of life against its detractors. This task requires, among other things, that free men have a secure understanding and appreciation of the what and the why of their social faith. The apologists and publicists for communism and fascism have much too easy a time when they set out to convert free men who lack this understanding and appreciation.

To teach youths the democratic way of life is to make explicit what the distinctive ideals are which command the loyalties of free men, and to show how and why the American people have found the pursuit of these ideals to be good. To understand and appreciate democracy is to know the historical origins of its constituent ideals and practices, to perceive the evils which each was designed to remedy, and to gauge the betterment, in human terms, which each has brought about. Further, to understand and appreciate democracy is to gain an insight into the pains with which its fruits were won, the vigilance with which it must be guarded, and the price which must be paid for its loss.

To give young people a sure intellectual foundation for loyalty to their social faith is a labor beyond the capacities of the nonschool educational agencies. It requires systematic training in bodies of knowledge which only the secondary school is characteristically competent to provide.

But more than instruction in important bodies of subject matter is required of the school if it is to help its students build a sure foundation for loyalty to the democratic way of life. The school must also provide a democratic environment. Two considerations make this imperative: first, students cannot be expected to take seriously the democratic precepts which are taught by a school that consistently ignores or violates these precepts in its own organization and conduct; second, the beliefs, allegiances, and modes of conduct which the democratic way of life demands in its adherents can never be effectively learned by precepts alone—to be learned, they must be lived. If it provides an environment which is undemocratic or which presents a confusing mixture of democratic and undemocratic practices, the school may actually hinder its students from learning the democratic ideals expounded in the classroom. Good citizens are likely to emerge from only those schools where good citizenship is the rule of life.

Since the school is the institution most competent to teach the history and theory of democracy, since the public secondary school is designed to give each individual the opportunity to develop to the limit of his capacities, and since democracy can be learned only if it is lived, there is no good reason to doubt the validity of the following principle:

PRINCIPLE 4. | *If societal strength and individual well-being are best to be ensured, one of the top-level priorities of the public secondary school must be to teach youths to understand, appreciate, and live the democratic way of life.*

Teaching youths to understand, appreciate, and practice the principles of safe and healthful living

A society is not strong if it is comprised of men and women who suffer chronically from debilitating illness or whose physical strength is inadequate to the demands of daily life. A society is weakened if its members are maimed or killed as a result of accidents.

Safety and good health can be assured only if the principles of safe and healthful living are followed, yet our young people cannot apply these principles if they have not been taught them. They should not only know them but understand and appreciate the reasons for them. Such thorough knowledge comes, as we have seen, not from instruction alone but from practice.

Hence, if societal strength and individual well-being are best to be ensured, students must understand the principles of safe and healthful living, and they can gain this understanding only through systematic and rewarding practice. Many other educational agencies of the community, most notably the home, can help to bring such knowledge to our youths. But the school is the most competent to teach the principles of safe and healthful living, and only the home and the school can assure the systematic practice of them.

Obviously, young people must keep in good physical condition if they are to live long and active lives. They can best acquire physical strength through rigorous exercise in childhood and youth. Except for the secondary school, no agency in America can give young people *systematic* exercise in supervised and balanced programs of physical education, and only the secondary school is typically competent to teach them why this development is essential to their individual and communal welfare.

The school provides a physical environment which will be either healthful or harmful, either free or burdened with hazards to life and limb. Students whose eyesight is impaired by faulty school lighting, for instance, or who incur a debilitating disease in the classroom, are obviously being handicapped rather than helped by their association with the school. Because the secondary school is virtually a world in miniature, it presents many of the hazards which are found anywhere. Obviously it should take special pains to assure the safety of its laboratories, shops, playing fields, school buses, and so on.

Some secondary school teachers and administrators, and many critics in institutions of higher learning, make the mistake of thinking that the school is exclusively, or nearly exclusively, an institution for intellectual training, a mistake which probably derives from the emphasis in most of their own higher education. But the care of the body is just as important as the care of the mind; one without the other can lead to a radically one-sided education.

Since only the secondary school is competent to help youths acquire a secure intellectual foundation for safe and healthful living, and to provide the balanced variety of activities which the development of physical strength requires, and since the school may hinder more than it helps unless it provides a safe and healthful physical environment, we can be confident of the validity of the following principle:

PRINCIPLE 5. | *If societal strength and individual well-being are best to be ensured, one of the top-level priorities of the public secondary school must be to teach youths the principles of safe and healthful living, help them develop bodily vigor, and provide a safe and healthful physical environment.*

Providing direct study of all the other basic social processes

The three first-priority tasks of the American public secondary school have been stated in the three preceding principles. But these principles are directly related to only three of the basic social processes. What about the others? Should the public secondary school teach young people to make a living, to rear children, to provide for their physical security, to satisfy their spiritual and aesthetic needs, and to organize and govern?

We have seen (Chapter 3) why the school must give priority to only those educational tasks necessary to societal strength and individual well-being which it alone can perform more adequately than can any other educational agency. We have also seen that the secondary school is the only agency which is characteristically competent to teach youth to think and communicate effectively, and to understand and appreciate democratic ideals, democratic practices, and the principles of safe and healthful living. No such claim can be sustained in respect to the other basic social processes. Other educational agencies of the community, with some help from the school, can do a reasonably adequate job of helping our young people make themselves competent to carry on these other processes. The teaching of these processes should not be made a top-priority task of the public secondary school.

But this institution should not ignore or neglect the other basic social processes. Instead, it should contribute a great deal toward educating our youth to carry on these necessary functions of daily living. In fact, it must do so if it is to discharge capably its first-priority tasks. Let us re-examine these three tasks, one by one, to see why this is true.

No one can understand or appreciate the principles of American democracy simply by memorizing the words in which these principles are stated. To really understand these principles, young people must learn to apply them to actual living conditions—they must understand what these principles do and do not sanction in specific instances. Hence, since the principles of American democracy apply to all aspects of our daily life, our youths should learn how to apply them to making a living, strengthening the family, providing for society's physical security and for their spiritual, aesthetic, and recreational needs, and for social organization and control. If students are to understand these principles, they must also make a direct study of how they apply to thinking and communicating and to healthful and safe living.

In the same way, students cannot learn how to think and communicate in an intellectual vacuum. They must speak, read, write, listen to, and think about *something*. Since what students learn is a function of what they do, if they are to learn to think and communicate effectively about the basic social processes, they must study these processes—all of them—directly, and they must command the principles and skills of critical thinking and communication which are pertinent to each social process.

Finally, a student cannot adequately apply the principles of safe and healthful living unless he has been taught them in the context of the actual activities in which health and safety are issues.

In respect to these three fundamental social processes, the secondary school should strive to make its graduates "finished products" —as finished, at least, as their inherent capacities and levels of maturity will allow. In other words, the school's principal objective should be to turn out good citizens—citizens who understand and value the principles of American democracy and who are skilled in applying them to all aspects of daily living; citizens who think and communicate as effectively as possible in everything they do; citizens who apply the principles of health and safety in all aspects of their daily lives. If this is done, if our high school graduates are capable of these three things, then they will also know a great deal about making a living, rearing children, satisfying their spiritual needs, and so on, even though, in order to become finished products in these respects, they must rely considerably upon the educational services of the nonschool agencies.

All those who go directly from high school into the labor market should be helped in school to develop some salable skill, though a great deal of the work of equipping oneself to earn a living must be done after graduation from high school. Most or all of the courses in business education, industrial education, and agriculture are clearly vocational, but so are many courses in academic subjects. Students of the former subjects are preparing themselves to enter the labor market immediately after their graduation from high school, while students of the latter subjects are generally looking forward to occupations that require university training for which high school academic courses are the necessary antecedents. The vocational preparation of the college-bound students is only well begun by the time they have graduated from high school. To a somewhat lesser degree, this should also be true of the students who are enrolled in "vocational" courses. Except for jobs requiring unskilled labor, the high school cannot adequately prepare youngsters for occupations in the agricultural, business, homemaking, and industrial worlds without seriously neglecting its three primary tasks. Business, industry, and other agencies of adult education are generally equipped to continue the vocational education of young people who enter the world of work following high school graduation. For virtually all its students, then, the secondary school should not provide the "finished product" but should furnish a good beginning in vocational education; the community college, university (or some other agency of adult education), business and industry should continue and complete this task. The secondary school should, of course, accept the responsibility of helping to inform young people about these opportunities and encourage them to choose their vocations wisely.

The occupations in which somewhat over half of the people in this country engage require at most but a few weeks' training in vocational skills; these skills can best be learned on the job. To succeed in these (and in virtually all other) occupations, however, one must have good work habits and get along well with his associates—one must be reasonably punctual and dependable, follow oral and written directions when necessary, be tactful and considerate in dealing with others, avoid loafing on the job, and be loyal to the organization by which he is employed. These are all learned behaviors, none of which can be acquired in but a few days, weeks, or months, and all are behavior patterns that the school should deliberately help students to develop through all that it does. This is the most fruitful kind of vocational preparation which the secondary school can and should provide for all youth, and, except for work in the practical arts as part of a general education, the only kind which it should attempt with youths who are not interested in entering a profession, a semiprofession, or a skilled trade.

For those who are interested in and capable of preparing themselves to enter one of the professions, the secondary school should provide college preparatory work which will enable them to pursue this ambition successfully.

The semiprofessions are typically technical, and they characteristically require two years of schooling beyond the twelfth grade. Workers in these occupations far outnumber those in the professions. The youths who have the requisite interests and capacities to prepare themselves for these occupations should find in the secondary school technical courses for which a substantial grounding in mathematics and science is prerequisite and in which their learning is reinforced by required shop experiences.

The skilled trades are crucial in our daily lives. Contrary to the opinion many people hold, the preparation which business, industry, and organized labor alike require for entry into the skilled trades cannot be accomplished successfully by persons of less than average capacity to learn. For the many youths with the interest and capacity which this preparation requires, the secondary school should offer vocational courses which will prepare them for the apprenticeship training which business and industry require them to undergo before they acquire journeyman status.

Because expensive equipment is required, some large cities have found it desirable to set up separate vocational and technical high schools. Chicago is a good example. It has approximately forty high schools, of which seven and three are separate vocational and technical high schools, respectively. In these vocational schools students are prepared for any of twenty-four skilled trades. The technical high schools serve youths who plan to enter the professions of engineering and architecture.

Most of what our young people will need to learn in order to establish and maintain wholesome families should be learned through the adult education agencies of the community. This does not mean that the secondary school should not strive to help its students improve the quality of family living; it should. It should teach students to understand family relationships, to apply democratic premises to these relationships, to apply the principles of health and safety to the home, and to transmit the best that has been accumulated from the experience of the past in all these respects. These are tasks which many parents perform capably and with pride. The school should supplement the teaching of the home by providing laboratory experiences in home management and child rearing for girls and, to a lesser extent, for boys. But the agencies of adult education should be expected to complete the work, usually at a time in the lives of the students when they have become more aware of the problems of home and family. The school should assist these other agencies by making their services known and by directing former students to them.

To assure our physical security, we must provide for the wise use of our natural resources and for many other things as well—public sanitation, industrial safety programs, police protection, fire prevention and control, emergency aid in times of disaster, military readiness, and civil defense. Obviously, the secondary school which competently performs its priority tasks can offer but rudimentary training in any of these activities. Most of the vast work of education in these aspects of our welfare should be left to the adult education agencies of the local, state, and national governments.

The separation of church and state is basic to our way of life; it is mandated by certain of our democratic ideals. Our public schools, in ministering to the spiritual needs of our young people, should carefully avoid the promulgation of sectarian religious beliefs. The home, the church, and other character-building agencies are exclusively responsible for sectarian religious training. There is, however, a body of moral precepts which is sanctioned by the whole community; these should be taught by the public school. Honesty, concern for the rights and feelings of others, fair play, respect for proper authority, and above all a regard for the primacy of conscience and the dignity of spiritual experience—clearly these can all be taught by the public secondary school.

The public high school should enable its pupils to develop the understandings, appreciations, and skills which will yield aesthetic satisfactions, and it should give its pupils rudimentary training in the arts and crafts from which such rewards may be obtained. But at most the school should be expected to do no more than provide keys to the doors which open upon such abiding satisfactions. Many communities offer a large variety of agencies for adult education in the appreciation and practice of the arts and crafts, and many adults whose aesthetic interests were awakened during their secondary school years are active participants in these programs. Again, the school should assist the community's nonschool agencies by guiding its students to the out-of-school opportunities which will be offered to them for training in the arts and crafts which are readily available to them. Furthermore, the school can do much to accustom its students to the use of the public library, which in most communities is the center for adult interest in literature. There are, of course, communities in which the nonschool agencies for education in the arts and crafts are lamentably inadequate. Such a state of affairs always suggests that the community's schools are also inadequate: if the schools had provided a stimulating introduction to literature and the other arts, the citizens of the community, who once were the students in the schools, would feel the need to sponsor community programs for education and participation in the arts and crafts. Thus we see that our secondary schools should influence the formation of aesthetic awareness in our society.

When we consider the role of the secondary school in relation to the recreational aspects of our life, we encounter a somewhat similar situation. It is axiomatic that only those who have learned to play while they are young are likely to be able to play when they are older. Hence the school should conduct a program of sports and games which will stimulate a lifelong interest in such recreational activities. But the school should only be expected to help its students make a good beginning; it should teach only the rudiments of a balanced variety of sports and games. Most adults, if their schooling has been adequate in this respect, will sponsor and join community recreational programs, and most communities today, it seems safe to say, provide at least a reasonably adequate number of recreational facilities. To help youths appreciate this aspect of community life and to direct young people into the recreational activities for which they are fitted are important responsibilities of the public high school.

The maintenance of social organization and control—the last of the basic social processes to be considered in this section—occupies an extremely conspicuous place in our public life. Our political parties debate it endlessly, all manner of voluntary associations attempt to influence it in one way or another, all newspapers and most magazines devote much of their space to it, it is the subject of countless books and radio and television programs, and it is a usual topic of conversation everywhere. All this is indeed fortunate, for in a rapidly changing world the political education of the citizens of a self-governing society should never end. It should begin in early child-hood, expand during adolescence, and continue throughout adulthood.

Although the entire program of the American public secondary school should be devoted to developing good citizenship in all of its principal aspects, only a part—though a very important part—of the education for political citizenship needed by Americans should be supplied by the high school. We have already emphasized the fact that the high school is a place where democracy should be experienced in action. In addition, the high school should teach the principles and skills of political citizenship as they apply to our republic and give students guided practice in applying these principles and exercising these skills in the on-going affairs of the community. If this is done, high school graduates will be able to take an effective part in the activities of the many other agencies to which they should look for their continuing political education.

We have seen that societal strength and individual well-being depend upon the high school's ability to perform its three top-level priority tasks and that these tasks can be competently performed only if the school has its students make a direct study of all the other basic social processes. Our sixth principle, then, can be stated thus:

PRINCIPLE 6. | *To perform each of its top-level priority tasks most effectively, the public secondary school must have youths make a direct study of the problems of making a living, strengthening the family, and providing for physical security, spiritual growth, aesthetics, recreation, and social organization and control.*

Whom should the public secondary school serve?

The proposition that all human beings are of equal moral worth lies at the heart of the basic ethical postulates of our society. We believe that access to the good life should be equally available to everyone. Since the good life is equally accessible to all only if all young people have an equal opportunity to learn whatever must be learned in order to live the good life, our public secondary schools should be designed to serve equally well all the educable children of all the people. By educable children we mean all but that tiny fraction of youths (a) who must be cared for by special-purpose institutions because they are incapable of learning to feed themselves, to button their own buttons, to dispose of their body wastes, to acquire any vocational skill, or to cope with any of the other ordinary routines of daily living; or (b) who must be confined to some corrective or even penal institution. In other words, to achieve its high purpose the public secondary school must be designed to serve equally well all youths who will later be permitted to become husbands or wives, fathers or mothers, employees or employers, unsupervised consumers of newspapers, magazines, and radio and television programs, spenders of unsupervised leisure time, drivers of automobiles, voters, and the like.

Complete equality of educational opportunity has long been a recognized goal of our society. The Commission on Social Studies of the American Historical Association has written: [6] "Since the general welfare requires the free and full development of all social and creative talents in the individual, the denial of educational opportunity or the submergence of gifts because of circumstances of wealth, family, race, religion, or nationality impoverishes society and is therefore intolerable."

The American people are committed to self-government; they repudiate all doctrines of rule by hereditary or divine right and reject totalitarianism, dictatorship, and tyranny. They hold, on the contrary, that sovereignty resides with the people and that government derives its just powers from the consent of the governed. They are engaged in a perennial experiment in popular self-government based on the consent of the governed. Only if this is an informed consent can our experiment possibly succeed. This was clearly understood by the men who founded our free government.

"A popular government, without popular information, or the means of acquiring it, is but a prologue to a farce or a tragedy; or perhaps both," said James Madison. "Knowledge," he added, "will forever govern ignorance; and a people who mean to be their own governors must arm themselves with the power which knowledge gives."

"If a nation expects to be ignorant and free, in a state of civilization," wrote Thomas Jefferson, "it expects what never was and

[6] Commission on the Social Studies, American Historical Association, *Conclusions and Recommendations of the Commission*, Charles Scribner's Sons, New York, 1934, pp. 39-40.

never will be. Above all things, I hope the education of the common people will be attended to; convinced that on their good sense we may rely with the most security for the preservation of a degree of liberty."

"In a monarchy," said John Adams, "the few who are likely to govern must have some education, but the common people must be kept in ignorance; in an aristocracy, the nobles should be educated, but here it is even more necessary that the common people should be ignorant; but in a free government knowledge must be general, and ought to be universal."

"In proportion as the structure of a government gives force to public opinion," said George Washington, "it is essential that public opinion should be enlightened." He urged his countrymen to "promote, then, as an object of primary importance, institutions for the general diffusion of knowledge."

Modern scholars have repeated the sentiments of the founders. "Democracy could not work without an enlightened electorate," says Henry Steele Commager.[7] "Obviously," wrote George S. Counts,[8] "a government which presumes to rest upon universal suffrage must make provision for the political enlightenment of the masses." Both were speaking in praise of the American public school.

Obviously, to establish universal education it is not enough merely to provide a lot of schools. The schools must be administered and their programs must be designed in such a way that all students will be able to develop to the limit of their ability. Every educable child in our society must not only attend school but must find there the educational resources which will meet his needs and fit his aptitudes. Only then will our schools offer genuinely equal educational opportunities to all.

To conclude, our basic ethic requires that all children and youth have equal access to the public schools. The success of our experiment in self-government rests on universal education, which also requires equal access to the public schools. Since such access is obviously an empty thing unless the public secondary school serves all youths equally well, there is no good reason to doubt the validity of the following principle:

[7] Henry Steele Commager, "Our Schools Have Kept Us Free," *Life*, Oct. 16, 1950, p. 46.

[8] George S. Counts, *The American Road to Culture*, John Day Co., New York, 1930, p. 78.

PRINCIPLE 7. | *To promote the general welfare most fully, the public secondary school must serve equally well all the educable youths of the community.*

How should public secondary school teachers teach?

The instruction offered in public secondary schools must be well suited to the educationally significant differences among American youths or our seventh principle will be violated. But because the differences among students are so great and so many, this is no easy task. The difficulties were vividly portrayed by those who wrote the Harvard Report.[9] After noting that the rate of growth in secondary school enrollments from 1870 to 1940 was thirty times greater than that in the general population, the Report continued, in part:

> . . . In 1870 three-fourths [10] of those who attended high school went on to college. . . . Those who went to high school were therefore a fairly homogeneous group, on the whole children of well-to-do families looking forward to the learned professions or to leadership in politics or trade. . . . Instead of looking forward to college, three-fourths of the students now look forward directly to work. . . . The consequences of this transformation for every phase of the high school are incalculable and by no means yet fully worked out. . . .

> As the roundedness and self-sufficiency of an earlier partly rural way of life has disappeared, the school has necessarily taken on new functions. . . . Health, play, social life, avocations, help in the choice of a career all devolve increasingly on the school. . . .

> It is worth observing somewhat more exactly what this new part is which the high school has been called on to play. It is, in essence, the incomparably difficult task of meeting, in ways which they severally respect and will respond to, masses of students of every conceivable shade of intelligence, background, means, interest, and expectation.

"Masses of students of every conceivable shade of intelligence, background, means, interest, and expectation"—this is no exaggera-

---

[9] Report of the Harvard Committee, *General Education in a Free Society*, Harvard University Press, Cambridge, 1945, pp. 7, 8, 9, 21.
[10] The proportion now is about one-half.

tion. Virtually all American youth now enter the ninth grade, the freshman year in the traditional four-year high school. These huge numbers of students differ greatly in many respects—in what they are capable of learning, what they have already learned, and what they are ready to learn.

A student's innate intelligence determines very largely what he is capable of learning. Because we have not yet invented an entirely culture-free test of intelligence, great care must be employed in interpreting the results of our present tests for mental capacity: a low score may reflect the intellectual impoverishment of a child's early environment and not a low order of intelligence. In spite of this defect, however, our present intelligence tests yield the most dependable evidence of intellectual capacity that we have, and the results of such tests, given en masse, show that the mental ages of beginning high school students differ by as much as thirteen years: some have the mental age of a typical first-grader, some that of the average college freshman, and the rest are scattered at every level in between.[11]

Some idea of the changes which must be made in the traditional secondary school program in order to accommodate these disparities among entering students is suggested by the declaration of competent scholars that about half the school population is incapable of learning algebra as it has been taught in the past.[12] Obviously, a secondary school which ignores such evidence as this by requiring all its students to take the traditional algebra course is doing four things which make its educational procedures less effective than they might otherwise be. First, the school is frustrating a sizable number of its students by forcing them to attempt to do something which they patently cannot do. Second, it is frustrating its teachers by asking them to take on a job in which the possibility of success is automatically ruled out. Third, the school is forcing many of its students to waste time which might profitably be spent, for example, in a course in general mathematics. Fourth, the school is also wasting the time and energies of its teachers, which might be put to better use—perhaps, again, in teaching general mathematics to the students who cannot learn algebra.

[11] Illinois Curriculum Program, *The Nature of the School Population in Illinois*, Office of Superintendent of Public Instruction, Springfield, 1955, p. 19.
[12] *General Education in a Free Society*, p. 10.

What a student is capable of learning depends on a number of attributes in addition to his level of intelligence. We shall make brief mention of but six such attributes here, although this does not exhaust the list by any means. How well can the student see? How well can he hear? Is he seriously crippled in any way? Is he handicapped by some organic disability; by a serious heart condition, for example? Does he have an adequate diet, or is his energy potential low because he is improperly fed? Is he growing rapidly, or recuperating from some debilitating illness, so that he needs frequent and possibly extended periods of rest and relaxation? Is he burdened with some species of serious emotional maladjustment? It should be obvious that any boy or girl who is handicapped in any one or more of these respects cannot be expected to do (and hence to learn) what his more fortunate classmates are easily capable of doing (and hence of learning). If it is to serve all students equally well, the public secondary school must take into account all such differences in shaping its program of instruction, guidance, and other services.

We have mentioned that high school students also differ greatly in respect to what they have already learned. On standardized academic achievement tests, entering secondary school pupils range in performance from that typical of third-grade children to that characteristic of college sophomores.[13] Because their home and neighborhood environments differ, high school students also vary in their speech, manners, morals, hopes for the future, respect for formal education, and anticipations regarding school achievement— all learned responses.

High school students vary greatly in respect to what they are ready to learn. Readiness depends in part upon what the student is capable of learning and in part upon what he has already learned: neither the student of very low intelligence nor the student who has not previously studied arithmetic is ready to learn algebra. It also depends upon the student's level of maturation: a pre-adolescent boy is not likely to be ready to learn the etiquette of dating. Another factor is the student's emotional state: many cases of reading disability have been traced to psychic disturbances. Still another factor is the home and neighborhood environment in which the student has spent his earlier years: a student who has been conditioned by the speech of his elders to regard as acceptable such locu-

[13] *The Nature of the School Population in Illinois,* p. 19.

tions as "I knowed," "He shoulda went," "She usta could," "Them folks was," and the like, is obviously not ready for a course in advanced composition.

Obviously—because of the great differences in what youths are capable of learning, in what they have already learned, and in what they are ready to learn—no uniform approach to the problems of learning, no single pedagogical technique, and no single course of instruction can serve all the students of a given school grade equally well; they cannot arouse a willing response to the things which the school is obligated to teach, nor can they provide effective teaching for all students. To serve all students equally well, then, the school must adapt both its teaching procedures and the content of its instructional program to their varying states of readiness. It also can and should help develop its students' readiness.

If the school is to succeed in adapting its program to what students need, want, and are able to learn, teachers must make use of our knowledge of adolescent growth and development. The events of physiological growth which occur during the years of adolescence influence the feelings, interests, and motivations of the person who experiences them. The fact that adolescence is a period of uneven growth in various parts of the body often produces anxieties or temporary emotional disturbances which divert the student's attention from his academic duties. Adolescents of the same chronological age often manifest wide variances in their rates of maturation; the fact that many older adolescents are physically ready for the responsibilities of adulthood before our culture will permit them to assume an adult role often creates emotional blocks to learning which sympathetic teachers can do much to remove.

The period between childhood and adulthood is for many students a time of bewilderment and some anxiety, and teachers must understand these states of mind if our public schools are to carry out their responsibilities successfully. At the same time, however, adolescence impels many students to demonstrate to themselves and to those around them that they are capable of dealing with the problems of the adult world and of thinking and conducting themselves in mature ways. Teachers who can capitalize on this new-found pride and energy can often take the student's will to grow up and turn it into the will to learn.

So far, we have considered what must be reckoned with if the secondary school is to accommodate the educationally significant differences among its students. But there is a second major consideration which the public school must recognize and act upon if it is to discharge its full responsibility to its students and to society. Let us see what this consideration is and what it means.

Our knowledge of the learning process is a two-edged sword; it cuts two ways and can be used for either good or evil, for either democratic or tyrannical ends. The democratic way of life requires that we solve our problems by appealing to reason and balancing opposed opinions; as a noted philosopher has observed, democracy proceeds by unending inquiry and debate. In a dictatorship, however, the important decisions are made at the top and persuasion is based on indoctrination or, if need be, physical coercion. Independent judgment and critical thinking are necessities in a democracy, but subversive activities in a dictatorship.

In any given instance, teaching may be made to serve one or the other, but not both, of these purposes. Learning may be made so mechanical that students will develop little ability to think critically. Or learning may be made so meaningful that students will conceptualize at ever higher levels of insight and thus continually increase their ability to think critically and act wisely. Which path education will follow is determined by which aspects of our knowledge of the learning process the teacher applies. Here we shall discuss briefly a number of important precepts which we derive from the theory of learning as it is applied to education in a democratic society.

First, however, it might be well to explain our unavoidable use of the word *learning* as a technical term. Commonly, the word means *any acquired knowledge*, but there is no way in English, except by cumbersome circumlocutions, to indicate the special content or subject of an individual act of learning. Hence educators often speak of *a learning* and *learnings* when they wish to signify the specific thing or things which are learned in specific acts of learning.

Let us proceed, then, to our discussion.

Teachers should plan for desirable concomitant learnings

Assume that the direct learning sought in a given instance is a knowledge of some period of history, some principle in economics, or some formula in chemistry. The student who undergoes this process will acquire, not only the direct learning, but a series of concomitant attitudes toward the subject studied, the teacher, his fellows, himself, and so on. He may learn, for instance, to regard the subject as valuable or valueless, himself as a success or a failure, his teacher as a friendly counselor or a tyrant, his fellows as considerate or ruthless. Whether these ancillary learnings are desirable or undesirable, they will be acquired, and none will occur by chance. Each will be a consequence of the kind of experience the student had in connection with the direct learning in question. Moreover, in any teaching-learning situation, even the most passive, the student is certain to acquire skills—skill in working cooperatively with others or in dominating others, skill in studying or in getting by without study, and so on. Again, what is learned will be a consequence of the student's experience in the teaching-learning situation.

In short, every experience involves a constellation of learnings. Indirect learning of attitudes, values, information, skills, and modes of behavior is bound to accompany the acquiring of any direct learning. Only when the teacher bears in mind all the learnings which may potentially accrue from a given teaching-learning situation and plans his work accordingly is the total outcome of his efforts likely to be satisfactory.

Teachers should relate course material to students' goals

Students can confidently be expected to employ the means which seem to them consistent with the primary objective which they have in mind. If what the teacher asks them to do is not clearly related to their objectives, unfortunate consequences will usually follow; many students will try to do as little as they can and still get by. Since what students learn is a function of what they do, they will probably acquire habits of shirking and attitudes of distaste, at least toward the subject in question, as concomitant learnings—outcomes which no conscientious teacher can desire. Both direct and concomitant learnings of the kind sought by every good teacher will occur much more readily if the student perceives a desirable relationship between the teacher's objectives and his own.

Teachers should know students' needs, wants, and motives

Havighurst has helped us to see what some of the needs, wants, and motives of adolescent youths in America are. What he calls their "developmental tasks" are listed here. Some of these tasks arise from biological or psychological considerations and are usually self-motivated, and we find that most young people are actively concerned about them. All of these developmental tasks represent demands which are enforced by society.[14]

—Acceptance of their physique and acceptance of a masculine or feminine role.

—Development of new relationships with age mates of both sexes.

—Attainment of emotional independence from parents and other adults.

—Achievement of assurance of economic independence.

—Selection of an occupation and preparation for it.

—Development of intellectual skills and concepts necessary for civic competence.

—Recognition and achievement of socially responsible behavior.

—Preparation for marriage and family life.

—Discovery of values in harmony with an adequate scientific world-picture.

Havighurst [15] emphasizes the point that failure to learn these tasks "leads to unhappiness in the individual, disapproval by the society, and difficulty with later tasks." His observations suggest how important it is for the secondary school to give every possible assistance to young people in these crucial aspects of their education.

It is interesting and significant to note which of the categories of learning that we found to be essential to individual and societal well-being (see p. 22) are related to the developmental tasks of youth. Thinking and communicating, making a living, rearing children, building strong bodies, and behaving democratically—these are clearly related to their developmental tasks. School work related to these categories, therefore, may be expected to encounter comparatively few problems of motivation in most students. The relationships of the other basic social processes to the developmental tasks of youth, though they exist, are more tenuous, and teachers will have to point them out carefully to students if the value of school work in these phases of life's activities is to be made clear to

[14] Robert J. Havighurst, *Developmental Tasks and Education,* Longmans, Green and Co., New York, 1950, pp. 30-63.
[15] Havighurst, *Developmental Tasks and Education,* p. 6.

them. And of course it is society at large, as well as the individuals directly concerned, which benefits from the successful achievement of these developmental tasks by our youth.

Students should have some part in setting the goals of their learning, in planning ways in which these goals will be achieved, and in appraising their progress

It is axiomatic that whoever does the doing acquires the learning. If the teacher does all the planning and evaluating, obviously he is not helping his pupils learn how to plan and evaluate. Life is full of problems which one must solve in order to live successfully. To solve problems one must be able to plan, to do, and to evaluate what he has done. If the school is to help students learn how to plan and evaluate capably, it must give them experience in doing precisely these things in their classes and extra-class activities. Unless the school engenders in its students the disposition to plan and evaluate, and unless it teaches the principles and skills which these activities require, it is not doing what it should to encourage the practice of intelligent self-direction in out-of-school life.

When a student shares in planning an activity, he is more likely to understand its significance and hence to give it his best efforts. And if he himself shares in evaluating what he has done, he is more likely to acknowledge and to try to remedy his deficiencies.

There is still another consideration, one which also relates to the fact that what students learn is a function of what they do. If the teacher alone determines the course of action by which his students are to achieve their goals and if he alone evaluates their accomplishments, he is likely to find that his students have acquired as an indirect learning an attitude of dependence: they will have learned to rely upon someone else instead of upon themselves for the resolutions of their own problems. This is a kind of learning which cannot be squared with the requirements of a free society.

All this does not mean that pupils should determine the curriculum, or that they should replace the teacher in planning their instruction or in evaluating their work. As noted earlier in this chapter, the major goals which the curriculum should serve are determined by the needs of society and of individuals. The pupils should be helped to recognize that neither they nor their teachers can ignore the major goals of society or of individuals. But there is no one best way for all pupils to acquire the learnings which they need to reach these goals. Here choices must be made among alternative procedures. There is good reason to believe that the most efficient learning will result if pupils are encouraged to share with the teacher some part of the planning through which these choices among alternatives are made. In respect to evaluation, pupils should be helped to recognize that the ultimate judgment of their competence will be made by the community, not by their teachers or by themselves. Our society expects its members to be self-critical in respect to the competencies which they must possess in order to take part in community life. If pupils are encouraged to be self-critical in school, they are more likely to be self-critical after they have graduated into the community.

To help students develop worthy goals, and to link their work to these goals in the minds of the students by inviting them to share the work of planning and evaluation, are important parts of the master teacher's art. A teacher who does these things will win the willing co-operation of most if not all of his students, and he is unlikely to be troubled by any serious disciplinary problems.

It should not be inferred from what we have said, however, that the goals of the teacher and the pupil are the same. The teacher's goal is always a response by the learner, while the response will occur only if it serves some purpose sought by the student. The pupil's goal is never the response itself.

Students' satisfaction can be reinforced by social approval

Learning a principle or skill which enables one to solve a problem that is seen as genuinely important is in itself a satisfying experience. This suggests why good teachers use students' problems and interests to elicit a strongly motivated and favorable response to classwork. Also important, but no substitute, are the applause of one's classmates, the approval of the teacher, and the plaudits of the school and the community.

Students retain facts learned for the sake of their long-range goals

Students who learn facts for the sole purpose of passing a test soon forget them when the test is over. But when facts are learned and generalized for the sake of some less ephemeral goal, such as becoming a doctor, they may be remembered as long as this goal is actively sought. They will be remembered for the same reason that they were learned in the first place—because they support something that is consciously desired.

This is another compelling argument for linking the secondary school's program to the life purposes of youth. We repeat: to be most effective, the school must help its students develop worthy purposes which relate to the pursuit of a wholesome and well-rounded life, and then it must help them acquire and generalize the insights which are necessary to the pursuit of these life purposes. These generalizations and the facts which support them will be remembered because the students will continue to use them.

Learning should satisfy the desire for new experience

Few things are more inimical to learning than monotony. When there is the fun and excitement which a variety of learning experience affords, pupils' interests are more easily caught. Learning is exciting in the hands of the skilled teacher who brings such artistry to his work. Dull, drab classes dampen or kill the interest of the students. Without the teacher's interest, little that is desirable can be taught to anyone. If people are to gain in understanding, they—especially adolescent boys and girls—need new experiences. Teachers who understand this need and treat it systematically are usually the ones who will be remembered gratefully by their students long after their school days are over.

More than one sensory approach should be employed

Our organs of reception enable us to learn by seeing, hearing, feeling, smelling, and tasting. Students should be encouraged to use all of their senses in various combinations. Teachers in classroom, shop, and laboratory should be skilled in the use of audio and visual aids to instruction, and students should be given every opportunity to "experience" new ideas on school farms, camps, and field trips. Some pupils learn best through one sense, some through another. All of them should be trained to make the most intelligent use of their senses and to recognize the role of the senses in maintaining contact between the individual and exterior reality.

Direct experience should supplement verbal activities

Learning through the medium of language is necessary for nearly all that civilized man does. But many other kinds of direct experience contribute to learning, and these should be provided for high school students. Visiting a criminal court, for example, or helping to get out the voters at election time will give added meaning to what students have learned about these activities from their civics books and their teachers. A discussion of school citizenship comes to life when it is augmented by experience in governing the school, beautifying its surroundings, making visitors feel welcome, helping convalescent classmates keep up with their studies, and the like. Experimenting, collecting, surveying, constructing, and role playing afford still other direct experiences which can increase the fruitfulness of language as a medium of learning.

Content of instruction should be organized into meaningful problems

High schools, realizing that students learn more when material is meaningful to them, are turning more and more to what is called problem-centered instruction. Such instruction is offered both in standard courses, like English, mathematics, and science, and in the newer courses that appear under such names as unified studies, core courses, and common learnings courses.

Using as criteria the gains made on standardized achievement tests or the records of academic success in college, several studies have been made in which the achievements of students in these newer courses have been compared with the achievements of students in traditional high school courses. Whatever the criterion, the performance of students in the new courses has been found to be better, on the whole, than that of students in the comparison groups.[16]

[16] See, for example: Kermit A. Cook, "Effect of Two Patterns of High School Training on College Achievement," *School Review*, Vol. 59, Mar., 1951, pp. 164-7.

Kalamazoo, Michigan, Board of Education, *How Much Did They Grow?* General Information Bulletin No. 164, Sept. 1952.

J. Wayne Wrightstone, *Appraisal of Newer Practices in Selected Public Schools*, Teachers College, Columbia University, 1935.

J. Wayne Wrightstone and George Forlano, "Evaluation of the Experience Curriculum at Midwood High School," *High Points*, Vol. 30, Dec. 1948, pp. 35-42.

Teachers should teach for transfer of training

Several hundred studies dealing with the question of the transfer of training have been made since about 1890. As it is summarized in the *Encyclopedia of Educational Research*,[17] our present knowledge makes it quite evident that very little in the way of transfer will occur unless teachers deliberately aim for it.

Five things must be done to ensure the likelihood of transfer of training. First, the possibility of transfer must be pointed out to the students, so that they will realize that what they are learning now may be useful later in other situations. Second, teachers must use varied materials which involve actual samples of life situations as similar as possible to those to which it is hoped the learning in question will transfer. Third, teachers must help their students develop meaningful generalizations by enabling them to see each classroom topic as an illustration of a broad principle which is applicable to situations far beyond the classroom, and they must be certain that these generalizations are really understood, not merely verbalized, by the students. Fourth, students must be given guided practice in varied new situations in applying to real problems the generalizations they have learned. Fifth, teachers must evaluate the accomplishments of their students on the basis of what they do in the kinds of new situations to which their learning is intended to apply.

We have described three respects in which young people of high school age differ significantly and certain of the precepts which derive from what is known about the learning process. We have shown that these differences must be accommodated and that these precepts must be honored by its teachers if the American public secondary school is to fulfill its obligations. This is epitomized in our eighth principle:

PRINCIPLE 8. | *To promote the general welfare most fully, the public secondary school must make full use of what is known about the learning process.*

Who should control the public secondary school?

In the last analysis, the public high school is like our other great public institutions—everything it does depends finally upon the consent of the lay public. Sometimes this consent is only tacit or indi-

---

[17] Walter S. Monroe, ed., *Encyclopedia of Educational Research*, The Macmillan Co., New York, 1950, pp. 1483-88.

rectly expressed, but it is always there. Public consent is the ultimate sanction of the public school.

Under our form of government, public education is a function of the state. The public schools exist by virtue of laws enacted by state legislators whose members are elected by the people. If these legislators enact laws which displease the public, they will be replaced, in the normal course of political life, by persons who represent the will of the majority.

In nearly all states local boards of education are vested with broad powers to administer the public schools. The members of these boards are elected in most communities and in the rest are appointed by elected officials. Thus, directly or indirectly, the people may replace board members whose official actions displease them. No board of education can stay in office for more than a short time without the consent of the public.

State law usually stipulates that certain subjects be taught in the public high schools, e.g., English, civics, history, and physical education. In some states the law specifies that textbooks must be selected by special agencies for use throughout the state. Usually the law also establishes the qualifications for teacher certification and requires the local boards of education to select school superintendents.[18]

Local boards of education may, of course, do only those things which their state laws permit them to do. But certain additional powers are implied in these laws. Thus, school boards may legally add any subject to the curriculum which is not expressly forbidden by law. They may legally extend the qualifications for teacher certification by setting higher standards for the selection of teachers in their districts.

All of these things may be done legally by the laymen who constitute the boards of education, if they choose, without the benefit of professional advice. If they want to, they may select new teachers, determine promotions, and prescribe the teaching methods to be used in local schools—all without seeking or heeding professional advice. These are the legal prerogatives of the school board, and only the general public, through recourse to the ballot box, can

[18] Many school districts have no superintendent. Rural districts, for instance, may employ only one teacher for an ungraded school. But most larger, unified districts employ a superintendent, although he may be known under another title, e.g., principal, in some areas.

check the board's activities as long as it is behaving lawfully. Even if the board obtains professional advice in matters such as the selection of teachers and textbooks, the organization of the curriculum, etc., it is still responsible to the public.

But the fact that the public has the right to empower lay persons to administer the schools in all these important respects does not make such a procedure feasible or desirable. This is generally recognized in thousands of communities where we find good public schools. In such communities there is a widespread awareness of the proper division of functions between the lay officials and the professionally trained staff. It is recognized that although citizens have the power to resolve virtually every question pertaining to the school program, many decisions which affect that program can be wisely made only by trained and experienced persons.

One of the proper functions of the lay public is to determine, through its board of education, what age groups should be served by the public schools. For example, should there be a nursery school? A kindergarten? A junior college? Other programs of adult education? In seeking the answers to such questions, board members should solicit and study the recommendations of the professionally trained staff, but since the questions involve basic public policy, the decisions should rest with the board alone. In some such cases local law requires a public referendum before the board can act.

A second legitimate function of the lay public, acting through its board of education, is to determine broadly the subjects which shall be taught in the schools in addition to those required by state law. This also is a matter of basic public policy. We have already seen what abilities our young people must develop if humanity is to advance, and what part the school should play in developing them. It is the obligation of the professionally trained staff to make these things known to the board members and to the lay public. But the final decision rests with the public. Ideally, the professionally trained staff will present to the public all the principal considerations relating to the curriculum in such a way that an intelligent and thorough discussion can result. In this way the citizens of a community can be made to realize that their ownership of the school and its undertakings makes them responsible for assuring an educational program which meets the needs of the community and its youths.

In practice, however, policies respecting these matters are made or at least approved by the members of the board of education, who alone are legally empowered to provide funds for the operation of the school program. Actually, as we noted in an earlier paragraph, the final decision will be made by the public at large, for it can be expected to keep the members of the board in office only if it is persuaded that the educational program which the board sanctions has merit. Thus it is wise to encourage laymen to participate in school affairs and familiarize themselves with the reasons behind school policies. Then most will support the kind of a school program which is geared to the educational needs of the community and its youth.

We have suggested that the people of good school communities generally delegate certain functions entirely to the professionally trained staff. The people of such communities are aware that the expert knowledge of the teacher gives weight to his opinions on technical matters; that difficult technical questions are involved in such matters as recruiting and selecting qualified teachers, choosing instructional materials, determining teaching methods, and testing pupil achievement; and that these difficult technical problems should be left to the judgment of the professionally trained personnel.[19] Closely associated with the technical competence of teachers is their right to academic freedom, to teach the truth as they know it within their respective fields of scholarship. The people of good school communities support their teachers in the right to exercise this freedom, for they know that students are not free to learn the truth unless teachers are free to teach it.

In these communities the professional staff feels obligated to secure public consent to what it is doing by telling the public why the technical procedures employed in the school are effective in reaching the objectives which have been determined by the community. The professional staff strives to involve the public in sufficient study and discussion of these technical matters not only to show why the practices of the school promise to yield the desired results, but also to spread a feeling of public ownership of these practices.

In good school communities citizens and teachers alike recognize that a public appraisal of the achievements of the high school is inevitable and desirable. This appraisal should *not* be based on whether

---

[19] By professionally trained personnel we mean school administrators, supervisors, and classroom teachers, together with consultants from the state department of education, from universities, and from the community, i.e., doctors, dentists, public health officials, psychologists, businessmen, craftsmen, farm advisors, home demonstration agents, etc.

or not particular technical procedures are employed in the high school, but on whether or not the graduates of the school are proficient in the abilities which the school is expected to help them acquire. The professional staff of the school should encourage the citizens to make such appraisals and when necessary should help them to do so.

The relationships between the lay public and public school personnel which we have sketched in the preceding paragraphs are ideal. Nowhere have they been yet fully established in actual practice, but the ideal is no less valid for all that. It should guide our behavior; the closer we approach it the better our public schools will be. For these relationships must be established between lay citizens and professional personnel in the public schools if these institutions are to be *public* in the best sense; that is, if questions of public policy are to be resolved capably by the public and if the technical problems of executing public policy are to be handled expertly. Here is the principle which states this important truth:

PRINCIPLE 9. | *To make it a public institution in the best sense, the public secondary school must have its basic educational policies shaped by the lay public with competent professional advice, its technical operation determined and interpreted to the public by competent professional personnel, and its products appraised through joint lay-professional efforts.*

Summary

In the course of this chapter we have presented and discussed nine principles which underlie public secondary education in America. Each of these principles rests firmly upon one or more of the fundamental truths which were set forth in Chapter 3. For easy reference, these principles are restated here.

PRINCIPLE 1. | *The American public secondary school is obligated to promote the general welfare: to assist in teaching youths whatever they need to learn during adolescence in order to carry on those basic social processes on which the strength of the United States and the well-being of each citizen depend.*

PRINCIPLE 2. | *To promote the general welfare most fully, the public secondary school must build on the past but orient itself to the future.*

PRINCIPLE 3. | *If societal strength and individual well-being are best to be ensured, one of the top-level priorities of the public secondary school must be to teach youths to think and to communicate.*

PRINCIPLE 4. | *If societal strength and individual well-being are best to be ensured, one of the top-level priorities of the public secondary school must be to teach youths to understand, appreciate, and live the democratic way of life.*

PRINCIPLE 5. | *If societal strength and individual well-being are best to be ensured, one of the top-level priorities of the public secondary school must be to teach youths the principles of safe and healthful living, help them develop bodily vigor, and provide a safe and healthful physical environment.*

PRINCIPLE 6. | *To perform each of its three top-level priority tasks most effectively, the public secondary school must have youths make a direct study of the problems of making a living, strengthening the family, and providing for physical security, spiritual growth, aesthetics, recreation, and social organization and control.*

PRINCIPLE 7. | *To promote the general welfare most fully, the public secondary school must serve equally well all the educable youths of the community.*

PRINCIPLE 8. | *To promote the general welfare most fully, the public secondary school must make full use of what is known about the learning process.*

PRINCIPLE 9. | *To make it a public institution in the best sense, the public secondary school must have its basic educational policies shaped by the lay public with competent professional advice, its technical operation determined and interpreted to the public by competent professional personnel, and its products appraised through joint lay-professional efforts.*

Principles are guides to action, and the principles which we have enumerated are guides for American teachers in their professional activities. But principles are useful only to those who know how to apply them, how to analyze individual circumstances in which the principles should be made operative. In later chapters, therefore, we shall use these principles, deriving from them implications which should guide secondary school teachers who are confronted by the problems of their vocation.

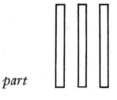

part III

APPLICATION OF PRINCIPLES

TO PROFESSIONAL PROBLEMS

chapter 5

IMPROVING THE HOLDING POWER

OF THE SECONDARY SCHOOL

The National Citizens Commission for the Public Schools once expressed the educational belief characteristic of Americans in these words: "The goal of our public schools should be to make the best in education available to *every* American child on completely equal terms." The Commission has now been succeeded by the National Citizens Council for Better Schools, which, we can safely assume, accepts the same point of view.

This purpose is implicit in what our better public secondary schools everywhere are doing. It has been made explicit in official pronouncements in many school systems, of which that in Saint Paul, Minnesota, is an outstanding example: [1] "The educational practices which the Board of Education seeks to foster proceed upon the assumption that all young people, whatever their capabilities, are educable in some manner and to some extent through high school age, and that it is a public duty to provide that education in such a manner as to do as much as possible for pupils of the most diverse capabilities and interests."

As we noted in Chapter 4, the goal which the Saint Paul Board of Education officially declares "a public duty" is in keeping with the belief that all human beings are of equal moral worth. We have seen why we can live up to this ethic only if we provide equality of educational opportunity and why we must educate all of our

[1] *School Code*, Board of Education, Saint Paul, Minnesota, 1954, p. 1.

79

people if our great experiment in democratic self-government is to succeed. For these reasons, we have seen, one of the basic principles of the American public secondary school is that it should serve equally well all the educable youth of the community. Now let us ask how fully this principle is being honored.

In spite of great gains, accomplishment falls far short of our goal

Only about one youth out of every fourteen attended high school in 1890; today virtually all youths enter the ninth grade and about 80 per cent are found in some one of grades nine through twelve. But although our accomplishment has been great, it is not as great as these figures make it appear to be. Only about three out of every five pupils who enter high school today remain long enough to graduate. Obviously, when less than two thirds of our youths are receiving a complete high school education, we still have a long way to go before we can say that secondary education is universal in our country. If education is ever to be universal, the holding power of the typical high school must be greatly improved.

There are several ways in which our public secondary schools can improve their holding power. In this chapter we shall present the findings of a number of factual studies which show quite clearly, we believe, what these needed improvements are.

The high school is not yet suited to young people with low academic aptitudes

An important group of studies has been made of the population of the typical American high school, and every reported study reveals that this population comprises not *all* children of *all* people, but instead an aristocracy of the more intelligent. Let us take a look at the findings of some of these studies.

The results of the Army Alpha Test, given in World War I, showed that about 65 per cent of the adults tested received the "average" or "less-than-average" ratings of C, C−, D, and D−. One would expect the same figures to be true for the whole population, including high school students. That is to say, if the high school displayed no selectivity on the basis of intelligence, approximately two-thirds of the nation's high school students would have been expected to score average or less-than-average on the Army Alpha Test. In 1922 Cobb [2] found that this was far from the case. He reported that 17.4 per cent of the entering high school pupils and 1.4 per cent of the seniors scored average or less-than-average on the Army Alpha Test. Obviously, Cobb's data show that in 1922 the chances were only about one in five that a youngster of average or less-than-average intelligence, as measured by Army Alpha, would even enter high school, and if he did enter, his chances of graduating were only about one in twelve.

Ten years later, the National Survey of Secondary Education [3] again revealed unmistakable evidence of selection by intelligence. The survey found that the median I.Q.'s of tenth-, eleventh-, and twelfth-grade pupils respectively exceeded the medians of the ninth-, tenth-, and eleventh-grade groups. The investigators who conducted this part of the National Survey said [4] that in their opinion progress toward intellectual democratization was being made. "It is not that intellectual selection is no longer operative," they wrote, "but that it is less operative than formerly."

A few years later, as a part of the New York Regents' Inquiry, an exhaustive study of the pupils who dropped out of high school was conducted. These investigators reported in 1938 that [5] "a marked tendency exists for the less academically able students, as measured by both aptitude test results and school marks, to withdraw at low grade levels. . . . The average [high school] graduate surpasses about 85 percent of withdrawing pupils with respect to academic potentiality, as measured by current intelligence tests. . . . Half of the withdrawing boys, and almost as large a proportion of the withdrawing girls, ranked in the lowest quarter of their respective classes. . . . The same type of boys and girls tend to drop out everywhere, leading to the obvious conclusion that persistence in school and success at academic tasks are intimately related." They also found [6] that the secondary school is progressively more selec-

[2] M. V. Cobb, "The Limits Set to Educational Achievement by Limited Intelligence," *Journal of Educational Psychology*, Vol. 13, Nov. and Dec., 1922, pp. 449-64, 546-55.

[3] G. N. Kefauver, V. H. Noll, and E. C. Drake, *The Secondary School Population*, U.S. Government Printing Office, Washington, 1933, p. 33.

[4] *Ibid.*, p. 26.

[5] R. E. Eckert and T. O. Marshall, *When Youth Leave School*, McGraw-Hill Book Co., New York, 1938, pp. 50, 51, 59, 60.

[6] *Ibid.*, p. 52.

tive in terms of I.Q. as one proceeds from the lower to the higher grades. The median percentiles on the Otis test attained by tenth, eleventh, and twelfth grade pupils were in each instance significantly greater than those attained by students on the next lower grade levels.

A 1941 study [7] based on the populations of twelve high schools in Maryland found that the chances of completing high school were three to one in favor of the pupil of high (110 or above) as compared with the pupil of low (90 or below) I.Q.

Charles M. Allen,[8] in a study of all pupils who withdrew from a sample of twenty-two four-year high schools in Illinois between the fall of 1943 and the spring of 1947, found that the school marks of 78 per cent of these boys and girls would presumably have placed them in the bottom one-fourth of their respective graduating classes if they had completed the full four-year program. In other words, the youngsters of low academic aptitude were the ones who dropped out of these schools.

In a National Child Labor Committee study [9] of the students who dropped out of high schools in various towns and cities of Indiana, Michigan, and Ohio in 1944-45 or 1945-46 similar evidence was uncovered. Only 9 per cent of the students who quit school while in the seventh grade had I.Q.'s of 95 or higher. The corresponding percentages for the eighth, ninth, tenth, eleventh, and twelfth grades were 16, 25, 46, 57, and 60. The median I.Q.'s of the seventh and eighth grade drop-outs were below 85, those for the ninth and tenth grades fell between 85 and 94, and those for the two uppermost grades were between 95 and 104.

Very similar findings were yielded by an investigation, sponsored by the Kentucky Association of Colleges, Secondary, and Elementary Schools,[10] of the students who dropped out of secondary school during the year 1948-50 in a stratified random sample of all

[7] Survey Committee, College of Education, University of Maryland, *A Program of Reorganization for the Public Secondary Schools of Prince George's County, Maryland*, University of Maryland, 1941, Ch. 2.

[8] Harold C. Hand, *Principal Findings of the 1947-48 Basic Studies of the Illinois Secondary School Curriculum Program*. Office of the Superintendent of Public Instruction, Springfield, Ill., 1949, p. 14.

[9] Harold J. Dillon, *Early School Leavers—A Major Educational Problem*, National Child Labor Committee, New York, 1949, p. 34.

[10] Stanley E. Hecker, *Early School Leavers in Kentucky*, Bulletin of the Bureau of School Service, College of Education, University of Kentucky, Lexington, 1953, p. 38.

types and sizes of junior and senior high schools in Kentucky. Fewer than 6 per cent of the boys and girls who dropped out while in the seventh grade had I.Q.'s of 95 or higher; in the eighth, ninth, tenth, eleventh, and twelfth grades, the corresponding percentages were 19, 19, 46, 51, and 69. The median I.Q. of the students who dropped out during the seventh grade was below 85, of those who left during the next three grades in the 85-94 range, and of those who quit school while in grades eleven and twelve between 95 and 104.

From 1950 to 1954 all ninth-grade pupils, about 2750 in all, who entered the public secondary schools of Saint Paul, Minnesota, were individually studied in order to discover the respects in which those who dropped out of high school before graduation differed from those who completed the twelfth grade. In every secondary school in the city, it was found that the median I.Q. of the early school leavers was appreciably lower than that of the graduating group. For the city as a whole, the median I.Q. of all dropouts was 94; of all graduates, 103.[11]

The available evidence, then, overwhelmingly indicates that Eckert and Marshall characterized the generality of secondary schools in this country when, in commenting upon the findings of the New York Regents' Inquiry, they said:[12] "On the average, the less competent a pupil has shown himself to be in meeting school tasks, the more quickly he is released to face adult problems. Those who will be least able to acquire socially useful habits, information, and points of view without formal instruction are those to whom the school has given least attention." In a society which, like ours, is committed to the proposition that all human beings are of equal moral worth and which, in consequence, is dedicated to the ideal of equality of educational opportunity, such a failure of the schools is clearly intolerable. It is intolerable in a practical as well as a moral sense. All citizens are taxed to support public education because public education is aimed toward making the community a better place in which to live. If it does not do so, there can be no justification for levying general taxes to support the schools. Obviously, the greatest societal good can never be achieved so long as our public

[11] Samuel H. Popper, ed., *Today's Challenge: Tomorrow's Citizen*, Office of Secondary and Vocational Education, Saint Paul Public Schools, Minnesota, 1957, pp. 24, 27.
[12] Eckert and Marshall, *When Youth Leave School*, pp. 67-68.

high schools continue to provide their least effective services to the group of boys and girls which most needs competent instruction. Too many of these students drop out of our educational system and grow into adulthood unprepared for the roles they must play in civic affairs, in occupational endeavors, in family life, in recreational programs, and so on. They are, in other words, living evidence that we need to improve our program of public education if we are to improve our society.

The high school is not yet suited to young people of low socioeconomic status

Numerous studies reveal that a student's socioeconomic status is an important factor in predicting whether or not he will finish his high school education.

In an investigation reported in 1922 in Bridgeport, Connecticut, Mount Vernon, New York, St. Louis, Missouri, and Seattle, Washington, George S. Counts [13] studied the socioeconomic status of the high-school population. If a student's socioeconomic status—which depends wholly upon his parents' status, of course—were not a factor in determining how long he remains in our educational system, Counts would have found that the number of students from each socioeconomic level was roughly proportionate to the number of citizens from each corresponding socioeconomic level. We say "roughly proportionate" because families of low socioeconomic status tend to have more children than families with a larger share of social and material benefits. Hence in a democratically constituted student body one would expect to find a somewhat larger relative number of children from poor families than from families of average or more-than-average wealth.

But this is not at all what Counts found. He found that the ratio of the relative number of pupils from the topmost socioeconomic bracket to that from the lowest was not one to one, but twenty-four to one. In other words, a boy or girl from a well-to-do family was twenty-four times as likely to attend high school as a boy or girl from a poor family. Counts also studied the question of continuance through high school. He found that the pupils from well-to-do

[13] George S. Counts, *The Selective Character of American Secondary Education*, University of Chicago Press, Chicago, 1922.

families were five times as likely to finish high school, once having entered, as pupils from poor families.

Ten years later this investigation was repeated in two of the four cities studied by Counts; no marked progress toward socioeconomic democratization was found.[14]

Two or three years before this repetition of the Counts study, E. G. Palmer conducted an investigation in Oakland, California,[15] based on two groups of students: Group A, about 250 in number, had continued in school beyond the age limit of compulsory school attendance; Group B, of a comparable size, had quit school as soon as it had become legally permissible for them to do so. She found that the pupils in Group A came predominantly from homes in the upper-income brackets and that those in Group B, with a few exceptions, came from homes low on the income scale.

In general, the findings of these early studies have been corroborated by all the more recent investigations of the socioeconomic composition of our high school population. In 1938 H. M. Bell [16] found that children from families in the highest socioeconomic level were eleven times as likely to enter high school as were children from families at the other end of the scale. He also found that eight out of every ten pupils from the top-income group graduated from high school, whereas only one out of every ten from the economically underprivileged families graduated. Once in high school, in other words, children from poor families were only one-eighth as likely to continue on to graduation as children from well-to-do families. Bell wrote, with understandable astringency, "The strongest single factor in determining how far a youth goes in school is the occupation of his father."

The findings of the New York Regents' Inquiry are in substantial agreement with those reported by Bell. In 1938 Eckert and Marshall [17] found that almost two out of every three pupils who had dropped out of school below the ninth-grade level were from families rated as poor or on relief. Of the high school pupils studied, the group that withdrew from school contained twice as many boys and girls

[14] Kefauver, Noll, and Drake, *The Secondary School Population*, p. 63.

[15] E. G. Palmer, *Pupils Who Leave School*, University of California, Berkeley, 1930.

[16] H. M. Bell, *Youth Tell Their Story*, American Council on Education, Washington, 1938, p. 63.

[17] Eckert and Marshall, *When Youth Leave School*, p. 72.

from poor or indigent families as did the group that continued to graduation.

In the 1938-1940 North Carolina Youth Survey, Lovejoy [18] found that a similar situation prevailed in the high schools of that state. His findings are in close agreement with those cited in the preceding paragraphs.

One can draw the same conclusion from the findings of a 1941 survey [19] of twelve Maryland (white) high schools. It was found that the chances of continuing on to graduation were more than twice (2.3 to 1 times) as good for ninth-grade pupils from families in the highest third of the socioeconomic scale as for those pupils whose families fell in the bottom third.

The findings of the 1943-47 study [20] based on twenty-two four-year high schools in Illinois similarly attest the privileged educational status of the upper socioeconomic groups in that state. Allen found that it was overwhelmingly the children from the low-income families who had withdrawn from these Illinois high schools. Of the total number who withdrew before graduation, 72 per cent were from families relatively low on the socioeconomic scale.

Although the data with which he worked were incomplete, Dillon reported that [21] "it is perhaps safe to say that semi-skilled work predominated" among the parents of the children who withdrew from the high schools in Indiana, Michigan, and Ohio which he studied in 1944-46. Presumably, this places most of the families of these children in the lowest third of the socioeconomic scale.

Finally, although his findings were inconclusive because of the inadequate data upon which they were based, Hecker [22] also concluded that the pupils who dropped out of high school in Kentucky in 1948-50 were predominantly from families in either the bottom half or the bottom third of the socioeconomic distribution.

The findings of all these studies which bear upon the socioeconomic composition of the student body in the typical American public secondary school give ample evidence of a vicious cycle to

[18] G. W. Lovejoy, *Paths to Maturity*, University of North Carolina, Chapel Hill, 1940, pp. 56-61.

[19] Survey Committee, College of Education, University of Maryland, *A Program of Reorganization*, Ch. 2.

[20] Hand, *Principal Findings of 1947-48 Basic Studies*, p. 15.

[21] Dillon, *Early School Leavers*, p. 21.

[22] Hecker, *Early School Leavers in Kentucky*, p. 30.

which Bell [23] has called attention. He has pointed out (1) that the socioeconomic status of the family determines how far up the educational ladder its children will go, (2) that the grade in school attained by the individual child determines in no small part the type of work he will pursue as an adult, (3) that the type of work he does will determine the socioeconomic status of the family he establishes, and (4) that this in turn will determine how far his own children will progress in school, the kinds of jobs they will secure, the socioeconomic status of the families they will establish, the length of time their children will remain in school, and so on.

Moreover, Newton Edwards [24] has pointed out that the denial of equal educational opportunity which is characteristic of much of our present educational practice results in consequences which are subversive of our democratic ideals. He warns that our schools, which ought to be our chief models of democracy, are in fact working inexorably, albeit unconsciously, toward more rigid social stratifications in our society, toward greater economic, social, and cultural inequalities, and toward a serious widening of class distinctions.

In summarizing their findings, Eckert and Marshall [25] expressed the same disquieting judgment: "On the average, the poorer a student is, the sooner he will leave school. Those who most desperately need what the school might offer because of their circumscribed home backgrounds and their limited ability to learn directly from experience are the least likely to receive it. . . . Within the schools of our democracy, an aristocracy, not alone of aptitude, but also of economic privilege, still exists to perpetuate class barriers."

At the same time, the truth of these observations about students with low aptitudes or of low socioeconomic status should not blind us to the fact that, in spite of these flaws in our educational system, the holding power of the American public school has greatly increased over the past quarter of a century. In 1920 only 31 per cent of those who entered the ninth grade remained in high school long enough to graduate. In 1930 the corresponding percentage had risen to 41, while in 1952 three out of every five (60 per cent) of the

[23] Bell, *Youth Tell Their Story*, p. 93.
[24] Newton Edwards, *Equal Educational Opportunity for Youth*, American Council on Education, Washington, 1939, pp. 151-52.
[25] Eckert and Marshall, *When Youth Leave School*, pp. 78, 85.

entering pupils graduated from high school.[26] These figures demonstrate that, within the complex of the social forces which impinge upon it, the public high school essentially doubled its holding power between 1920 and 1952.

Laudable as our progress in this respect has been, it has not been good enough. One of our basic principles stipulates not that only three out of five of our young people be graduated from high school, but that *all* our youth be equally well served by our system of public education. (Of course, parents may send their children to private high schools if they wish to do so—some desire a school which will provide sectarian religious training—but it should never be necessary for parents to resort to private education because their children cannot share equally in the normal processes of public education.) Why, we must ask, do young people of low academic aptitude and those from low-income families drop out of high school in proportions so far in excess of their relative number in the whole student population?

Why a disproportionate number of the youths of low academic aptitude leave high school

In Chapter 4 we noted the extremely difficult task which confronts the modern high school, and we quoted the authors of the Harvard Report, who spoke of this task in these words: "It is, in essence, the incomparably difficult task of meeting, in ways which they severally respect and will respond to, masses of students of every conceivable shade of intelligence, background, means, interest, and expectation." And in support of this observation we noted also that the mental ages of the students entering a typical high school today range from that ordinarily found in the first grade to that expected of a college freshman, and we saw that their scores on standardized tests of academic achievement ranged from the third grade to the college sophomore levels.

This does not mean that entering students of every high school differ so greatly, but the differences in mental equipment among the students of any entering class in a public high school will be great

[26] Office of Education, U.S. Department of Health, Education, and Welfare, *Statistics of Public Secondary Day Schools 1951-52*, U.S. Government Printing Office, Washington, 1954, p. 7.

enough to cause many educational maladjustments unless the school's program is organized to prevent them. And similar differences can be expected in most of the many other educationally significant characteristics of high school youth. Furthermore, these differences will increase, as the distance between a slow and a fast horse will increase during the length of a race, the longer the students continue in school.

It is principally because the typical high school has made only some of the necessary adjustments in its program that such grossly disproportionate numbers of pupils whose academic aptitude is low leave school before graduation. Too commonly such pupils are offered only the kind of school subjects which have little meaning for them. Too often they are held to standards which they are incapable of achieving; thus the law which requires them to attend school forces them to confront impossible standards. As a result they are branded as failures, and their frustration in the face of this manifest injustice often leads them to drop out of school as soon as the law will allow them to do so—or sooner if they can contrive it.

These observations have been substantiated with almost monotonous uniformity by the various studies [27] which have been made of early school leavers. These investigations have shown that the majority of these young people leave school during or at the conclusion of the school term in which they attain the legal school-leaving age. This seems to prove that most of these students would have preferred to leave school earlier; i.e., that what schooling they did receive was against their will. Girls are generally believed to be more tractable than boys, and it has been found that in fact boys are more apt to drop out of high school than girls are. And all of the investigators who have looked into the matter have reported that low or failing grades had characterized the academic standings of most youths who quit school before their graduation.

The reasons which many early school leavers themselves give for dropping out of high school also show that they had experienced

[27] Eckert and Marshall, *When Youth Leave School*, pp. 39-44, 89, 178-79.
Hand, *Principal Findings of the 1947-48 Basic Studies*, pp. 13, 14.
Hecker, *Early School Leavers in Kentucky*, pp. 32, 35, 36, 39-43.
Dillon, *Early School Leavers*, pp. 23, 26, 27, 35, 43.
Leonard P. Ayers, *Laggards in Our Schools*, Charities Publishing Company, New York, 1909, pp. 12-13.
E. L. Thorndike, *Elimination of Pupils from School*, U.S. Government Printing Office, Washington, 1907, p. 9.

the repeated frustration of low, even failing, marks or that their high schools had not offered work which they believed to be valuable to them. Dillon [28] found, among the early school leavers whom he interviewed, that of the approximately 1000 who were willing to tell why they had quit high school about 70 per cent gave as their primary reason an answer which reflected these dissatisfactions. Among these reasons were "not interested in school work," "could not learn and was discouraged," "was failing and didn't want to repeat a grade," and "disliked a certain subject." Of the approximately 3000 reasons given, these four accounted for somewhat over a third and constituted by far the largest category.

In Hecker's study [29] of various Kentucky high schools, interviews were held with about 1400 early school leavers. All told, the interviewees responded with about 3550 reasons, but as in the Dillon study, one or another of the four reasons noted in the last paragraph accounted for slightly more than a third of all the reasons given. And again the category of "dissatisfaction with school" constituted the largest single block of reasons.

Of the reasons given for dropping out of high school in the Saint Paul study, over 40 per cent reflected some kind of dissatisfaction with school.[30]

A study of 440 early school leavers was conducted in Louisville, Kentucky, under the auspices of the United States Department of Labor.[31] These young people were interviewed and asked their reasons for dropping out of school. In this case almost half the reasons given had to do with dissatisfaction with school. No other category included more than a fourth of the reasons given. When they were asked why they were dissatisfied with school, the interviewees said most frequently that they were discouraged by failing school marks, dissatisfied with the courses offered in school, disconcerted by unsympathetic teachers or ineffectual teaching methods, or that they just disliked school in general. Much improvement is needed in a school if students such as these are to benefit from a high school education.

[28] Dillon, *Early School Leavers*, p. 54.
[29] Hecker, *Early School Leavers in Kentucky*, p. 51.
[30] Popper, *Today's Challenge*, p. 20.
[31] E. S. Johnson and C. E. Legg, "Why Young People Leave School," *Bulletin of the National Association of Secondary School Principals*, Vol. 32, No. 157, Nov. 1948, pp. 15-18.

Why a disproportionate number
of the youths of low socioeconomic status
leave high school

Why are students of low socioeconomic status so likely to drop out? Five hypotheses will be examined in this section. The first is that the financial costs incidental to high school attendance may be greater than many lower income families can afford. The second is that many youths from such families find themselves excluded from the extra-class activities of the school, and consequently do not feel that they belong. Third, many of these youths come from homes and neighborhoods in which education beyond the rudimentary level is not highly valued, often from parents who encourage them to drop out of school as soon as possible. Fourth, most high school teachers lack an adequate understanding of these young people. And fifth, many of these boys and girls drop out of school because they want or need to earn money in a full-time job as early in life as they can.

Children of lower income families
simply cannot meet the costs incidental to high school attendance

This hypothesis has been tested in several studies, and we shall review the principal ones here. The first of these studies of which we have any record was conducted by the author of this book during the years 1931-1937. Nine high schools, variously located in California, Connecticut, Massachusetts, Michigan, New York, and Ohio, were involved in the investigation. These schools varied in type and size from village schools of 125 pupils to large city schools with enrollments of over 2,000. In the smaller schools every pupil was included in the study, and in the larger schools random samplings—never less than one out of every six pupils—formed the basis of the investigation. Each student included in the study was asked to keep an accurate daily account of all the money he spent in connection with high school attendance, *excluding* costs of food, clothing, shelter, and transportation. These accounts were submitted each week. In the six schools located east of the Mississippi the study ran for an entire year; in one California school data were collected for the first semester only; and in the other California schools the study was carried on for a single eight-week period midway through the first semester.

In 1931, before the data of this study had been collected, a group of about 150 high school principals scattered through nearly all of the forty-eight states were asked to estimate what a typical student at their respective institutions spent during a year to defray the costs of attending school; costs for food, clothing, shelter, and transportation were excluded. The estimates given by the principals ranged from $3.50 to $15.00. The average estimate was about $7.50. We shall see later how far from accurate these estimates were.

High school costs are "reasonable," "heavy," or "prohibitive" only in relation to the purse of the family which must pay them. Hence it becomes necessary to note briefly the state of the American family purse in the mid-1930's if the findings of our school survey made in 1931-37 are to be interpreted correctly. Kreps,[32] a noted economist, has analyzed the national family income during these years as follows. About 26 per cent of all American families received total incomes of $750 per year or under, with an average of $470. Kreps called these people "the starvation fighters." An additional 37 per cent of American families during these years received annual incomes ranging from $750 to $1,500. These families were described as "continually fighting poverty." Thus we see that for more than three-fifths of the families in America during these hard Depression years any cash cost whatever for attendance at school was either prohibitive or extremely burdensome.

It is against this background of inadequate family income that we now report the findings of our pioneer cost study in American high schools. In the six high schools east of the Mississippi the average yearly expenditure per pupil was—not $7.50 as the high school principals had supposed—but $125. The median was $115. For freshmen, sophomores, juniors, and seniors, respectively, the averages were $95, $117, $135, and $154. *No pupil reported an annual expenditure of less than $25.*

In the California city in which the study ran only eight weeks two schools were included, a senior and a junior high school. In the senior high school the average eight-week expenditures were $52 for boys, $51 for girls. Let us calculate an approximate average expenditure for the full school year by multiplying these figures by 4.5; we arrive at an estimate of about $230. The comparable averages for

[32] Theodore Kreps in Stanford Education Conference, *Social Education,* The Macmillan Co., New York, 1939, p. 127.

junior high school boys and girls were $30 and $32, which would yield an estimate of about $140 for the entire school year.

In the other California community, in which the study extended over the first semester only, the results ran from a low of $5 to a high of $226 for the one-semester expenditures of high school students. The median was $41. If one doubles these findings to secure an estimate for the year, the results are a high of $452, a Q_3 of $134, a median of $82, a Q_1 of $52, and a low of $10.

In this community the study was extended by classifying each pupil's family according to the Alba Edwards socioeconomic scale. It was found that the average estimated annual expenditures (observed data for one semester multiplied by two) in the different classifications were: professional, $154; proprietor, $130; clerical, $124; skilled, $112; semi-skilled, $52; and unskilled, $54.

When one looks at these figures in conjunction with the drop-out figures given earlier in this chapter, two things become apparent. One is that many of the parents in the low income families simply cannot find the money to keep their children in high school, and the drain on the family budget becomes increasingly acute as the children progress from the ninth to the twelfth grade. Second, many boys and girls from poor families don't want to stay in high school when it means that their poverty, i.e., the poverty of their parents, will prevent them from maintaining themselves on a social level with their fellow students. In other words, young people want to keep up with the Joneses as much as older people do, and in school this means continuing expenditures for a multitude of goods and services which are important to the adolescent sensibility—admission fees for athletic contests, parties, dances, dramatic performances; dues for student body, class, or club memberships; fees or special assessments for homemaking, mechanical drawing, woodworking, laboratory science and other courses; charges for gym clothes, lockers, towels, domestic science uniforms, band and orchestra instruments and uniforms, athletic equipment, rooter's caps, class sweaters, rings, keys, pins; expenditures for various tag and ribbon drives, ROTC medals, school excursions, textbooks, workbooks, pens, pencils, paper, ink; subscriptions to the school yearbook, newspaper, magazine, handbook; costs of photographs for the school yearbook and for graduation, graduation announcements, diploma fees, commencement caps and gowns, and so on.

The fact is that our supposedly free public high schools are loaded with "hidden" tuition charges. In Illinois, for instance, the problem has been recognized. The Illinois Curriculum Program has prepared a manual [33] which enables local high schools to discover how big these hidden tuition charges actually are in each of a number of categories. The manual contains directions and materials which were originally prepared by Curtis M. Howd and were used in a study which he conducted in about eighty Illinois high schools in the school year 1947-48. Howd's study disclosed a considerable variation among the yearly costs per pupil for the different subjects offered in Illinois schools. Table 1 shows how these costs ranged when tabulated according to the textbook-procurement method followed by the school.[34]

Two important conclusions can be drawn from the data tabulated here. One is that the per-pupil costs are generally much lower in the schools in which textbooks are free or rented, though they are not low enough to eliminate a burden on students from poor families. The second is that the hidden yearly tuition costs are higher for some subjects than for others. The most expensive are the practical arts and vocational and business education courses—precisely the subjects which youngsters from low-income families particularly need, since most of them, because they cannot afford to go to college, will enter the labor market with only the vocational training which they have acquired in high school. The college preparatory subjects— foreign languages, mathematics, sciences, and social studies—cost less, even though they attract students whose families can better afford to pay the charges.

Similarly, the cost of participating in extra-class activities varied a great deal.[35] Class dues ran from $1.00 to $5.00 a year. A few schools imposed a general student body fee which ran as high as $16.70 annually. Class pins and rings ranged from $3.50 to $24.00. Subscriptions to the school yearbook ran from $1.00 to $3.50, and to the school paper from $.20 to $2.00. To attend the school parties, dances, and picnics or banquets which were held during the school year would cost as much as $5.10, $17.00, and $12.00, respectively. In a

[33] Harold C. Hand, *How to Conduct the Hidden Tuition Costs Study,* Office of Superintendent of Public Instruction, Springfield, 1949.
[34] Harold C. Hand, "Hidden Tuition Charges in High School Subjects," *Educational Forum,* Vol. 13, No. 4, May 1949, pp. 441-48.
[35] Harold C. Hand, "Hidden Tuition Charges in Extra-Class Activities," *Educational Forum,* Vol. 14, No. 1, November 1949, pp. 95-103.

TABLE 1   *Hidden tuition charges in high school subjects*

	Textbook Practice			
SUBJECT	PURCHASED BY PUPILS	RENTED TO PUPILS	SUPPLIED FREE	NO TEXT-BOOK USED
Art	x	x	x	$0.00–14.80
Business education	$0.90–26.35	$0.25–16.00	$0.00– 4.30	x
English	1.00–24.00	.40– 7.75	.00– 3.00	x
Foreign language	1.10–10.15	.20– 3.80	.00– 4.35	x
Mathematics	1.00– 6.75	.25– 3.05	.00– 2.40	x
Music	x	x	x	.00–15.75
Physical education—boys	x	x	x	.00–16.80
Physical education—girls	x	x	x	.00–14.55
Practical arts—boys	1.25–39.50	.30–22.95	.00–26.00	x
Practical arts—girls	.75–35.15	.25–41.80	.00–38.30	x
Science	.85–10.25	.30– 9.80	.00– 7.00	x
Social studies	1.40–10.05	.25– 6.35	.00– 2.30	x
Vocational subjects	1.00–39.50	.30–34.50	.00–21.90	x

few schools, however, these social affairs could be attended for a total of less than $1.00 a year.

Admission to athletic contests, dramatic performances, and concerts either was free or cost less than $.50 a year in a few schools. In others these annual costs ranged from $2.00 to over $7.00 for each separate group of activities—a considerable sum in all.

In a few scattered schools, pupils were not required to pay anything to take part in dramatic activities, play in the school band or orchestra, sing in the chorus, or serve on the staff of the school paper or yearbook. In other schools these costs were very high—as much as $12.50 per year for dramatics, $265.00 to play in the band, $165.00 to play in the orchestra, $6.00 to sing in the chorus, and nearly $5.00 to take part in the publication of the school newspaper or yearbook.

Similarly, in a few schools it cost nothing to take part in intramural or in interscholastic sports programs. In a quarter of the schools, however, pupils had to spend from $4.00 to as much as $100.00 each year for each sport in which they participated. Intramural sports cost as much as $17.65 for boys and $45.00 for girls per year.

The cost of belonging to high school clubs almost defied analysis. To belong to Future Distributors, for instance, might cost a pupil as little as $1.50 or as much as $33.80 per year. It cost nothing to belong to a Movie Operators Club in three-fourths of the schools, and no more than fifteen cents in any. For twenty of the thirty-six clubs which were studied, the median costs ran from $1.00 to $19.30. For half of the remainder, the median costs were between $.50 and $.90 per year.

The cost of graduation was found to be relatively high in most schools. Announcements cost from $1.00 to $8.00. Graduation pictures were not free anywhere and cost as much as $20.00. Caps and gowns were supplied free in less than one-fourth of the schools; in half the schools the rental charge was beween $1.75 and $2.25. Name cards cost from $.50 to $2.00. Other costs incidental to graduation (flowers, memory books, graduation fees) varied from $.25 to as much as $10.00.

Moreover, there were a good many miscellaneous costs—locker fees, towel fees, yearbook photographs, insurance, charity drives and other solicitations, school sweaters, briefcases, notebooks, pencils, pens, gifts for teachers, and so on. In the median school these additional costs totaled about $25.00 per year.

How burdensome all these costs may be on the family purse, and hence how they may presumably affect the holding power of the high school, was made clear in a 1949-50 study in Wisconsin.[36] This investigation was conducted in a carefully chosen cross-sectional sample of all the high schools in that state. The income of the family of each of the pupils involved in the study was determined by consulting the state income tax returns on file in the office of the Wisconsin Department of Taxation. These families were then grouped on the basis of the occupations of their chief breadwinners, and the median annual net income for each group was computed. The families classified under the heading of Business Owners and Managers headed the list; they had a median net income of slightly over $4000; the average expenditure of the pupils from these families was a little over $150 for the school year 1949-1950. The families classified under the category of Domestic Workers stood (except for the Unemployed and Pensioners' group) at the bottom of the list; their median net income was below $1600 and the average expenditure of their children was about $115. The figure of $1600 is well below the amount needed to support a family at the level of minimum comfort and decency, so to spend a single dollar for school expenses means meat off the table. Obviously, genuine self-sacrifice was required of such families if their children were to obtain a complete high school education. Add to all this the fact that there are usually more children in the lower- than in the upper-income families and it is obvious that heroic efforts are often required to find the funds to enable many youths to attend the supposedly free public secondary school.[37] It is no wonder that such a large number of young people from low-income families drop out of school.

A poll conducted recently among secondary school students in four cities in Illinois, Michigan, and Missouri [38] has shown that the students themselves are aware of the high costs of attending high

[36] Russell T. Gregg and Raymond E. Schultz, *Personal Expenditures for High-School Education*, School of Education, University of Wisconsin, 1951, pp. 20-21.

[37] Raymond E. Schultz, "Can Parents Afford to Send Their Children to High School?" *School Review*, Vol. 60, Oct. 1952, pp. 285-91.

[38] Data on file in office of Harold C. Hand, College of Education, University of Illinois.

school and that in many cases they find these costs truly burdensome. The responses given by the students to two questions asked them by the investigators are tabulated in Table 2.

TABLE **2**   **Student evaluations of the costs of attending high school**

QUESTION: *How do you feel about the amount of money you need to take part fully in school life?*

REPLY	CITY A	CITY B	CITY C	CITY D
Altogether or far too much	65%	52%	49%	37%
About right	26	39	40	53
No opinion or no reply	9	9	11	10

QUESTION: *Does the amount of money required make it too hard for students who don't have much money to spend to take part as much as they should in what goes on at school?*

REPLY	CITY A	CITY B	CITY C	CITY D
Yes	65%	63%	53%	52%
Uncertain	21	20	26	29
No	13	16	20	17
No opinion or no reply	1	1	1	2

As these tabulations show, from about two-fifths to two-thirds of the students agreed that the amount of money required of them was too much, and from about half to two-thirds were of the opinion that the high costs of attendance in high school made it too difficult for students with lean pocketbooks to take part as fully as they should in the activities of the school.

The findings reported by Dillon [39] and Hecker [40] corroborate the belief that a considerable number of early school leavers are motivated by financial anxieties. Of the nearly 1000 young people who were willing to tell Dillon why they had quit high school, about one-fifth (21 per cent) gave first importance to financial considerations. In the study by Hecker exactly 20 per cent of the interviewees mentioned financial problems first.

Dillon's and Hecker's studies were made between 1944 and 1950, relatively prosperous years throughout America—unemployment figures were low and family incomes were higher than they had ever been before. But even during these prosperous times, as we have seen, one out of every five school leavers said that he had dropped out of high school primarily for economic reasons. It seems reasonable to expect that the percentage of school leavers motivated by economic considerations would be even greater during years of general economic hardship.

Many children from low-income families
are excluded from participation in extra-class activities

This hypothesis, related to the one we have just discussed, has been the subject of several studies. In the school year 1936-1937 Wright [41] investigated the extent to which participation in extra-class activities was associated with socioeconomic status in an Oregon high school of about 1500 pupils. He first classified the family of each pupil according to the Alba Edwards socioeconomic scale and computed the percentage of the student body which fell into each of the six classifications. These he called his "basic percentages." Then he recorded the "participation story" of each pupil for the year. The study was based on the assumption that, if no welfare factor were operating, the proportion of students from each of the six classifications who "belonged to," "took part in," or "went to" the various extra-class activities of the school could be expected to approximate the "basic percentage" for that particular socioeconomic group in the total high school population.

[39] Dillon, *Early School Leavers*, p. 50.
[40] Hecker, *Early School Leavers in Kentucky*, p. 47.
[41] David Wright, *Participation in Extra-Class Activities According to Economic Status*, unpublished master's thesis, Stanford University, California, 1937.

The study included all the various student organizations and activities of the school. The socioeconomic levels of the families represented on the membership lists of such organizations as the following were recorded: athletic teams, clubs, literary societies, music organizations (band, orchestra, glee club, etc.), Hi-Y and Tri-Y, school publications, student governing body, and traffic and safety squads. Similarly, a record was made of the welfare level of all pupils who attended school parties and dances, went to football, basketball, and other athletic games or events, purchased student body or activity cards, ran for student body offices, served on the staff of school publications, staged dramatic productions, and so on.

All told, forty-one activities were used for comparisons with the basic percentages. In thirty-two of the forty-one activities the participation of students from the lowest socioeconomic level ranged from 20 to 100 per cent below expectation. In seven activities Wright found that these less privileged students were completely frozen out; in eighteen others their participation was 60 per cent below the reasonable expectation. In only six activities, or about one out of every seven, were they represented in proportions equal to their relative number in the total student body. Over all the activities studied this bottom group on the scale averaged 40 per cent less representation or participation than their basic percentage would lead one to expect. The two highest socioeconomic groups, on the other hand, had about 35 per cent more representation or participation than would have been the case if all socioeconomic groups had been proportionately represented in the extra-class activities of the school.

Wright's study was repeated two years later [42] in a large California high school. The findings of this second study were even more disappointing than those of the first.

Another important study of participation in extra-class activities was conducted in 1946-1947 by Graham Pogue [43] under the auspices of the Illinois Curriculum Program. Thirteen high schools chosen to represent down-state Illinois were included in this investigation. Pogue asked each of the students of these schools to tell how much

---

[42] Elizabeth J. McElroy, *Participation in Extra-Curricular Activities as a Welfare Level Phenomenon*, unpublished master's thesis, Stanford University, California, 1939.

[43] Harold C. Hand, *Principal Findings of the 1947-48 Basic Studies of the Illinois Secondary School Curriculum Program*, Office of the Superintendent of Public Instruction, Springfield, Illinois, 1949, pp. 23-27.

he valued the extra-class activities offered and to fill out an inventory which recorded his extra-class activities during the school year. Additional data were secured on the sex, age, grade in school, location of home, acceleration-retardation, and socioeconomic status of each student.

To reveal how much their extra-class activities meant to them, the pupils were asked to assign relative "satisfaction ratings" to commercial activities (public dances, motion pictures, etc.), extra-class activities in school, home activities (parties and games at home, etc.), noncommercial activities (Scouts, YMCA, church events, city recreation department affairs, etc.), school subjects, and unplanned activities (e.g., the activities which arise when one starts out with a friend to look for something interesting to do). Extra-class activities were ranked second only to commercial activities in this appraisal. These high school students greatly valued the extra-class activities in their schools, and there is no reason to think that most high school students everywhere do not feel the same way.

Pogue was interested in discovering precisely who, in terms of age, sex, grade in school, location of home, acceleration-retardation, and socioeconomic status, was taking part in extra-class activities—or, more accurately, to what extent participation in extra-class activities was associated with these factors. The interesting result of Pogue's study was that nothing was found to have any noticeable bearing on participation in extra-class activities *except* the socioeconomic status of the student's family. When this factor was held constant, all the others were seen to be chance variables.

But what a difference the socioeconomic status made! Pogue divided all the pupils into upper, middle, and lower thirds on the basis of socioeconomic status. Then he divided the median number of extra-class activities reported by students in the upper third of the scale by the corresponding number for the students from the lower third of the scale. Obviously, if socioeconomic status had had no bearing upon participation in extra-class activities Pogue would have found a one-to-one ratio between them. But as we have already indicated, his findings were far different.

Let us review them in some detail. He divided all the extra-class activities into one or another of three categories: primary group, secondary group, and leadership participations. Under "primary group participations" he included all activities in which the student was a continuing member of a group; examples are membership on any of the school's athletic teams, playing in the school band, serving on the staff of the school paper, belonging to the camera club, taking part in a dramatic performance, putting on a dance, etc. "Secondary group participations" referred to short-term activities in

TABLE 3

Pogue study of student participation in extra-class activities *

PRIMARY GROUP PARTICIPATIONS		SECONDARY GROUP PARTICIPATIONS		LEADERSHIP PARTICIPATIONS	
1.1 to 1	A	1.1 to 1	C	1.4 to 1	H
1.7 to 1	B	1.2 to 1	A	1.7 to 1	A
2.2 to 1	C	1.2 to 1	D	1.7 to 1	L
2.2 to 1	D	1.4 to 1	H	1.7 to 1	B
2.4 to 1	E	1.5 to 1	I	1.8 to 1	C
2.9 to 1	F	1.6 to 1	B	1.8 to 1	F
2.9 to 1	G	1.7 to 1	E	1.9 to 1	D
3.0 to 1	H	1.7 to 1	F	2.1 to 1	E
3.1 to 1	I	1.8 to 1	G	2.5 to 1	K
3.6 to 1	J	2.4 to 1	K	3.1 to 1	G
3.7 to 1	K	2.4 to 1	M	5.0 to 1	M
6.5 to 1	L	2.5 to 1	L	5.7 to 1	J
?	M †	3.1 to 1	J	6.5 to 1	I

* The median number of activities of each type reported by pupils in the upper third of the socioeconomic scale was divided by the median number reported by students in the lower third of the scale. The letters in italics designate the schools.

† The median for the pupils in the lowest third was zero in this school.

which the students "receive" something "produced" by others; examples are going to a dance or an athletic contest, reading the school paper, attending a school play, etc. All captaincies, chairmanships, presidencies, and other student activities of a directive nature were classified under the category "leadership."

Table 3 shows the ratios which Pogue found in the thirteen schools.

There can be no question that participation in extra-class activities was a welfare level phenomenon in the schools where Pogue's study was made. The student from a family in the upper third of the socio-economic scale was far more likely to engage in primary group, secondary group, and leadership activities [44] than were most of his schoolmates from the least favored homes.

Other studies, for instance those by Dillon and Hecker, suggest very strongly that there is a close linkage between nonparticipation in extra-class activities and the decision to drop out of high school before graduation. Dillon [45] found that among the approximately 800 early school leavers for whom data could be secured, nearly three-fourths (73 per cent) had taken part in no extra-class activity. Hecker [46] found that nearly two-thirds (62 per cent) of the slightly more than 1,000 early school leavers for whom he could find such information had not participated in any extra-class activity. In both studies the early school leavers were asked what changes in the high school might have induced them to remain in school. Greater participation in extra-class activities was the response which ranked third in one study, fourth in the other.[47]

In analyzing the factors which cause students from economically unfavored homes to drop out of school in such disproportionate numbers, we have discussed two explanations. The first is that the cash cost of attending high school and taking part in the normal student life is greater than many pupils can afford to pay. The second and related explanation is that pupils from families low in the socio-economic scale typically participate in far fewer extra-class activities —the activities from which students derive both fun and prestige— than do students from more favored homes, and therefore feel excluded. It doesn't take much imagination to grasp the plight of the student whose school life is encumbered by these disadvantages. How weak must be his sense of identification with the school society, how distressing must be his frustration when he is unable to enjoy the pleasures or even the company of his schoolmates, and how inviting must seem an escape which can be achieved by the simple act of quitting school!

Obviously, these factors alone are enough to make leaving school seem very attractive to a good many children from low-income

[44] Hand, *Principal Findings of the 1947-48 Basic Studies,* pp. 25-27.
[45] Dillon, *Early School Leavers,* p. 44.
[46] Hecker, *Early School Leavers in Kentucky,* p. 44.
[47] Dillon, *Early School Leavers,* p. 57.
Hecker, *Early School Leavers in Kentucky,* p. 53.

homes. Unfortunately, there is a third factor, set forth in the opening paragraph of this section, which may be even more conducive
to early school leaving.

*Adults of the lowest socioeconomic stratum
often view the school with indifference or hostility*

Characteristically, their own schooling was brief and too frequently
unhappy; they discern little advantage in schooling beyond the
rudiments; and they frequently prefer—or, in some cases, urgently
need—to have their children on somebody's payroll rather than in
high school. Although there are many exceptions, most boys and girls
who live in such an environment receive virtually no encouragement
to finish high school. Many are encouraged to drop out of school
as soon as the law will allow them to, or sooner if they can contrive it.

It is easier to understand these parents' attitudes when one notes an
authoritative description of the typical conditions in which people
on the lowest economic level live. Writing in 1928, when the wave
of prosperity which preceded the Great Depression was reaching its
zenith, a noted welfare economist [48] wrote about the "poverty level,"
a group which, even in those good times, comprised "several millions" of persons:

> The homes of people on this level are overcrowded shacks or
> shanties with no modern conveniences, furnished from the
> wreckage of better homes or with cheaply made goods. Food
> is limited in amount and poor in quality. There are no savings
> and no insurance. Health is precarious and the death rate rela-
> tively high. Necessary medical service is lacking or obtained
> from free clinics. These families are often the breeders of tramps,
> delinquents, and criminals. Schooling of children on this level
> is limited to the compulsory period or less. The better culture
> is practically absent. Amusements or recreations involving cost
> are prohibited. Occupations consist of the roughest unskilled
> labor. Knowledge is lacking of how to prepare for or obtain
> access to the better paid employments. The chief bread-winner
> may be dead or a runaway from his family.

The author carried his descriptions up the scale progressively to
the level of "bare subsistence" and that of "minimum health and effi-

[48] P. H. Nystrom, *Economic Principles of Consumption,* The Ronald Press
Company, New York, 1928, Ch. 12.

ciency" before he came to the level of "minimum comfort" which most people probably regard as the typical American standard of living. Above this come the "comfort" level, the "moderately-well-to-do," the "well-to-do," and at the top the "luxury" level.

Many teachers do not understand these young people

Many high school teachers come from middle-class origins; very little in either their experience or their training has qualified them to understand the environmental influences, the needs, or the motivations which characterize life at the low end of the economic scale. In consequence, the school program offered by these teachers is too often unappealing to children from such a background.[49] Very often these children—and others, for that matter—must see little connection between what they are asked to study in school and their life outside the school.

Many of these young people want or need to earn money from a full-time job

Many young people from low-income families find the beginning wages of the jobs that are available to them when times are good too alluring to make the prospect of continuing in school without money attractive, or in some cases, even feasible. Their decision to leave school is unwise, of course, even from the financial point of view. This has been suggested by the findings of the President's Commission on Higher Education.[50] The Commission compared the earnings of those who had dropped out of high school with the earnings of those who had graduated from high school but had not gone on to college. It was found that the percentage of graduates who eventually earned annual incomes of $3000 or more was twice as high as that of nongraduates. Other variables seem not to have been controlled in this comparison, and so we can conclude no more than that high school graduation is one of the probable causal factors, undoubtedly a very important one. Those who drop out of school invariably learn that the lack of a high school diploma is a serious handicap in today's labor market.

[49] For elaborations of this point see: W. L. Warner, et al., *Who Shall Be Educated?* Harper & Brothers, New York, 1944, Ch. 9.
[50] Gail Kennedy, *Education for Democracy*, D. C. Heath & Company, New York, 1952, p. 7.

How to increase the holding power of the secondary school

So far in this chapter we have devoted our attention to a diagnosis of some of the shortcomings of the American public secondary school, the shortcomings which weaken its power to hold our adolescent youth during the full period required for a high school education. Obviously, these shortcomings must be remedied if the holding power of the high school is to increase. But before any workable remedies can be applied, the school must meet two preconditions.

The most fundamental of these—it is so fundamental that without it we can expect very little improvement of the school's holding power—is that the faculty of the school must be dedicated to the principle of universal public secondary education. The high school is not likely to serve all youth equally well unless the teachers themselves believe that this is what the high school should do. Today most experienced and successful teachers do believe in equality of educational opportunity. Young teachers who begin their first teaching assignment in an established school find that nearly all of their older colleagues are firmly committed to this principle, even though their daily practices in some respects may contradict it. The fact that the holding power of the American high school has doubled during the past quarter of a century and is still increasing seems to suggest that most teachers believe in universal secondary education and have tried to take at least some of the steps which will put it into effect in all of our schools.

Yet voices are being raised in America urging our people to make the public high school a *selective* rather than a universal institution. In some cases this urging takes the form of recommendations for a single rigorous standard of achievement for every school subject—a practice, already too common, which dooms many young people of low academic aptitude to the frustration of failing marks no matter how hard they may study. Such a practice does not benefit the very capable student, either: he may be rewarded for achievements which have cost him little effort and hence are no index of self-development. Proponents of the selective high school have suggested that the last two years of the school program be restricted further by the use of externally set examinations which would rigorously weed out a considerable proportion of the students whose aptitudes for the traditional academic regimen are low. This kind of advice is welcomed by some influential elements in our population, people who perhaps see in it a way to keep down school taxes despite the increasing birth rate. It is welcomed, too, by some college and university professors and others who seem to think that the public high school's sole admissible function is the preparation of our most capable young people for higher study.

The question of whether public secondary education should be selective or universal is not merely a matter of public opinion. It involves a fundamental moral choice. The level of formal schooling achieved by the individual will help determine the work he will later be able to undertake, and hence the income which he and his family will enjoy and his usefulness as a member of our society. A teacher who refuses to do everything he can to assure the continuance in school of as many young people as possible is deliberately committing these young people—and the children who will be born to them—to a lower standard of living than they might otherwise be able to attain. In terms of the concomitants of welfare status, such a teacher is committing his nonacademically oriented students and their children to less in the way of food, clothing, shelter, cultural advantages, economic security in old age, health, and years of life than they would enjoy if they were enabled, through additional formal education, to occupy a higher rung on the occupational ladder. By definition, therefore, no conscientious teacher in a democracy who is aware of the relationship between educational level and occupational status can condone any practice which threatens the holding power of the public high school.

The tasks to which teachers should rededicate themselves are suggested by the questions which have been raised by a noted educational sociologist: [51]

> Schooling experience thus lies between that which prevails at the family welfare level and that which . . . may obtain at the level of subsequent adult living.
>
> Can we believe that American schools are enriching the personalities of children from all these welfare levels and making life more abundant for them? For those who come from the culturally impoverished levels, can we suppose that the schools are compensating for their losses and leveling up their attainments to compare more favorably with the standards of the more fortunate? Are they removing stigma of low status—ignorance, superstition, and credulity; ugly speech, slovenly ap-

[51] P. E. Davidson in Stanford Education Faculty, *The Challenge of Education*, McGraw-Hill Book Co., New York, 1937, p. 22.

pearance, and boorish manners; distorted views of life and conduct? Are they helping these prospective workers to equip themselves for the better grades of labor? Are those at the middle levels being made acquainted with their occupational and other opportunities, receiving a marketable equipment for labor service, and learning of better ways of using their modest resources? Are the schools assisting the children at the more fortunate levels to utilize their unusual circumstances to enhance social well-being, and to avoid wasteful and frivolous modes of living? Are children from all levels being helped to discover the finer values in the social heritage so abundantly supplied them and to seek and qualify for some measure of helpful social leadership in a world beset with evils and menaced by the prospect of catastrophe?

Are all the children on all these levels being encouraged to find themselves embraced within a democratic fellowship, committed by its historical ideals to the attainment of a high common productivity and a better standard of living for all, to a just and reasonable sharing of the common heritage and resources of the national community, and to finer personality for each and all as the supreme objective of its operations?

As we have said, the first requirement for increasing the holding power of the high school occurs precisely in this matter of dedication to the principle of universal education. Unless its faculty is committed to this ideal, no high school is likely to carry out a program which will improve its holding power.

There is a second necessary precondition: The holding power of the local school must be evaluated and made known not only to the teachers but to the pupils, the parents, and the general public. Better yet, pupils, teachers, and general public should cooperate actively in appraising the situation, since they will then feel a sense of ownership and will be more strongly motivated to do something about it.

In most high schools, unfortunately, no one knows what the holding power of the school is. This, we believe, is true largely because most school faculties are so dedicated to the ideal of universal secondary education that they believe, without bothering to look for the evidence, that the holding power of *their* school is good. Obviously, teachers who think their school is already performing adequately are not likely to worry very much about improving it. The author recalls, for instance, a fairly large high school in which this kind of wishful thinking prevailed. Almost everyone believed that the school's holding power was very great. Consequently, most of the teachers thought that there was little reason to change the current practices of the school. One or two teachers, however, were Doubting Thomases; they reasoned that, in the absence of local data to the contrary, the statewide holding power figure for their state (about 50 per cent) was presumptively true of their own school too. They led a holding-power investigation in their own community which found that only 48 per cent of the students who entered their high school (not counting deaths or transfers to other schools) graduated four years later. (The best materials and directions now available for conducting such a study, incidentally, are issued by the Office of Public Instruction, Springfield, Illinois.[52]) When this information was made known, the complacency of the faculty quickly diminished. Most of the teachers became convinced that something needed to be done, and they were eager to begin the doing.

In a well-designed holding-power study, one discovers not only how many pupils have dropped out, but their sex, the socioeconomic levels of their families, their academic aptitudes, their school marks, the extent of their participation in extra-class activities, and the point in their school careers at which they decided to quit.

These findings lead, or at least should lead, to factual studies designed to find out the reasons for their leaving. If, as is almost invariably the case, the preliminary investigation shows that the students who have dropped out come predominantly from families low on the socioeconomic scale, then a costs study will be desirable.[53] The facts revealed by a costs study generally shock teachers, pupils, and parents alike. Usually even a quick look at the figures convinces everyone that school costs must be signally reduced if all students are to take a full part in the life of the school. Once such a conviction takes root, ways are usually found to reduce the costs—perhaps by defraying them with school revenues. This is one of the first things that must be done to help boys and girls from poor families remain in high school.

[52] Illinois Curriculum Program, *How to Conduct the Holding Power Study of the Illinois Curriculum Program,* rev. ed., Office of the Superintendent of Public Instruction, Springfield, Illinois, 1955.

Similar materials and directions under the title of *A Guide for the Study of Holding Power in Minnesota Secondary Schools,* Minnesota State Department of Education, St. Paul, Minn., 1952.

[53] Materials and directions for conducting such a study are published under the title *How to Conduct the Hidden Tuition Costs Study,* Office of the Superintendent of Public Instruction, Springfield, 1949.

If the findings of the holding-power study reveal that the students who have left school are those who had taken part in very few if any of the extra-class activities, a study of participation in extra-class activities will be desirable. People most commonly ask, in this connection, whether the youngsters from low-income families who are still in high school are likewise being excluded from these activities.[54] As we have already seen in this chapter, the answer in all the investigations which have been conducted so far is yes. The discovery that this is happening in their school is invariably so repugnant to teachers, pupils, and townspeople that steps are quickly taken to provide a remedy. If more children from low-income homes are to be induced to remain in school, the school must offer a program of extra-class activities in which those children can participate freely and thereby feel that they belong to the school community.

The holding-power study will also reveal that the children of less-than-average academic aptitude comprise a large majority of the early school leavers. Any teacher of perception and conscience will be led by these findings to question the adequacy of his school's attempts to adjust the instructional program and related practices to the individual differences among the students. Frequently, the result of such questioning is the adoption of double or triple tracks in English, mathematics, science, and other courses, and the arrangement of groupings within classes. It also frequently leads to serious dissatisfaction with the single standard and to revisions in the marking and reporting system of the school. In any case, if the holding power of the high school is to increase, individual differences among students must be far more widely recognized and accommodated than they are today.

A faculty which recognizes its holding power problem will welcome a follow-up study of graduates and school leavers to determine what they think about the value to them of what has been taught in the school. Such a study conducted by a large number of Illinois high schools[55] found (a) that teachers, parents, other laymen, and pupils currently in school substantially agreed that the high school should help pupils with problems relating to making a living, de-

---

[54] Materials and directions for making such a study are published under the title *How to Conduct the Participation in Extra-Class Activities Study*, Office of the Superintendent of Public Instruction, Springfield, 1949.

[55] Kenneth B. Henderson, *Principal Findings of the Follow-Up Study of the Illinois Secondary School Curriculum Program*, Office of the Superintendent of Public Instruction, Springfield, Illinois, 1951.

veloping their personality, spending personal income wisely, living healthfully and safely, spending leisure time wholesomely and enjoyably, taking an effective part in civic affairs, preparing for homemaking and parenthood, and using educational opportunities, and (b) that the teachers and the recent graduates agreed that far too little of such help was being given. The findings of this study led the faculties in many of these schools to reorient their instructional programs to prepare students for the principal life-activities of young adults, and to make the relevance of the instruction clearer to the pupils currently in school. To improve the holding power of the high school, then, it is necessary to demonstrate to many pupils that there is a worthwhile relationship beween what is being taught and the activities of daily living in the community.

Studies of early school leavers usually reveal that most of them feel that they were not well known by their teachers, and that they had been given little educational or vocational information or counseling by their school. This suggests five additional tasks which most high schools must accomplish if their holding power is to be increased. First, each teacher must become personally acquainted with each of his pupils and make him feel important in the teacher's eyes. Second, the guidance program must be improved; each pupil must receive the counseling he really needs, even when he himself is not sure what his problems are. Third, a good cumulative record system is essential if teachers and counselors are to know and help their pupils. Not only must there be a detailed cumulative record for each pupil, but these records must be used regularly and wisely by teachers and counselors.

Fourth, the pupils who are likely to drop out of school should be detected and helped to remedy their troubles before it is too late. Here are the characteristics which Dillon [56] found to be the "symptoms of vulnerability":

1. Fairly consistent regression in scholarship from elementary to junior to senior high school.
2. Frequent grade failures in the elementary school.
3. High frequency of grade or subject failure in the junior and senior high school.
4. Marked regression in attendance from elementary to junior to senior high school.

[56] Dillon, *Early School Leavers*, p. 82.

5. Frequent transfers from one school to another.
6. Evidence of a feeling of insecurity or "lacking of belonging" in school (here participation in extra-class activities is an important indication).
7. Marked lack of interest in school work.

Most of these "symptoms of vulnerability" are readily apparent; the teacher can acquaint himself with the others from a study of records. Every high school faculty should see that students who manifest any of these symptoms to a significant degree are identified, that a diagnosis of the probable cause is made in each case, and that the proper remedies are applied.

The public high school must undertake a fifth and final task if it is to increase its holding power. We have placed this undertaking last for two reasons. First, it is by far the most difficult of all the things which must be done. Second, it is, if not the most important, at least equal in importance to any of the others. We have already noted that many parents in the low socioeconomic group place little value on education and are commonly indifferent about their children's attendance at school or even eager to have them drop out and begin contributing to the support of the family.

We have been careful to say that there are many fortunate exceptions to this generalization. Certainly no one should ever conclude without adequate evidence that a given student's parents are guilty of this misjudgment. In more cases than we like to admit, however, the educational welfare of students from families of low socioeconomic status is jeopardized by the attitudes which play upon them in their homes and neighborhoods. The fifth task of the school, then, is as difficult to accomplish as it is obvious to prescribe —it is to re-educate the parents. They should be led to understand the value which a completed high school education will have for their sons and daughters. Such parents, unfortunately, seldom visit the school or attend the meetings of Parent-Teacher Associations and other community-school organizations. Hence the school should aim at those parents careful programs of interpretation and enlightenment. The teacher who pays an informal visit to the home, if possible in the company of the boy or girl of the family, is probably making the most direct and most promising approach.

Bread-and-butter considerations usually weigh the most heavily in such homes. If the parents can be helped to realize what is implied for their children by the prediction of the U.S. Department of

Labor's Bureau of Labor Statistics that by the time these youngsters are in their thirties there will be jobs for 25 per cent fewer unskilled workers than at present, some modification in their views toward formal schooling may result. Also, too many of these parents feel that the school isn't really interested in them or in their children, a notion that personal visits by their youngsters' teachers might help to dispel.

Summary

This chapter has emphasized the improvements which must be made in the American public secondary school if our educational system is to perform the task which is required of it by the ideal upon which we have built our democratic way of life. This task, as every public school teacher is obligated to remember, is to serve equally well all the adolescent children of all the people of the community.

chapter 6

MAINTAINING GOOD

SCHOOL-COMMUNITY RELATIONS

We observed, in connection with our discussion of the last basic principle set forth in Chapter 4, that everything which the public secondary school seeks to accomplish is in the last analysis determined by public opinion. This is one of the reasons that experienced teachers, school administrators, and school board members value few things more highly than good relations between the school and the community.

A relationship is good when the community supports the school's program and appreciates the efforts made by teachers and school officials to serve the community. Mutual confidence characterizes the outlook of teachers and townspeople alike. The problems which inevitably arise in the course of providing for the community's educational needs are met in a spirit of cordial cooperation. Under such circumstances teaching as a profession benefits the community and satisfies the teacher.

But if the relations between school and community are not good, the school staff will be in almost constant trouble. The public will lack confidence in what the school is doing. The best that can be hoped for from a dissatisfied community is indifference, with an accompanying lack of support for the school program. But smoldering resentment or overt hostility is more likely. It will spring from certain sectors of the community and spread to others, causing gossip and harmful rumors. The community will splinter into pro- and anti-school factions. Dissension, petty recriminations, and the other marks of intracommunity squabbles will characterize the towns-people's behavior. In such an atmosphere the teacher is scarcely likely to find his career a happy or productive one.

School superintendents and principals, therefore, prize the teacher who can help produce and maintain good school-community relations. The members of school boards, who are usually caught in the midst of any community dispute which arises in connection with the schools, are eager to bring such teachers to the staffs of their schools. Conversely, neither school administrators nor board members are likely to want to retain the services of a teacher whose presence jeopardizes the relationship between school and community. No matter how good a scholar the beginning teacher may be, no matter how skilled he may be in the arts of instruction, he can scarcely hope for an appointment on tenure or a recommendation to take to another community if he is inept in his public relations.

Application of the Golden Rule

The Golden Rule lies at the heart of good public relations everywhere, and as we observed in our discussion of the fourth basic principle presented in Chapter 4, it is particularly applicable to the American way of life. We observed that the ethical precept which is fundamental to American democracy is the conviction that all men are of equal moral worth, and that the dignity and integrity of every person should be respected everywhere and always.

This is what Americans believe, and they believe it most of all when it is applied to children, either their own or their neighbors'. The insightful teacher realizes that every child is the most highly cherished "possession" of someone in the community and as such must be unfailingly treated as a person of worth. Nothing is more corrosive of parental confidence and good will, and nothing is more destructive of good school-community relations, than an action of any member of the school staff which appears, in the eyes of the community, to demean a pupil. Only if the citizens of the community are convinced that the teachers, counselors, supervisors, administrators, clerical workers, custodians, and bus drivers are genuinely concerned about the welfare of the children in their charge can good relations possibly continue between the school and the townspeople. Everyone employed by the school, especially the teachers, should be openly dedicated to the spirit of the Golden Rule and should apply it to all dealings with the school's students. Many other conditions must be satisfied in order to assure good public relations, but this one is absolutely fundamental. Unless it is fulfilled, the others can never be of much avail.

Teachers can demean pupils in many ways. These practices are more common than we like to think, and they inevitably produce an adverse effect on the relationship between school and community. Of all the actions of an unpopular teacher, probably the one that is most bitterly resented by students is the use of sarcasm. To be sure, a teacher's patience is often sorely tried, particularly if he is burdened with classes that are too large and with a schedule of teaching and extra-class duties that is too heavy. The temptation to stoop to sarcasm may be great: it offers a quick and easy release to taut feelings. But the use of sarcasm can never be justified. It is an affront to the dignity of the individual; it destroys the bond between teacher and pupil and usually produces ugly reverberations in the community.

Every normal boy or girl wants to be treated as a person who is as worthy as other people. Yet some teachers permit themselves to have favorites among their pupils. This is resented by pupils and their parents and therefore undermines school-community relations.

Teachers who treat adolescents as if they were little children offend the high school pupil's sense of his own dignity and integrity. Probably this is not an offense that is committed very often by secondary school teachers, but when it does occur it creates another cause of ill feeling between the community and the school.

Teachers who hold grudges against particular students (in the author's experience, they are not encountered in many schools) are perhaps the most destructive of student morale. A pupil who feels that one of his teachers "has it in for him" can often persuade his parents to feel the same way, with the result, of course, that they become antagonistic toward that teacher and perhaps toward the whole school.

Insecurity as well as resentment may be engendered by the teacher whose temperament is changeable—say, warm, pleasant, and approachable one day and cold, disagreeable, and aloof the next. Not many teachers have such a fault, but those who do can create a great deal of ill feeling in their community.

We all like to be treated with consideration and sympathy by others. The pupil and his parents have a right to expect that his teachers will behave benevolently, or at least inoffensively, toward him. Opinion polls which have been conducted by the author among high school students and their parents give abundant evidence that most secondary school teachers do in fact treat their students fairly. But the occasional teacher who is inconsiderate can seriously injure the good relations which have been established by his more professional colleagues.

Further, every normal person likes to be regarded as reasonably important. Teachers occasionally demean their pupils by treating them as relatively inconsequential persons, too young or too inexperienced to amount to anything. Sometimes by his offhand manner a teacher can unintentionally offend his pupils; they may interpret such a teacher's behavior as a sign of disdain. When this happens, the result is unfortunate.

So far we have been engaged in the rather distasteful job of noting the ways in which teachers occasionally demean or humiliate their students. But in addition, there are certain ways in which a whole school, acting as a single agency, may violate the spirit of the Golden Rule, thus separating the school from the community. Three of these ways are sometimes major sources of public disaffection.

First, many schools require or permit financial charges in connection with the school's courses or extra-class activities, thus making it difficult and in some cases impossible for children from economically unfavored homes to participate in the school's full program. To be compelled by law to attend a school which excludes one from many of the activities which one's more fortunate fellows enjoy is, of course, an affront to one's feelings. This practice, which is much more widespread than many of us realize, cannot be reconciled with the spirit of the Golden Rule. We have discussed the problem at some length in a previous chapter, so we shall note here simply that this practice in any school seriously jeopardizes the relations between the school and a large segment of the public.

Second, many schools offer a curriculum which satisfies the needs of only a part of the student body. Again, this is a matter which is discussed in detail elsewhere in this book. We shall say here only that such a practice, by forcing many pupils into a program which appears useless to them and to their parents, arouses widespread resentment and greatly injures the school's public relations.

Third, some schools hold all pupils to a single minimum standard of achievement. As we observed in Chapter 4, the abilities of pupils at any high school grade level differ greatly. We have observed that the mental ages of pupils may vary by as much as thirteen years in the ninth grade and by even more in the later grades. Consequently one should not be surprised by the fact that achievement, measured in traditional academic terms, varies no less widely. To hold two ninth-grade pupils, one with the mental age of a fifth-grader and the other with the mental age of a high school senior, to the same standard of achievement is destructive of good school-community relations as it is unfair. No matter how hard he may study, the first pupil will bear the stigma of failure; he is simply incapable of performing at the level of the average ninth-grade pupil. Parents are likely to be embittered when they are compelled by law to send such a child to a school where he will be branded as a failure in spite of his best efforts. The precocious youngster, on the other hand, will excel in the tasks of the average ninth-grader with little effort—hence with little self-development. The bright student is invited to dawdle and waste his abilities, and his parents will resent it; often, in fact, the pupil himself will resent and scorn the school's program. The single standard of achievement, especially when it is applied to courses which are required of all pupils, is an out-of-date absurdity which will injure both the pupils and the reputation of the school in the community.

Establishment of a good educational program and the means to make it known to the public

The first basic principle discussed in the fourth chapter of this book states that the basic task of the American public secondary school is to help the youths of America learn whatever must be learned during adolescence in order to assure their present and future well-being and the well-being of the society to which they belong. Most Americans support compulsory education laws and pay for school programs which extend well beyond the period of compulsory attendance because they want their children and their neighbors' children to get an education which will benefit both the children and the community. They are certain to be displeased if they find that the schools are providing an education which does not include the things that they think are beneficial.

The citizens expect their high school to produce young men and women of good character. They expect these young people to become good citizens, dedicated to the ideals of American democracy and ready to take part intelligently in civic affairs. They expect the high schools to give these young people a reasonably good preparation for their next steps in life—gainful employment or further education in college. They expect these young people to be helped to make a success of marriage, homemaking, and child rearing. And finally they expect their children to learn in high school how to live healthfully and safely and how to spend their leisure time wholesomely. To do these things, as we have seen, the young people must learn first of all how to think and communicate effectively. These expectations of the citizens must be satisfied by the school, at least to a degree which the citizens feel is reasonable. Otherwise, it is vain to hope for good school-community relationships.

Thus the provision of an effective educational program is fundamental to good relations between the school and the community. But simply providing a good program is not enough. The citizens themselves must be convinced that the program is good, that it is producing the desired results. This means that the school must publicize each phase of its work, not—as is too often the case—merely athletics, music, and dramatics. Many of our better school systems publish well-illustrated reports [1] which describe the many important things that the schools are doing; the reports show, for example, how pupils are being prepared for good citizenship, for healthful living, for success in work or college, and for the wholesome use of leisure time. Schools staffed by men and women who are alert to the importance of good public relations often use the radio, television, and the community and school newspapers to give the citizens accounts of the significant work being done in all departments of the school. The intelligent classroom teacher can accomplish a great deal by making use of any of these means of communication with the public.

But perhaps the best way to convince the citizens that the school's educational program is a good one is to show them good results. There are a number of ways in which schools can show that their work has been genuinely effective. Achievement tests, for instance,

---

[1] See, for example: George N. Wells, *We Grow*, Board of Education, Bloomington, Ill., 1955.
Benjamin C. Willis, *We Build*, Board of Education, Chicago, Ill., 1956.

will demonstrate the progress of the pupils in many areas of learning. Or the school may conduct a self-survey based on the evaluative criteria supplied by the Cooperative Study of Secondary School Standards [2] and release the findings to the public. Follow-up studies of graduates who are now in college or engaged in other adult activities are obviously useful. The school can demonstrate its seriousness by studying children who have dropped out of school, in order to discover why they left and what improvements in the school will prevent others from leaving. Lay citizens of the community should be involved as much as possible in both types of follow-up studies, for through such involvement they can learn to recognize the real problems of education, the good work that is being done by the school, and the need for their help if the school is to be made even better. Needless to say, classroom teachers must help administer achievement tests, self-surveys, and follow-up studies if these are to be used to promote good public relations.

Another proof of good results is afforded by the pupils themselves, who are, after all, the most constant intermediaries between the school and the public. A pupil who is articulate about what he has learned can do a great deal in the course of his daily life to impress the achievements of the school upon the adults with whom he comes in contact. Unfortunately, some pupils are anything but articulate; they tend to forget, not what they have learned, but the fact that they have learned it. Consequently, classroom discussions which accentuate and remind the students of what they have learned strengthen their self-confidence and give them a more or less systematic basis for their comments about their school to parents, neighbors, and other laymen of the community.

The example set by teachers

What we know about how young people learn and what they should learn (matters which are related to several of the basic principles which were discussed in Chapter 4) implies that the example set by teachers must seem commendable to the community. Laymen generally sense that many of the most important things which pupils learn, particularly their attitudes and values, are "caught" as much as they are taught. One can learn by imitation. Conse-

[2] American Council on Education, *Evaluative Criteria of Secondary School Standards*, Washington, 1950.

quently, most citizens will never agree that their school is educating their children well unless the teachers characteristically exhibit, both in and out of school, socially desirable behavior. Because they want worthy models for their children to follow, most people want teachers who consistently typify the qualities which they themselves approve and which they want their children to acquire. For most parents, the most important thing about a teacher is not his knowledge of his subject or his skill as an instructor, but what he *is*. They are interested in the whole complex of his personality, because they know that this will markedly influence their children's behavior. Consequently, the public relations of the school will suffer if an appreciable number of the citizens feel that the teachers are unworthy models for the youth of the community.

This creates no problem for the conscientious teacher who is working in a community where the prevailing sentiment favors the development of wholesome character. Unfortunately, in some communities large and influential elements of the population hold and express beliefs which are antithetical to the fundamental concepts of American democracy, and they want the youth of the community to share their values. Racial discrimination and religious bigotry are anti-democratic modes of behavior which teachers sometimes encounter in this way. Under these circumstances, what is the teacher to do? The answer is not easy. On one hand, good relations between school and community, even in a community where a distorted sense of values prevails, are essential to the educational process; on the other hand, the teacher cannot be expected to oppose his own convictions in a way subversive to American society. In the end, of course, the teacher should decide that his allegiance to American democracy is more important than good public relations in the local community. By being tactful, he can usually adhere to his convictions and offer a model worthy of his pupils' emulation without arousing the animosity of the community. The long-run relations between school and community will be improved by teachers who are worthy models, conformable in all ways to the American ideal.

Although this requirement seems unreasonable to some teachers, especially when they see parents and other adults who consistently belie in their own behavior the qualities which they say they would like the youth of the community to acquire, the lay citizens are still right in insisting that teachers must be among the community's primary models for youth. Values are learned, but usually not as arithmetic or history is learned. They are learned most frequently by a process called "internalization"—the taking into oneself of qualities possessed by somebody else.

Certain conditions, which are apparent even without formal psychological studies, must be met before pupils will internalize values: first, the pupil must want to be like the person who is the "carrier" of the values, and second, the carrier must consistently typify those values. Consequently, most people usually hope that their children will have teachers whom they will want to imitate. Such parents justifiably demand that the teachers consistently typify the qualities which they want their children to acquire.

Teachers, on the other hand, are also justified when they point out that all adults are really teachers and that the learning process for children would be far more effective if all parents and other citizens exemplified the qualities which they profess to admire and want their children to learn. Teachers are on sound ground when they insist that children will not learn values most effectively until the home and community combine with the school to provide a permanent and universal environment of good behavior. But all this does not absolve the public school teacher from his own responsibility for practicing the good qualities which our young people must acquire if we are to assure the health of American democracy.

State laws frequently stipulate that "conduct unbecoming a teacher" is a legitimate cause for dismissal. In interpreting these laws, the courts have uniformly held that teachers are expected to typify in their behavior the values which are generally held in this country, particularly those values which support the total social interest.

This does not mean that the courts impose any unreasonable limitations on the personal lives of teachers or that teachers should accept such limitations if local attempts are made to impose them. Behavior like that normal to most of the respected citizens of the community is probably allowable for teachers under most circumstances. But teachers lead open lives, in a sense; their personal lives are always on display before the most susceptible element of the community—the youth. Even things which other adults may do with impunity will sometimes make a teacher an unworthy model for his students and hence contribute to poor relations between the school and the community.

"Psychological ownership" of the school program by the citizens of the community

The citizen who feels closely, responsibly, and possessively identified with the program of the public school is most likely to support it. The more he feels that it is *his* program, the more staunchly he will support it. If the school's program is to win the whole-hearted support of the lay public, the citizens of the community must feel that it reflects their desires; they must view every part of it as theirs; they must feel responsible for it. Only then are they most likely to cooperate with the teachers, to defend the school against unwarranted criticism, and to provide the funds necessary for its development.

Almost every high school in this country is in a rather sorry fix so far as this business of "psychological ownership" is concerned. In fact, one cannot even say that in many of them the whole school program is the psychological property of the entire faculty, much less of the citizens of the community. Even worse, in very few of the high schools that have two or more teachers in one department do all the teachers feel identified with the entire departmental program, to say nothing of the courses offered by other departments. To the contrary, the typical teacher feels that he "owns" only the courses which he is actually teaching.

The reason for this unhappy state of affairs is almost self-evident. To feel responsibly identified with any undertaking, one must have taken part in its inception, its development, and its evaluation. But the teacher of English, for instance, has usually done these things only for his English courses, not for all the courses in his department and certainly not for those in the other fields. The involvements of the teachers of art, agriculture, foreign languages, home economics, industrial education, mathematics, physical education, science, and social studies have generally been restricted to the particular subjects which they themselves teach. A splintered faculty, each member of which is dedicated to his particular program, cannot feel a psychological commitment to a single, comprehensive program. And the lay public, having been excluded almost altogether, feels almost no psychological ownership at all.

This has put the high school in an extremely vulnerable position, the consequences of which may become well-nigh disastrous within the next few decades. The children have already been born who will swell the present high school enrollment by about 30 per cent in 1960 and by about 70 per cent five to ten years later. Obviously, high school revenues must be sharply increased if the present quality of instruction is to be maintained; they must be increased even more sharply if the quality of instruction is to be improved. Since the likelihood of any appreciable amount of federal aid for operational purposes seems quite remote, these increased revenues can probably be obtained in most states only if the local citizens are willing to vote for higher school taxes. If we could be sure that most citizens felt individually responsible for the programs of their high schools, we would be sure of the outcome of such a vote. But given the present divorcement of the public from the high schools, and the over-all increase in taxes which is expected during the coming years (to pay for national defense, the care of a rapidly aging population, and the like), we cannot be at all sure that our lay citizens will support vital increases in school revenues at the polls.

We will be particularly uncertain if the unjustified attacks which have recently been made on the public schools continue. By an unjustified attack we mean one based on premises contrary to the fundamental precepts of American democracy or violating ordinary rules of evidence. Examples of the former are proposals that American public schools should educate only young people of a certain proved intellectual capacity rather than all our educable youth, or criticisms based on the premise that the public school should teach sectarian religious doctrines or that it should evade all controversial issues.

The ordinary rules of evidence provide, among other things, that all pertinent evidence—contextual evidence included—must be considered, that no inference or conclusion can be regarded as valid which is contrary to the preponderance of the relevant evidence, and that issues must not be misrepresented nor evidence distorted. For example, a rule of evidence is violated when a critic selects from a textbook a sentence unfavorable to, say, labor, ignoring other more numerous and stronger statements which balance the effect of this one sentence, and then asserts on the basis of this partial evidence (which he presents as if it were the whole truth) that the school which uses the textbook is antilabor.

The charge that the public high schools are now teaching the standard subjects of general education (English, foreign languages, mathematics, science, social studies) to far fewer youths than they did five decades ago grossly violates the rules of evidence. The report of an interview was published under the title "We Are Less Educated Than 50 Years Ago" in the November 30, 1956, issue of *U.S. News and World Report,* a magazine read by a great many people in the business and professional worlds. Let us examine the factual aspects of the report of this interview in some detail. The statistics quoted in it were neatly summarized in an eye-catching graph on page 71 of the article cited. Table 4 shows, without the colorful pictographs employed, what this graph said.

TABLE **4**   *Misleading statistics on education*

Among all of the country's high schools—

ONE HALF offer no courses in physics

ONE QUARTER offer neither physics nor chemistry

NEARLY ONE QUARTER offer no geometry

Year after year, these subjects are taught to a shrinking proportion of students. In the last year alone, 1,500 high schools dropped some or all of their science and mathematics courses.

As a result here is the record of 56 years:

	IN 1900	NOW
Percentage of high-school students taking science	84%	54%
Percentage of high-school students taking mathematics	86%	55%

The gentleman who was interviewed said that the enrollment data given above were U.S. Office of Education figures. Although he did not mention this fact, the data respecting the proportions of schools in which chemistry, geometry, or physics is not offered are to be found in another U.S. Office of Education bulletin.

Now let us ferret out the rules of evidence which were violated in this graph—and in the interview, no less. To begin with, all the percentages given in the right-hand column are quite misleading.

They make it appear that during their high school careers 46 and 45 per cent of today's high school pupils take no work in science and mathematics, respectively, whereas the U.S. Office of Education enrollment statistics for 1950 (the most recent available) actually show that the figure is much smaller in both instances. Let us illustrate by considering the 1950 figures for mathematics. The U.S. Office of Education reported [3] that 27, 13, 13, and 2 per cent of *all* pupils registered in *all four grades* of the high school were enrolled in algebra, general mathematics, geometry, and trigonometry, respectively, in the *one* grade in which they happened to be located in 1950. What the gentleman who was interviewed obviously did was to add up these four figures to get his 55 per cent figure which he said in the interview was the "percentage of all American high-school students" who are taking any work in mathematics these days. Now let us see why his figure is misleading in the extreme.

In the bulletin already cited, the U.S. Office of Education reported that 31, 27, 23, and 19 per cent of all the pupils enrolled in all of the public high schools in 1950 were found in the ninth, tenth, eleventh, and twelfth grades, respectively. Another bulletin [4] broke down the algebra and geometry enrollment figures just noted: elementary algebra, a ninth-grade subject, 20 per cent; intermediate algebra, an eleventh-grade subject, 7 per cent; plane geometry, a tenth-grade subject, 10 per cent; solid geometry, a twelfth-grade subject, 3 per cent. General mathematics is a ninth-grade offering, but about one-fifth of the pupils who take it do so when they are in the tenth grade. Solid geometry and trigonometry are classified by the U.S. Office of Education as twelfth-grade subjects.

One must take the *one year* enrollment data supplied by the U.S. Office of Education and apply them at *each* of the *four* years of the high school in order to determine what percentage of American high school students are taking work in mathematics these days. More than this, one must do so in a statistically representative high school; i.e., one in which 31, 27, 23, and 19 per cent of all the pupils are enrolled in the ninth, tenth, eleventh, and twelfth grades, respectively. The enrollments in such a school are presented in Table 5.

[3] *Statistical Summary of Education, 1949-50*, U.S. Office of Education, p. 22.
[4] *Offerings and Enrollments in Science and Mathematics in Public High Schools*, U.S. Office of Education, p. 17.

TABLE 5 **Students enrolled in a high school with proportionate grade enrollments typical of those reported for 1950**

GRADE	NUMBER OF PUPILS	PER CENT OF PUPILS
9	155	31
10	135	27
11	115	23
12	95	19
Total	500	100

The U.S. Office of Education reported that 20 per cent of all the pupils in this school took elementary algebra in 1950. These 100 pupils, except for a few repeaters, were all ninth-grade youngsters. The U.S. Office of Education also reported that 13 per cent, or 65, of the 500 youths in this school were enrolled in general mathematics in 1950. Four-fifths, or 52, of these youths were in the ninth grade. If there were no repeaters, then, we see that 152, or 98 per cent, of the 155 ninth-grade pupils were enrolled in mathematics in 1950. Let's call this 95 per cent to allow for the probable repeaters.

In like manner, it can be shown that 49, 30, and at least 16 per cent of the tenth-, eleventh-, and twelfth-grade pupils were enrolled in some mathematics course in 1950.

What we have seen here is that only about 5 per cent of the pupils enrolled in the typical public high school today take no work in mathematics during their high school careers. The faulty interpretation of the person who was interviewed made this figure appear to be about nine times greater than the figures reported by the U.S. Office of Education show it to be. His gross misinterpretation, a serious violation of the rules of evidence, gave the present-day high school a completely undeserved black eye.

The same observation is warranted in respect to the enrollment situation in science. Well over 90 per cent of our public high school pupils who entered in 1950 were enrolled in some science course before they graduated four years later.

Still another of the rules of evidence was grossly violated when, on the basis of enrollment statistics for 1900 and for 1950, the interview was advertised as showing that "We are less educated than 50 years ago." When one says that "we" are less educated today than "we" were fifty years ago, he is referring to *all* of us today and to *all* of us fifty years ago. Within the context of the interview we are discussing, the reference is to *all* youths of high school age today and to *all* youths of high school age in 1900. The U.S. Office of Education bulletin which supplies the enrollment figures which were misused in the interview says clearly that only 8 per cent of all youths of high school age were enrolled in the public high school in 1900, and that this figure had risen to 64 per cent in 1950—yet the inference drawn related to 100 per cent at both dates when it was declared that "We are less educated than 50 years ago."

No one can compute what percentages of the public high school pupils were taking work in mathematics and science in 1900, for we do not know what proportion of these youths was enrolled in each grade. But we do know that only 8 per cent of all youths then aged fourteen to seventeen were then attending the public secondary school, and we have good reason to believe that the typical ninth-grade class was four or five times larger than the typical senior class. It seems most likely, then, that not over 15 per cent of the youngsters around 1900 were ever enrolled in any public high school subject, mathematics and science included. In 1950, however, we know that no fewer than 83 per cent of all the fourteen-year-old youths in this country were enrolled in the ninth grade of the public secondary school. From the figures we have given above (95 and at least 90 per cent), it can be seen that nearly 80 and about 75 per cent of all the fourteen-year-olds in this country were enrolled in public high school courses in mathematics and science courses, respectively. When 80 and 75 are divided by 15, we get ratios in the order of five to one. So far as the comparative enrollment data for these two subjects are indicative, then, it is apparent that "we" are today much more rather than less educated than "we" were fifty years ago.

Now let us return to the figures in the right-hand column of Table 4, given on page 125. These figures are correct, but they relate to *schools* and not to *pupils* and turn out to be very misleading.

Some of our public high schools enrolled fewer than ten pupils in 1950, whereas others had enrollments in excess of 5,000, so it is important to know how many students were enrolled in the schools in which chemistry, geometry, or physics was not offered. One of the U.S. Office of Education bulletins cited above says very plainly—in bold face type, in fact—that the high schools involved here were all small institutions, that the equivalent of fewer than 2 per cent of all the public high school pupils in this country are enrolled in the schools which taught neither chemistry nor physics, and that only the equivalent of 2 per cent are found in those in which geometry is missing. It also says that the survey covered one year only, and that the smaller high schools commonly teach chemistry and physics in alternate years. About 16 per cent of all public high school pupils are enrolled in that approximate one-half of the institutions in which physics was not being taught the year the survey was made. It is a reasonable presumption that about half of these pupils would have the opportunity to take physics sometime during their high school careers.

We see, then, that from less than 2 to about 8 per cent of our high school pupils are denied the opportunity to study chemistry, geometry, or physics, as the case may be. This is a distressing situation, and one that should be remedied as quickly as possible. But the problem is by no means of the magnitude suggested by the statement that from about a quarter to a half of all our high schools fail to offer these important subjects. Yet not a word was said in the interview to indicate that it is the smaller high schools in which these deficiencies are found.

Nor was anything said in the interview about the almost catastrophic shortage of beginning teachers in these subject fields. The numbers of new teachers of mathematics, chemistry, and physics who accepted teaching positions in the fall of 1955 were sufficient to supply but one for every 19, 119, and 250 schools, respectively.[5] The article creates the impression instead that mathematics and science courses are not being offered in all our secondary schools because school administrators and professors of education are "confused" regarding the purposes of secondary education.

One part of the message given near the middle of Table 4 remains for us to analyze: "*Year after year*, these subjects [chem-

[5] NEA Research Division, "The 1956 Teacher Supply and Demand Report," *Journal of Teacher Education*, Vol. VII, No. 1, Mar. 1956, pp. 33-79.

istry, geometry, physics] are taught to a shrinking proportion of students." This statement is technically true, for the gains in the enrollments in these subjects have not kept pace with the gain in the total enrollment of the public secondary school. But within the context of the conclusion drawn from the interview ("We are less educated than 50 years ago") it is completely misleading. To infer that schools today educate less well than they did in 1900, enrollment data for the two periods must be related to the total number of youths of high school age living in this country then and now. From 1900 to 1950 the number of boys and girls aged 14 through 17 increased by 37 per cent. Enrollments in chemistry, geometry, and physics increased by 929, 387, and 195 per cent, respectively, during the same period. These figures yield ratios of 25 to 1, 10 to 1, and 5 to 1 when gains in enrollments are divided by the gain in the growth of total population of high school age youths. This does not mean that we should be complacent about the numbers of youths who are taking these subjects today. But these ratios do indicate that there is no justification whatsoever for saying, "We are less educated than 50 years ago," so far as the comparative enrollments in these three high school subjects are concerned.

We have given only one example of the many unwarranted attacks which have been made on public high schools in recent years [6]— unwarranted because they are either grounded on undemocratic premises or based on bogus proofs adduced through violations of the rules of evidence. These attacks have done nothing to strengthen the confidence of the public in its schools. That some confidence has been destroyed may not displease those whose primary interest in educational matters is to prevent any increase in school taxes.

Had the teaching profession in times past successfully involved the lay public in planning and assessing the high school program, two things would now be true which are unfortunately not true. First, the lay public would know what is going on in the schools and would immediately recognize as spurious much of the criticism directed toward our public educational system, in which case the criticism would do little damage. Second, the perpetrators of unwar-

[6] For other examples of current criticisms of public schools, together with analyses of their validity, see: C. Winfield Scott and Clyde M. Hill (editors), *Public Education Under Criticism*, Prentice-Hall, Englewood Cliffs, New Jersey, 1954.

ranted attacks on the schools would become extremely unpopular with the lay public and would be made to feel this social disapproval. In other words, citizens who felt that the high school program was really theirs would see in unwarranted attacks on the school a reflection upon their own intelligence and integrity, and they would respond by repudiating the originators of the attacks. This manifestation of social disapproval would go a long way toward improving the climate of public opinion in which American schools must exist.

But the lay public feels virtually no psychological ownership of the program of the public high school. The typical lay citizen does not feel himself to be under attack when the program of his school is unjustly condemned. Instead, he feels that the attack is directed only at the members of the teaching profession, which, in a sense, is true, for it was chiefly the teaching profession which was involved in shaping the instructional program in the first place.

Furthermore, the lay citizen does not see that the attack is unfair. To recognize an unjustified criticism for what it is, one must be acquainted with the facts. Chiefly because they have been involved far too little in school affairs, most lay citizens today do not know what the facts about their high schools really are.

The student who was preparing himself to become a teacher fifteen or twenty years ago heard much about "selling the schools to the public" or "interpreting the schools to the public." These were catch phrases which clearly betrayed the inadequate concepts of the educators of that time. The idea then was that the teachers and professional educators should determine the aims and lay the plans for the school program and afterwards persuade the public to approve what had been done. It would be difficult to imagine a more effective way of making the lay citizen believe that the school program was not his program, that he had no responsibility for it. Manifestly, this is *not* the way to create psychological ownership of the school program. Unless the lay citizen feels that he or his representatives have helped determine what the program is to be, he can scarcely be expected to feel himself closely identified with it or responsible for it. Consequently, the emphasis among educational leaders today is on *involving* the lay public in educational planning rather than on "selling" or "interpreting" the schools to the public.

The procedure followed in the Local Area Consensus Studies,

sponsored by the Illinois Curriculum Program, seems to be one of the most promising yet devised for creating a sense of psychological ownership among lay citizens, pupils, and teachers. These projects deal in turn with each of the instructional fields (music, science, mathematics, etc.) and with each of the service areas (guidance, library services, etc.) which are ordinarily included in the high school program, and each project calls upon all teachers (or, in very large schools, their delegates) and a large number of representative lay citizens and older pupils to help shape the purposes, assess the present strengths and weaknesses, and plan the future development of each aspect of the high school program.

Public opinion polling can also create a sense of psychological ownership among the members of the lay community. To ask the public how it feels about the way the schools are being administered is to intimate that the schools really belong to the people and that the teachers and administrators recognize their accountability to the lay community. And to accept and act upon the results of the poll, whenever they include potentially fruitful suggestions, is to acknowledge tacitly the public's partnership in the administration of the school. By using the materials contained in a book prepared by the present author,[7] American towns, cities, and counties have conducted many such polls during the past several years. In addition, there are many commercial market research organizations which can conduct competent opinion polls on questions relating to the public schools.

A poll conducted by a market research organization is tailor-made to meet the needs of the particular community which hires the organization. This is a great advantage, but it has its price. Such polls are so expensive that usually only our larger cities are able to afford them. The poll materials contained in the book which we have cited cost much less. These materials afford the means to question parents, teachers, and pupils on matters which have been found to be important to good school-community relations. Among the judgments which are solicited in this way are those which relate to the efficacy of what the school is teaching, the inadequacies of the present program, the considerateness with which pupils are treated, the level of pupil achievement, how well the pupils are

---

[7] Harold C. Hand, *What People Think About Their Schools*, World Book Co., Yonkers, N. Y., 1948.

known by their teachers, the satisfactoriness of discipline in the school, the pupils' workloads, and the adequacy of the help which pupils are receiving with their schoolwork.

The decision to take opinion polls or use the procedure embodied in the Local Area Consensus Studies rests, of course, with the school board first of all; then the survey is carried out by the whole school. But the individual classroom teacher who is concerned about the problem of improving school-community relations can help to start the ball rolling. He can urge the use of these devices in his conversations with the head of his school. He can help to persuade his fellow teachers that such methods of approaching the problem of improving school-community relationships are desirable. And, once the poll has been sanctioned by the board of education, he can volunteer his services for the work that must be done in conducting the poll and collating its results.

There are other immediate things which the classroom teacher can do to bring parents more into partnership with the school. He can visit the homes of his pupils, become acquainted with their parents, discuss with them the plans for the courses in which their children are enrolled, and ask them for their suggestions. He can make parents welcome as visitors to the school and to his classes, and use these visits as the basis for later conferences with them. Furthermore, he can take an active part in the school's Parent-Teacher Association or, if such an organization does not exist, urge that one be formed.

If they are welcomed, as they should be, by teachers and school administrators, Parent-Teacher Associations can do a great deal to engender the kind of psychological ownership upon which the well-being of public education depends. So can lay advisory groups which are invited to help in specific school projects. The growth of these lay advisory groups was stimulated by the work of the National Citizens Commission for the Public Schools; and its successor, the National Citizens Council for Better Schools, has continued this important work with no less vigor. Other important organizations which are doing much to improve the quality and increase the degree of lay-professional cooperation in support of the public schools are the American Association of University Women, the American Federation of Labor, the Chamber of Commerce of the United States, the Council of Industrial Organizations, the General Federation of

Women's Clubs, the National Association of Manufacturers, and the National School Board Association.[8]

Some idea of the important work which these organizations are doing is suggested by the following excerpts from their official declarations. Here, for instance, are the chief items in the current Action Program [9] sponsored by the more than eight million members of the National Congress of Parents and Teachers:

> 1. Promote understanding of the purposes and functions of the [public] schools.
> 2. Help build curriculums that will prepare young people to live in the complex world of today.
> 3. Support up-to-date and realistic systems of educational finance.
> 4. Attract and keep teachers who have the vision, the insight, and the skill to help children and youth utilize fully their natural talents and powers.
> 5. Create opportunities for the development of mutual confidence and understanding between the parent and the teacher.

The National Citizens Commission for the Public Schools stated its basic principles in these terms:

> 1. The problem of its children's schools lies at the heart of a free society. . . .
> 2. The goal of our public schools should be to make the best in education available to every American child on completely equal terms.
> 3. Public school education should be constantly reappraised and kept responsive both to our educational traditions and to the changing times.

With these basic beliefs in mind, the National Citizens Commission for the Public Schools set for itself two immediate goals: [10]

> 1. To help Americans realize how important our public schools are to our expanding democracy.

[8] Nelson B. Henry, ed., *Citizen Cooperation for Better Public Schools*, 53rd Yearbook of the National Society for the Study of Education, Part I, University of Chicago Press, Chicago, 1954.

Herbert M. Hamlin, *Citizen's Committees in the Public Schools*, Interstate Printing Company, Danville, Ill., 1952.

[9] National Congress of Parents and Teachers, *Action Program*, Chicago, pp. 2-3.

[10] *Education Molds Our Future: Better Schools Build a Stronger America*, Highlights Report of the National Citizens Commission for the Public Schools, New York, 1951, p. 4.

2. To arouse in each community the intelligence and will to improve our public schools.

A recent publication of the American Association of University Women states its policy on education in this way: [11]

> A.A.U.W. branches work for better public schools; for community understanding of school needs, adequate school budgets, conditions to attract good teachers, well-qualified school boards.

The reports of the Executive Council and of the Annual Convention of the American Federation of Labor on Education in 1951 contain these statements: [12]

> Today . . . we must do more than merely urge more funds for education. We must analyze and evaluate the programs through which these funds are administered. . . .

> We recognize that a layman cannot determine technical professional procedure in education any more than he can properly do so in any other profession or trade like medicine or law or building construction. But he can, as a layman, judge the results of such training.

Since 1921 the American Legion has joined with the National Education Association in promoting American Education Week. Among the purposes of the program are these two: "To increase public understanding and appreciation of the schools" and "To secure the active participation of the people in improving the schools." [13]

The public education program of the General Federation of Women's Clubs is in part described in the following statements: [14] "Know your public schools and cooperate with school leaders to solve local problems." "Secure well-qualified teachers by making salary schedule and social position attractive." "Study attacks against the public schools by: *first*—discovering the source and reason for the attack; *second*—separating facts from half-truths and falsehoods; *third*—cooperating with school leaders to strengthen and improve your public schools at local and state levels."

Although a good many professional educators believe that the United States Chamber of Commerce and the National Association

[11] *A.A.U.W. Fact Sheet*, Jan. 1953.
[12] American Federation of Labor, Washington, 1951, pp. 5-6.
[13] National Americanism Commission of the American Legion, *Americanism Manual*, p. 27.
[14] *Our American Heritage: Education to Preserve*, General Federation of Women's Clubs, Washington, p. 1.

of Manufacturers did not consistently support public education in the earlier periods of their history—a view which is not contradicted by the record—both of these organizations have in recent years issued pronouncements which are favorable to the improvement of the public schools. In its 1952 policy statement the United States Chamber of Commerce declared: "In addition to tax payments and contributions, business should assist education by making available, whenever feasible and requested" such aids as "consultant service," "contributions of equipment and facilities," "summer employment" for teachers and students, and "such other support as may be mutually determined." And one of the stated objectives of the National Association of Manufacturers is [16] "to bring about closer cooperation between industry and education to the end that each may understand the other's problems and contribute jointly toward their solution."

The National School Boards Association maintains close working relationships with the United States Office of Education, the National Education Association, the National Council of Chief State School Officers, and the American Association of School Administrators.[17] It is an active and influential agent in helping lay and professional groups cooperate for the betterment of public education.

These examples of the stated aims and methods of our important nonprofessional organizations in the field of education demonstrate that the citizens of this country are interested in establishing better school-community relations and are willing to assist in improving the public school enterprise. All these organizations are active, not only nationally, but on the state, and often on the local, level. As the results of the 1955 White House Conference on Education,[18] together with those of the more than 3,500 local, county, and state meetings of laymen and professional educators which preceded the national conference, show, there is abundant reason to believe that great gains can be made in solving the problems of public education

[15] *Education Policies of the Chamber of Commerce of the United States,* Government Printing Office, Washington, 1957.

[16] *Handbook of National Association of Manufacturers Activities and Services for Education-Industry Cooperation,* National Association of Manufacturers, New York, Oct. 1952, p. 4.

[17] Nelson B. Henry, ed., *Citizen Cooperation for Better Public Schools,* pp. 223-4.

[18] *Report of the White House Conference on Education,* Superintendent of Documents, U.S. Government Printing Office, Washington, 1956.

through joint lay-professional study and action, if the teaching profession will merely meet the public halfway.

Cooperation with local units of national organizations— highly desirable, but not enough

As we have indicated, much should be done to strengthen the public schools through cooperation with the local units of the influential national organizations which we discussed in the preceding section. But helpful as this may be, it is not enough. The public school cannot rely merely upon cooperation with the citizens who are already organized in particular groups, at least not if the widespread sense of participation in the education program which is so important to the maintenance of good public schools is to be obtained.

Many communities have no chamber of commerce, no chapter of the American Association of University Women, no bodies of organized labor, no unit of the General Federation of Women's Clubs, and so on. In some villages and towns there is not even a Parent-Teacher Association, and unfortunately the P.T.A., even in communities where it has flourished, has seldom succeeded in attracting members from the lower socioeconomic brackets.

Even in our larger towns and cities, the school can usually reach no more than a minority, though perhaps an appreciable minority, of the adults in its neighborhood by cooperating exclusively with the local units of the large national civic organizations. In other words, large numbers of people everywhere simply do not belong to any of these organizations or perhaps to school-related organizations of any kind. In our larger as well as our smaller communities, therefore, the establishment and maintenance of good school-community relations require that something much more far-reaching be done to secure the involvement of lay citizens in the school program. The systematic procedures detailed in the Local Area Consensus Studies sponsored by the Illinois Curriculum Program constitute one promising way of bringing about this involvement. Similarly, the local opinion poll is a very useful approach. The formation of Home Room Mothers and Dads' Clubs has frequently produced new understanding and a new lay participation in school affairs. Visiting days, though of limited value, may also stimulate townspeople to think about school problems. The Parent-Teacher Association can be exceedingly valuable, and where a local branch does not exist, one should be organized. Teachers should give it their full support and should urge all parents and other citizens to participate. Many a P.T.A. has dissolved or become moribund because its teachers failed to take an active part in its work. Conversely, many a P.T.A. has been revitalized when the teachers demonstrated their willingness to take a strong hand in the group's work.

All these ways of involving lay citizens in the work of the school are valuable—indeed, they are indispensable. But the most valuable of all remains the individual contact between the teacher and the parents of his students, and this is what good teachers have always contrived to bring about. The heart of the matter is succinctly put in the title of a lively and useful pamphlet: "It Starts in the Classroom." [19]

Summary

Public opinion is the ultimate determinant of whatever the public secondary school in America accomplishes, and in consequence, good school-community relations are of the utmost importance. Teachers who can help bring about such good relations are highly esteemed by school administrators and boards of education—and, incidentally, by the community at large.

The adherence to the spirit of the Golden Rule by teachers is the prerequisite for good school-community relations. Unfortunately, some teachers sometimes demean their pupils, and the practices of some schools as institutions may unintentionally violate the sensibilities of its students.

A good educational program is a second requisite for good school-community relations, and this program must be made known to the public. The citizens of the community will be favorably impressed by proof of the school's effective performance; this evidence of good performance can be secured in various ways.

Furthermore, the example set by teachers must be found by the people of the community to be a desirable one, a fact which imposes no serious burden on conscientious teachers in most communities.

Finally, the entire program of the school must somehow be made the psychological property of the community at large. We hope that we have succeeded in making it clear that this task of inducing

[19] National School Public Relations Association, 1201 Sixteenth Street, N.W., Washington 6, D. C., 1951.

in the citizens of the community a sense of ownership of the purposes and program of the public school is frontier territory, still virtually unexplored, for most of our public high schools. Indeed, at the present juncture of our educational progress, this aspect of the work which must be done next offers our greatest opportunity to the inventive young minds who are now entering the teaching profession.

chapter 7

ESTABLISHING AND MAINTAINING

GOOD DISCIPLINE

In order to learn how good discipline may be established and maintained among high school students, one must first make sure that he knows what good discipline is. What is it that students do who are well-disciplined? Why is it that the teacher who provides a regimen suited to the learner possesses the key to good discipline? In this chapter we shall attempt to answer both of these questions.

According to the dictionary, the word *discipline* may be defined in three ways: the regimen suited to a learner, the exercise of control, and the correction of wrongdoing through reproof or other punishment.

All parts of this definition relate to the role of the pupil. Since this is a book about secondary education, the pupils with whom we are concerned are the adolescent boys and girls who attend secondary schools. Everything which the secondary school does in respect to discipline should take account of the educationally significant characteristics of adolescents. Adolescents present types of problems in respect to "learning," "control," and "correction" which are not commonly encountered when one is dealing with little children or with adults. Consequently, we shall call attention to the characteristics of adolescents which are especially significant in the establishment and maintenance of good discipline, and we shall consider what each of these characteristics suggests that the teacher ought to do.

Like all other behavior,
that which results in good discipline must be learned

In Chapters 3 and 4 we stated that the ways in which human beings conduct themselves constitute the sum of their learned behavior patterns and that persistent changes in these patterns can be induced only through learning. The modes of behavior which result in good discipline in the secondary school are no exception; like all other modes of behavior, they must be learned. Hence the key to good discipline lies in helping students to learn these ways of behaving—in providing, that is, the "regimen suited to a learner" which results in the ways of behaving which yield good discipline.

One might think that these things would be self-evident, yet some teachers apparently do not sense them. Many teachers who are made miserable by disciplinary problems are the architects of their own misery; their troubles ensue from their mistaken belief that discipline denotes *only* the "exercise of control" and the "correction of wrongdoing through reproof or other punishment." They have not yet realized that neither effective control nor wholesome correction is possible without the "regimen suited to a learner." Teachers who are rarely bothered by disciplinary problems are almost without exception those who recognize all three meanings of discipline, and particularly the first. They have learned that if they succeed in providing the regimen suited to a learner, their classes will seldom be disturbed by problems of control or cases of wrongdoing. Let us see why these things are true.

First, let us observe what it is that high school pupils do when they are well-disciplined. Since the purpose of the secondary school is to facilitate learning, no class is under effective control unless the pupils in it have good work habits. According to Principle 4 (Chapter 4) the public secondary school in this country is an educational agency of a democratic society. This means that its pupils are under effective control only if they treat one another and their teachers considerately, maintain good order, obey proper authority, and behave honorably—and do these things, not because they have been forced to, but because they choose to—because they have been helped to realize that these modes of behavior are essential ingredients of the democratic way of life and are therefore requisites for intelligent self-direction in such a society. Nor are pupils under effective control unless they are regular and prompt in their class attendance, except when circumstances beyond their control force them to be absent or tardy.

What do pupils who have been wholesomely corrected for wrongdoing actually do? Aside from its occasional use to help a youngster discover the limits of permissibility, generally speaking, reproof or any other form of punishment is wholesome only if the dissatisfaction it induces is internalized by the pupil, that is to say, if the pupil directs this dissatisfaction toward himself. And this is exactly what the wholesomely punished pupil does. If he does not direct his dissatisfaction toward himself, if instead his anger, let us say, culminates in a blind resentment of others, then his punishment has not been wholesome. No punishment is likely to satisfy this test of wholesomeness unless the pupil not only knows that what he has done is wrong but is distressed because of it. Punishment is wholesome when it reinforces conscience, when it helps the conscience to prevail over the part of the youngster's personality which prompted the wrongdoing.

Punishment will probably not be wholesome unless two conditions have been satisfied. First, the pupil must understand that his punishment is a consequence of his wrongdoing, not an annoyance which someone has invented simply to hurt him. Second, the pupil must feel that he is secure in the regard of the person who does the punishing, that this person really likes him, believes in him, and does what he does, not in anger, spite or revenge, but in the belief that the wrongdoing was the result of a lapse in the pupil's self-control and in the expectation that the punishment will give the pupil the help which he needs to regain this control.

Why is it that the teacher who provides a regimen suited to a learner possesses the key to good discipline? This is the second question we should consider in order to show why it is that teachers who concentrate on providing the kind of regimen suited to a learner encounter almost no disciplinary problems, while those who concentrate on control and correction are usually plagued by a seemingly endless succession of disciplinary problems. To begin with, the mode of pupil behavior which must prevail if a class is to be well controlled is always *learned* behavior. In many cases, this behavior is not only difficult for pupils to learn but is more than even many mature adults have acquired. The modes of behavior which result in prompt and regular class attendance, fruitful study skills, good work habits, considerate treatment of others, good order, respect for proper authority, and honorable conduct are not built into our nervous systems. To the contrary, as we have pointed out, they must be *learned*. And so must certain other ways of behaving which the community expects its adolescents to practice, ways of behaving which result in the exercise of intelligent self-direction and the maintenance of self-control. Since effective classroom control is possible only when high school pupils behave in these ways, since these ways of behaving must all be learned if they are to be put into action, and since these learnings have been only partially acquired by most pupils before they begin going to high school, providing a regimen suited to learners of these ways of behaving is the only method by which the high school teacher can effect good control in his classroom.

Wholesome punishment is related to the provision of a regimen suited to a learner. Since, aside from its sparing and judicious use to make clear to the errant student the limits of permissibility, punishment is wholesome only when it reinforces the dictates of conscience—i.e., only when the pupil agrees that what he has done is wrong and directs against himself the dissatisfaction which arises from the punishment for his wrongdoing—the sense of right and wrong must be present in the pupil *before* his punishment can become wholesome. The knowledge of right and wrong, and the desire to do what is right, are learned; after they have been learned, they become the learner's conscience. The person who does not possess a sense of right and wrong can acquire it only through learning. As many case studies of delinquent children have shown, punishment is a poor way to teach boys and girls to distinguish right from wrong and to choose what is right. This knowledge is usually learned by internalization (see p. 28). The persons whose values the youngster wants to internalize must be worthy models if this internalization is to result in a sound sense of right and wrong.

Since, aside from its occasional use to define the limits of permissibility, punishment can be wholesome only when it is directed toward pupils who already possess reasonably well-developed consciences, the teacher who wants punishment to be wholesome must first make certain that the pertinent ideas of right and wrong have already been inculcated in the minds of the pupils for whom the punishment is intended. If they have not been inculcated, the wise teacher knows that they must be learned—i.e., that he must provide the regimen suited to a learner of what is right and what is wrong. This regimen should include provisions for associating the pupil with worthy persons whom he wants to imitate and whose ideas of right and wrong he will therefore internalize, i.e., learn (see p. 28).

Punishment, either physical or mental, may inhibit a socially disapproved response—that is to say, keep a pupil from misbehaving—but punishment alone cannot teach him to behave properly. It can teach him only that certain modes of behavior subject him to the risk of painful consequences; it can teach him only what not to do, not what to do. One acquires a knowledge of socially approved responses only if the proper conduct which this knowledge sanctions produces satisfaction. By definition, punishment is the infliction of pain, and no normal person derives satisfaction from pain. Therefore, no teacher can teach proper conduct through punishment alone. A teacher must make proper behavior rich in satisfactions for the pupil. The pupil must see that good conduct is more rewarding than misconduct, for what he believes will be most satisfying to him determines what he will do.

Teachers who experience serious and continual problems of discipline are either overlooking these facts or, if they do recognize them, are employing in their efforts to teach good behavior a psychology of learning which their common sense would forbid them to utilize in teaching mathematics, science, English, or whatever their special subjects may be.

Many high school pupils have imperfectly learned the modes of behavior which result in good discipline

Secondary school pupils differ greatly in respect to what they have previously learned (see Principle 8, Chapter 4). Some are advanced, some greatly retarded, while most tend to cluster around the average for their age group. This is true for all kinds of learning, whether it is formal training in English, science, mathematics, and the other academic subjects, or whether it is the kind of training in behavior which results in good discipline. Almost every teacher is aware of these differences in his students' knowledge of his special subject of instruction, but some teachers overlook the differences which apply to discipline.

Any sensible teacher of high school mathematics, for instance, would dismiss as preposterous any suggestion that the mathematical knowledge which he has been hired to teach was instilled in his pupils at birth. He knows that the newborn infant is completely innocent of the attitudes, skills, concepts, and modes of thought which constitute a knowledge of mathematics. He knows that these ways of behaving must be learned, that this learning is difficult for many young people, that it can be accomplished in most cases only with the help of good teaching, and that even if the elementary school training which his pupils have already received was very good, there are certain to be vast differences among these pupils in respect to their competence in mathematics when they enter high school. Consequently, he would think it absurd to believe that the new pupils who appear in his high school classes should manifest a uniformly high degree of proficiency in mathematics. And he would regard it as even more outlandish to believe that these high school pupils are blameworthy if they exhibit a less than perfect knowledge of mathematics at the end of the course.

What we have said about our hypothetical mathematics teacher applies equally well to teachers of all high school subjects. Most teachers are reasonable in their expectations regarding the academic attainments of their new students; few teachers will condemn a pupil because his accomplishment when he enters a new class is low. And without exception teachers will recognize that the desirable behavior which they wish to induce in their students as the synthesis of knowledge in a given subject can be brought about only by good teaching, by providing the regimen suited to a learner of the subject in question.

But when it comes to the modes of behavior which pupils must practice if the classroom is to be well controlled, these same teachers may respond quite differently and, for that reason, encounter no end of serious disciplinary problems. These teachers expect—or act as if they expect—all their pupils to come to high school in an advanced stage of self-discipline. They think that all their pupils should already have acquired effective study skills and good work habits. They seem to expect all their pupils to have learned to be considerate, to maintain good order, to conform to proper authority, to behave honorably, to exercise intelligent self-direction, and to practice good habits of punctuality and self-control. Some high school teachers not only have these completely unreasonable expectations, but also seem to be unaware of the fact that when pupils persistently misbehave they probably do so because they had an inadequate or faulty prior education, and that the remedy lies in their further education or re-education. The disciplinary problems which confront high school teachers who overlook these facts are largely the result of their own misconceptions.

But this is not all. Teachers who overlook the fact that pupils must learn the modes of behavior which make for effective classroom control err in still another respect: they assume that pupils who do not measure up to their unrealistic expectations are blameworthy. Consequently, they punish these pupils for not doing what the pupils have never learned to do, or for doing things which they have been taught to do by a faulty prior education in the home or neighborhood. This only compounds the errors and frequently makes the situation in the classroom so explosive that the peace of the school and the tenure of the teacher are threatened.

The dunce cap and the rod were once standard school equipment. They were used freely by teachers who were attempting to teach the correct way to solve an algebraic equation, for instance. The force of ridicule or physical pain was thought to assist the pupil's mental processes. But now we know that pupils do not make mistakes in mathematical computations because they are willfully obtuse or unskillful. Such mistakes are the result of faulty learning and hence—in most cases, at least—of faulty teaching. And so today we regard the pupil whose "mathematics behavior" is improper, i.e., erroneous, not as an incarnation of the devil, but as a learner who has been victimized at some prior point in his education. We no longer try to shame him or beat the devil out of him; instead, we, as teachers, give this particular learner of mathematics the treatment that is appropriate to him: we supply him with the proper regimen. This is the enlightened point of view which must be transferred to the problem of classroom management if the teacher is to attain effective classroom control. This is the point of view and the practice which characterizes teachers who maintain good discipline in their classrooms.

Discipline evolves best from classroom activities which pupils have helped to plan

The high school teacher whose classroom presents no serious problem of control and whose pupils are rarely guilty of wrongdoing is the teacher who (see Principle 8, Chapter 4) recognizes that the most stable and usually the best classroom control results when the pupils engage earnestly in their activities. Such a teacher knows enough about the psychology of adolescence to realize what the chief interests of his pupils are likely to be. This teacher is careful to clarify the aims of the course, to demonstrate how they are related to the lives of the pupils in his class, and to encourage the pupils to share with him the responsibility of deciding how the class may best realize these aims.[1] This cooperation comes slowly and haltingly at first. But when the pupils are convinced that the teacher really means what he says about shared planning, nearly all of them will participate, and the units of work which result will come very close to being the "psychological property" of the entire class.

This device of shared planning, which induces in the students a sense of involvement, of psychological ownership, is probably the most effectual means known to high school teachers for the maintenance of good discipline. This applies to all three aspects of discipline. The incentive to learn is usually strongest and most enduring when students are invited to participate in planning their classroom work; similarly, experimental research has demonstrated that individuals are far more likely to carry out group decisions than those which they have made alone; moreover, because their peer culture (see pp. 149-50) is supremely important to them, adolescents are particularly susceptible to group commitments. If the aims of the group dominate the interest of all the members of the group, then the achievements of the individual which support these aims will be

[1] It may be desirable to emphasize here the framework within which we believe teacher-pupil planning should take place. As we have indicated in the text, we assume that every course—and every extra-class activity as well—in the high school program has been put there to achieve some worthwhile objective, and that it is the proper business of the teacher to see that these objectives are realized. Pupils, in our opinion, should be invited to pass judgment on these objectives only when the immediate end in view is the revison of the curriculum, and then, as we have pointed out elsewhere, we believe that lay citizens as well as pupils and teachers should participate in establishing the revised program of instruction. Otherwise, we believe that the teacher should present the objectives of the instructional program as received from constituted authority and demonstrate how these objectives promise to benefit the pupils in the class. But we are convinced that there is no single royal road to learning, that there are many possible ways, equally fruitful, for a given class to proceed toward the objectives which have been established for it. It is in choosing among these alternative ways that we believe teacher-pupil planning should be employed as fully as the capacities and capabilities of the pupils will allow. Here good resource units prove their value in the hands of capable high school teachers (see Chapter 11).

greeted by group acclaim, and nothing is more satisfying than this to any normal adolescent. This, then, is a regimen suited to a learner *par excellence*. Control is inherent in group-centered activity; to "get out of line," as the pupils themselves might say, is to flout the will of the group, to risk being a nobody or a "square," something which normal adolescents are not likely to do. Correction, when it becomes necessary, is for the same reason an inherent or a built-in function of the group-centered activity. In his skill in converting the aims of his instruction into the self-determined aims of his pupils lies the real secret of success of the teacher who is free from disciplinary troubles.

When a teacher makes classwork the psychological property of his pupils, he is acting as a disciplinarian in the most effective sense. To bring about this sense of psychological ownership he can (in addition to explaining the aims of his course, showing how these aims can be correlated or identified with the needs of the pupils, and inviting the pupils to contribute to the planned course of activity which will achieve these aims) do three things, which we shall discuss here briefly.

First, the teacher can incorporate pupil guidance in his instructional program: he can guide as he teaches (see Chapter 9). Such a conception of the teacher's role implies a much closer relationship between teacher and pupil than that which was customarily required by the pedagogy of the old school. The teacher must know the student's capacities, special abilities, interests, and needs and must shape his teaching to conform to them. He must observe the nature and quality of the student's accomplishments and reactions, and he must use this new knowledge of the student to guide the reshaping of his instructional program, which should be followed by further observations, further reshaping, and so on in an unending spiral of benefits to the student. Obviously, to do these things the teacher must become an ever more perceptive and sympathetic master of adolescent psychology; it is precisely this accomplishment which unfailingly makes for good discipline in the classroom.

Second, the teacher can employ comparatively long-term units of work, to introduce the possibility of dealing with larger and more meaningful topics or problems. These are usually easily broken down into subtopics, or subproblems, which the students may then choose or be assigned to study in accordance with their various capacities, interests, and needs. Such organization of work improves the quality of both instruction and discipline.

Third, the wise teacher not only makes his classroom as interesting and attractive as possible, but invites his students to help keep it that way and tries to see that their contribution satisfies them. Students who have secured books, magazines, clippings, cartoons, specimens, charts, pictures, and the like acquire a sense of ownership and pride which promotes good conduct in the classroom.

Wise teachers employ many techniques to maintain good discipline

There is no bag of tricks which the teacher can use to secure good discipline. Tricks can result in temporary outward conformity, which masks fear, resentment, and sometimes hatred, but they never result in a regimen suited to a learner, in effective control, or in wholesome correction. Good teaching—teaching which makes sense to the class and which proceeds upon a course that the pupils themselves have helped to plan, thus committing themselves to the teacher's aims—is the only dependable recipe in the long run for securing good discipline.

However, there are other factors which bear upon the establishment or maintenance of good discipline. Some techniques and devices are either demanded or sanctioned by the basic principle which relates to the conditions necessary for effective learning (see Chapter 4). Techniques derived from these factors are commonly employed by successful high school teachers to help establish and maintain good discipline. Let us analyze, first, the techniques and devices which help establish good discipline and, second, those which help maintain it.

A number of the techniques which make for good discipline derive from a recognition of one factor: that the adolescent peer culture greatly influences the behavior of high school students. The beliefs and modes of behavior common to a group of adolescents constitute their peer culture. Normal adolescents want to break away from their former infantile dependence on adults, but the problems raised by this desire are extremely perplexing to youngsters. For this reason, most adolescents feel unsure of themselves and need to find security somewhere. They almost always find it in group approval, i.e., in the sense of acceptance which comes from conformity to what their "gang" thinks, wears, says, and does. This makes the peer culture the most important single element in the lives of high school pupils. Every good teacher knows that the authority which these young people most willingly accept is that which resides in their peer group. Hence he knows that he must be acceptable to the group if he is to exert much influence upon any individual within the group. If he is rejected by the group, he knows that no pupil can accept him without running the awful risk of being disapproved by his fellows. Hence the teacher will strive to make himself acceptable as a leader of the group. If he succeeds, his influence in the establishment and maintenance of good discipline can be very great indeed.

To win this acceptance is always one of the chief concerns of the teacher who is a good disciplinarian in all three senses. To achieve this acceptance he does many things. He scrupulously respects the standards of the group, at least those which are socially creditable; he neither invites nor tolerates informers; he gives no cause for any pupil to be suspected of being a "teacher's pet" or a "model" pupil; he puts no individual in any position in which he will appear to be puerile, a "sissy," or an eccentric; in short, he does nothing to injure the chance of any boy or girl to win and keep acceptance in the peer group.

Such a teacher will also identify himself with the desirable aims of the group and make himself helpful in the group's efforts to achieve these aims, even outside of the classroom. So far as possible he will offer his assistance to the solution of such problems as making friends, dating, learning desired social skills, improving personal appearance, acquiring status in extra-class activities, or choosing a vocation or a college.

The wise teacher, in other words, will do his best to respond sympathetically to the behavior which is exhibited by adolescents during this difficult period of their growth, trying though this behavior may be. He realizes that social experimentation intrigues adolescents, and that it is as necessary for their development as getting into the water is for ducklings. Consequently, he knows that his classroom will be, not only a forum for learning and acquiring intellectual skills, but a place for experimenting with ways of making friends, winning the favor of the opposite sex, achieving popularity, attaining status with the group, influencing others, testing one's associates, rewarding one's friends, and the like. He knows that what appears to be senseless giggling, shoving, and poking is a normal concomitant of growing up, especially in early adolescence. He is aware that building castles in the air is a normal function of the adolescent imagination. He recognizes the absurdity of expecting anyone, and especially an adolescent, to work at top speed all the time; he knows that fluctuations in work performance, sometimes very pronounced, are bound to occur. He appreciates the fact that tensions sometimes mount rapidly in adolescents and that as a result they need to blow off steam. More than this, the wise teacher will train himself to accept the fact that he will sometimes be treated with rudeness, defiance, and even contempt which he does not deserve.

Unlike the foster mother hen who goes into a dither because the ducklings in her brood cannot be kept out of the water, and unlike some teachers who have little understanding of adolescents, the teacher who wins the acceptance of the boys and girls in his high school class takes all these things in his stride. Of course he does not allow his class to run wild. He does not allow any pupil to impose unreasonably upon him or the other members of the group, because he knows that if he refrains from making proper educational demands on his students, they will take this to be evidence of his lack of concern for their welfare.

The wise teacher realizes that a pupil's need to resolve some problem of winning group acceptance, or of acquiring status, or of achieving self-esteem may be as important to this boy's or girl's wholesome development, at a particular moment, as the subject matter of his class, and consequently the teacher makes no issue of these small acts of social experimentation which occur in his classes even though they may interfere somewhat with his work of instructing. The wise teacher recognizes giggling, for instance, as a release of inner tensions, and good-natured shoving and poking as unconscious expressions of affection or rapport; he does what he can to ease embarrassments and overlook antics which do not disrupt the group. Furthermore, the wise teacher provides for a certain amount of moving about in his classroom, tries to pace the work to coincide with the attention span of which his pupils seem capable, varies the routine of the class to avoid monotony, is understanding when tensions erupt, and deals good-naturedly with the pupil who has expressed his tension or impatience in a minor act of misconduct. And finally the wise teacher understands why he is sometimes the victim of unpleasant treatment which he does not deserve; he knows that the offender is probably having trouble adjusting to the adult world and that his ensuing resentment is vented against the adult closest at hand, the teacher; unless the episode threatens to destroy his good relations with the rest of the class, the teacher accepts such instances of ill treatment, though he will of course try to keep them from becoming too frequent and to provide by his own example a model of more becoming behavior.

Certainly one of the most important things a teacher must do if he is to win acceptance from the adolescent group is to treat all high school boys and girls as young adults. Normal adolescents want ardently to be done with their infantile past, and they long to be considered young men and women. The wise high school teacher intimates in every way he can that he looks upon his associates in the classroom not as children but as young men and women who will conduct themselves in an adult and intelligent way. If students feel that the teacher treats them as young adults, they will respond enthusiastically to his attitude; nothing is more attractive to the adolescent mind. The result is that the teacher's attitude becomes a strong influence toward good discipline. But if the teacher who voices this expectation then treats high school students as he would little children, the results may be disastrous. Pupils will instantly see that a teacher who treats them as children is acting in bad faith when he asks them to behave like grown-ups, and a teacher who does not keep faith with his class cannot expect to have good discipline.

Another very powerful technique which leads to the establishment of good discipline might be called the "put it up to the group" approach. A teacher who has not won acceptance from his pupils will not be able to do this; any problem of pupil conduct which he presents to the group will be viewed as his problem, not theirs, and they will be inclined to sit back and let him solve it if he can. But if the teacher has been accepted by his pupils, any problem of pupil conduct which he might bring up would stand a good chance of being seen by the students as their problem—one which concerns the welfare and self-esteem of the whole group, and one which they should resolve. Because of the authority of the adolescent peer group, the resolution of the problem which is produced by the decision of the group is very likely to be one which all of the pupils will feel obligated to support. In the rare instance when one pupil fails to conform to the decision, the necessary correction of his wrongdoing will be supplied by the group itself, usually in the form of openly expressed disapproval.

Another technique which makes for the establishment of good discipline consists in organizing classwork into a sensible routine. When the pupils don't know what is going to happen next, they may enjoy the suspense for a time, but ultimately the uncertainty will breed feelings of insecurity and eventually dislike. A poor routine means disorder. When pupils do not know what is expected of them, they can scarcely be blamed for not knowing how to behave appropriately. Although they relish innovations from time to time, pupils dislike continuing uncertainty. They will show their dislike by behavior which does not make for good discipline. Both to establish and to maintain good discipline, therefore, at least a moderately well-organized routine is necessary. This is what every wise teacher will take pains to establish. He will avert monotony by introducing occasional novelties, but he will be sure that the basic routines of the class are sufficiently stabilized to give his pupils a sense of security. Pupils must feel that in general they can count on what is going to happen.

We turn now to a consideration of various techniques commonly employed by good high school teachers to reinforce the modes of pupil behavior which produce good discipline, once that discipline has been established.

What may be called the "tut-tut" signal is perhaps the most frequently used of these techniques. Everyone knows what it is. A pupil is just beginning to do something which will threaten class discipline, he is about to do something distracting, for instance, or something which will annoy another pupil; his momentary impulse is about to prevail over his conscience. The teacher, seeing this, frequently need do no more than catch the pupil's eye in order to alert him to his impending loss of self-control. The pupil reasserts his self-control, and the threatened distraction or disturbance does not occur. Or perhaps the teacher may resort to an almost imperceptible sign of dissent, a nod or some other inconspicuous signal. This device, it should be noted, will not establish good discipline. But it can and frequently does help maintain the good discipline which the teacher has already established.

This is true, too, of what may be called a special form of the "tut-tut" signal. In this case, the teacher simply moves to or past the vicinity of the pupil who is about to lose his self-control. Nothing is said. There is not even any implied threat in the teacher's presence. But the teacher's nearness tends to make the pupil more self-conscious and hence more perceptive of what is going on inside himself. If good discipline has already been established, this is all that most pupils need in order to recognize their imminent loss of self-control and avert it.

What we may call the "osmosis treatment" is another technique which good teachers often find useful. The pupils in a typical high school class will invariably be at different levels of behavioral development. There will nearly always be one or more who do not behave in ways which result in good discipline in the classroom. Consequently, good teachers, who are often accustomed to dividing their classes into groups for instructional purposes, will assign the pupil whose behavior problems are serious to a group in which the accepted mode of conduct is what the teacher desires. Provided the poorly trained pupil feels himself accepted by the group and admires and wants to be like one or more of its members, he will usually internalize many of the group's attitudes and responses. Hence this device helps establish better discipline in the class group as a whole. Note, however, that good discipline must already have been established among most of the members of the class if this "rubbing off" process is to take place in the proper direction.

A fourth technique depends on the fact that virtually every secondary school classroom contains one or more "stars," that is, boys or girls who are especially admired and respected by the other pupils. The behavior these very popular students exhibit will be imitated by the other members of the class. If this behavior is conducive to effective classroom control, then the teacher will encounter few disciplinary problems. But if these very popular students behave poorly, then there will be many disciplinary problems. The wise teacher finds out as quickly as possible who these "stars" are. If they already behave well, he takes pains to see that they continue to behave well; if they do not, he makes a special effort to make them desirable leaders of the group. This might be called the "bell-wether" device. It can be used not only to maintain but to improve the discipline of the class.

Even when good discipline has been established, trying moments will occur from time to time. The high school teacher who has developed a good sense of humor and enough inner security to be able to laugh at himself will weather these occasional storms. He can head off a potentially troublesome incident by turning it into a joke on himself; in fact, this is a technique which many good teachers have used to neutralize situations which might otherwise have destroyed the good discipline they had established.

The "changing gears" technique is used by all good teachers. The wise teacher, as we noted above, knows that there are limits to the attention span of his pupils, and he is shrewd in estimating what these limits are from day to day. He knows that the good discipline which he has established will be endangered if he allows his pupils to continue too long at one task. When he sees that tension is beginning to mount, he is ready with interesting suggestions for something different to do or for a different way of performing the assigned work.

Every wise high school teacher also knows how to use the technique of pretended unawareness. He simply ignores examples of individual behavior which threaten the self-control of the group. By doing this he sets an example for the class, and if he is liked and admired by his pupils, most of them will follow it. Later the teacher will deal privately with the pupil who has caused the difficulty and help him to solve his behavior problem. Note that the teacher regards the errant pupil, not as a problem, but as a person with a problem.

The "face saving" technique is another which good teachers commonly employ to maintain the good discipline which they have already established. Suppose that a high school pupil in a class in mathematics does something which if continued would be contagious, i.e., would lead others to lose self-control, too. The teacher offers some plausible explanation which rationalizes what the pupil has done—he might say, for instance, "Oh, you don't quite understand this step in the problem; here, let me help you"—which enables the pupil to recover his self-control without losing face before the rest of the class, but which clearly indicates the teacher's disapproval of the pupil's breach of good conduct.

Every wise teacher uses what might be called the "ounce-of-prevention" technique. Suppose that the class is scheduled to undertake in the near future some activity which is apt to provoke a general loss of self-control. The teacher, by foreseeing this, can do much to prevent it if he takes the trouble to talk out the problem with his pupils in advance. His purpose here is to create in the minds of his pupils a prior image of what their behavior should be, so that when the time comes they will conduct themselves according to this image rather than according to some spontaneous impulse. Examples of the kind of activities for which the teacher may prepare in this way are a visit of the high school class to a business or industrial establishment, a class picnic or other social event, a survey of some aspect of school or community life—in short, any experience which is new to the class.

A "how well did we do" session at the conclusion of a successful unit of work can reinforce good discipline, provided that the center of attention is the project itself, and not the conduct of the pupils engaged in it. When students look back at the factors responsible for the success of an undertaking, they usually see that the good conduct of members of the group has been a major one. In this way no pupil suffers a loss of face and there is at least implied group acclaim for right conduct. But the teacher should let the pupils themselves express this acclaim. Expressions of appreciation by pupils for the good conduct of their fellows are much more likely to induce contagion than any words which the teacher can pronounce, however sincerely.

Classroom teachers are not competent to diagnose or treat all behavior problems

From time to time there is apt to appear in any high school class a pupil whose personality is so warped by emotional illness or by the miseducation he has received from an extremely inadequate home and neighborhood environment that his case is entirely beyond the competence of any ordinary teacher. The wise teacher recognizes the symptoms of mental or emotional illness, even though he cannot diagnose them. He knows that he must refer to competent psychiatric authority any pupil who is seriously withdrawn, or who persistently lives in a world of make-believe, or who reveals extreme and continuing feelings of persecution, just as he would refer a pupil with a rash or a fever to competent medical authority. The wise teacher, moreover, will not permit the behavior of a seriously miseducated pupil to jeopardize the welfare of the other pupils in his class. He will, if necessary, exclude the miseducated pupil from his class in order to prevent this. If the demands of the necessary re-education are beyond his capabilities or if they require him to neglect or endanger the welfare of the other pupils, he will continue to exclude the miseducated pupil from class until he has been treated and recommended for readmittance by competent authority. And when the pupil is readmitted to class, the teacher will, of course, be guided in his future treatment of the pupil by the prognosis of the counselor.

The basic commitments of the American people are honored by good teachers

It will be recalled that the basic commitments of the American people (see Principle 4, Chapter 4) are the rules of the game in our democratic society. Consequently, it is the responsibility of the American public secondary school to help incorporate these rules of the game into our young people's moral equipment. Good teachers realize that the type of discipline for which they should educate should always be consistent in every respect with these basic commitments of the American people. In addition to striving for the greatest good for the greatest number, these teachers respect the dignity of each student in every way, and they make fairness and equality of treatment a rule from which they never deviate. Although they insist upon proper order, good teachers try to make this self-imposed by helping their students to understand what the components of good order are and to see why it is important to their own well-being to learn to behave in an orderly way of their own free will.

Teachers who maintain good discipline avoid certain serious mistakes

Some teachers do things which destroy good discipline. What are these things? Let us look at some of them. All are violations of the points in the psychology of learning discussed in Chapter 4.

Boredom is fatal to good discipline. Most students can tolerate very little of it. If they are bored, the things they will do to overcome their boredom seldom make for good discipline. The wise teacher knows this, and he never permits his class to remain bored for long. Instead, as we observed earlier, he does his best to make the work of his course interesting and varied. He knows that serious boredom is more likely to occur in two groups of pupils, those who are the most and those who are the least capable, and consequently he takes these groups particularly into account in his planning. And one should remember that most good disciplinarians—i.e., teachers who seldom have serious disciplinary problems—are themselves persons whom adolescents find interesting.

As we noted in the preceding section, the teacher who maintains good discipline is the teacher whose class is well organized. But it must not be overorganized. Overorganization is nearly as destructive of good discipline as lack of organization is. A superfluity of petty rules makes most high school pupils feel that they are being treated like infants. Quite properly, they resent this. The more daring pupils will openly spurn these petty restrictions; most of the others will invent devious ways of evading or neutralizing them. None of this avoidance behavior is apt to lead to good discipline. The good teacher seeks a golden mean between too little and too much organization. Furthermore, he knows that the degree of organization which is suited to one class will be altogether too little or too much for another, and he makes his plans with these differences in mind. In addition, he relaxes his organization in a given class as the pupils grow in their ability to direct themselves.

Closely related to the question of organization is that of overdirection. Either too much or too little direction by the teacher will create poor discipline. Again, what the good teacher does will vary from class to class. He will do what must be done to maintain good control in each class, but no more. Furthermore, he will offer his directions in the form of questions ("How would it be if we do it this way?") or of suggestions ("It might be better if you do it this way"). And of course he invites his pupils to work out their own solutions to the behavioral problems which may arise.

This means that the good teacher is tactful. Tactlessness creates poor discipline, just as it creates poor social relations in any sphere. All high school students are quick to resent a tactless remark, and many of them will respond by adopting the teacher's tactless manner. Hence, the good teacher is careful to consider how his words will sound to another.

An inconsistent teacher is another enemy of good discipline. If he is exacting today and lenient tomorrow, approachable one day and distant the next, and so on, his problems of discipline are apt to be vexing and relentless. Teachers whose own personalities are emotionally unstable obviously will tend to heighten the insecurities which normally characterize the development of their adolescent pupils. Conversely, the high school teacher who can maintain good discipline is usually a person of balanced and stable emotional responses. His pupils can predict what he will do; they are confident of his behavior.

Moreover, good high school teachers, though they are often persons of rather more than average personal dignity, do not overreact when they are affronted, intentionally or unintentionally, by their pupils. They do not allow even the most exasperating pupil's conduct to upset their self-control. In other words, they do not permit their egos to become involved. The teacher who takes offense at the crudities of his pupils will seldom achieve success either in teaching them the socially approved modes of behavior or in bringing about constructive control of his classes. The teacher who permits his ego to become involved in the intentional or unintentional provocations of his students is likely to yield to a temptation, which, above all others, will destroy good discipline. He will permit his desire for revenge to dictate what he does; in other words, he will retaliate. Nothing less than an atmosphere of open conflict can result. In this kind of guerilla warfare whatever good discipline may have been established is certain to vanish. No teacher should permit himself this kind of personal involvement. Though he should make himself one of the group in many respects, he should stand apart, and above, when it comes to questions of personal vanity.

Summary

Discipline signifies three things: a regimen suited to a learner, effective control, and correction when it is truly necessary. Good teaching affords our best guarantee of discipline in all three senses. The peer culture is very important to boys and girls of high school age. The secondary school teacher must be accepted by the group if he is best to influence the individuals in the group. A teacher can use certain techniques to win this acceptance, and certain other techniques to help establish good discipline once he has been accepted. These techniques were examined in this chapter, as well as techniques used by the teacher to maintain good discipline already established in the classroom and some of the mistakes teachers make which destroy discipline.

Teachers should not forget that the public high school as an institution is supported for the education of youth, not for the comfort or convenience of teachers. Some of what is done in the name of discipline by the few teachers who have overlooked or forgotten this precept, verges on temper tantrums. Good discipline can never be either established or maintained through such means. The only secure pathway to the establishment and maintenance of good discipline is the provision of a regimen which is suited to the adolescent learner engaged in acquiring the modes of behavior which result in good discipline, both in the school and elsewhere. This pathway is never smooth or untroubled, yet it is the only path by which teachers can both help their pupils learn the modes of behavior which result in discipline, and earn for themselves the respect and gratitude of their pupils.

chapter 8

VITALIZING THE EXTRA-CLASS ACTIVITIES

OF THE SECONDARY SCHOOL

In this chapter we shall apply the basic principles of American public secondary education to the extra-class activities program of the school. Everything we say will be based on the presupposition that all extra-class activities are part of the school's *educational* program. We believe that extra-class activities are as much a part of the school curriculum as are the regular subjects of instruction.

This belief can be justified in several ways. First, since the school is intended to be an educational institution, everything that it does, including all the things which its teachers or pupils are permitted to do in its name, should educate. Second, the educational program of the school necessarily includes all of the school situations in which learning occurs. Third, students learn everywhere, not just in classrooms; thus they are being educated, for good or ill, in the school's extra-class program.

In appraising the educational value of any part of the high school program, the following three questions should be asked.

1. What learnings is it intended to bring about?
2. Who is to acquire these learnings?
3. What measures have been taken to ensure that what is to be learned will in fact be learned?

The answers to these questions should be in harmony with the basic principles of public secondary education. We shall apply these basic principles to each of these three questions within the context of extra-class activities.

What learnings
should the extra-class activities program
be designed to produce?

The fundamental obligation of the public secondary school is to promote the general welfare by helping young people to learn whatever they must learn during adolescence in order to engage successfully in the basic social processes upon which the strength of the nation and the well-being of its citizens depend. To fulfill this obligation, the school must give top priority to helping its students make themselves as competent as possible to carry on three of these basic social processes (see Chapter 4). In order to do this the school must help its students to make a direct study of all the rest of these processes.

A direct learning never takes place without concomitant learnings (see Chapter 4). Whatever direct learning one acquires (e.g., that the angles of a triangle total 180°) is always accompanied by one or more concomitant learnings (e.g., that mathematics is a pleasure or a bore, that one is a success or a failure in the study of mathematics, that one's fellows are considerate or ruthless, and so on). The direct learnings which one acquires are determined by the nature of the subject matter in question; in chemistry one does not learn what one learns in mechanical drawing. But in all courses the concomitant learnings may be very much alike. In either chemistry or mechanical drawing one may learn to heed or ignore the feelings of others, to be self-confident or diffident, to regard oneself as socially accepted or rejected, and so on.

These two considerations, based on our previous discussion, warrant a number of generalizations about what students should learn through extra-class activities.

Every extra-class activity should provide
desirable direct and concomitant learnings

The extra-class activities which the secondary school sponsors, no less than its subjects of study, should be so conceived and so conducted that they provide direct learnings relating to the proper purposes of public secondary education. It is true, of course, that some direct learning results from participating in any extra-class activity, but this learning may be unrelated to the purposes of the school or even antithetical to them if the faculty member sponsoring the activity is inept at handling it.

Moreover, students who participate in any extra-class activity, whether the activity is planned wisely or poorly or not at all, are bound to acquire many concomitant learnings. When the faculty of a school neglects its extra-class program, these concomitant learnings are very likely to be undesirable. They may be the unintended consequence of events whose significance high school pupils are too unsophisticated to comprehend. For example, an extra-class activity may entail a cost in dues or other expenses for the student. The sum involved may be trifling for most students, yet crucial for a few. Being excluded for such a reason is an experience which, if repeated and especially if coupled with a lack of scholastic success, very often leads the student to believe that he doesn't belong in school. This is a concomitant learning, and once it is fixed in the student's mind there is a good chance that he will become an early school leaver. Desirable concomitant learnings are part of the school's responsibility and they are generally acquired only if the faculty sponsors of extra-class activities deliberately strive for them.

Collectively, the extra-class activities offered should provide direct learnings respecting all the basic social processes

If the public secondary school program is to make students as proficient as possible to carry on all of the basic social processes, the extra-class activities program must be deliberately planned to provide direct learnings respecting these processes; this cannot be left to chance. The scope of the secondary school's extra-class program will be broad enough only if each basic social process is "represented" by a balanced variety of activities related to it.

There should be extra-class activities, appealing to students, which will teach them to think and communicate effectively (Principle 3), such as:

Assemblies (especially those patterned on the town meeting)
Choral reading groups
Debate teams
Departmental clubs (especially those in English, foreign languages, history, mathe-matics, science, social studies, and speech)
Discussion groups
Dramatic clubs
Literary societies
Parliamentarians' clubs
Public forum groups
School publications

Effective thought and communication should be the deliberate aim of sponsors not only in these activities but in all others that are offered by the school. What this means is that teachers, both in and out of the classroom, should never forget that helping young people learn to think and communicate effectively is a top-level priority task of the public school and therefore of every faculty member each time he is in contact with his students.

These observations are equally applicable to the task of teaching students to understand, appreciate, and practice the democratic way of life—another of the public school's first-priority responsibilities (Principle 4). The school should include in its extra-class activities program a balanced variety of the activities which afford valuable direct learnings in democratic thought and action:

Assemblies to commemorate national heroes
Clubs organized for the study of local and regional affairs
Departmental clubs in history and civics
Parliamentary law groups

Public forum organizations
School elections
School service clubs
Student councils
Various forms of student participation in community services

In addition, every extra-class activity must be conducted in a way that is consistently democratic if students are to be taught how to live democratically (see pp. 43-45). Democratic attitudes and habits are concomitant learnings which the school should try to create in all that it does.

The third top-level priority task of the public high school (Principle 5) is to teach young people the principles of safe and healthful living, help them develop bodily vigor, and give them a safe and healthful physical environment. Direct learnings related to this necessary work of the school are furnished by such extra-class activities as:

Assemblies devoted to good grooming, health, safety, and so on
Boy Scouts
Camp Fire Girls
Clean-up weeks
Departmental clubs in home economics, hygiene, science, and so on

First aid groups
4-H Club
Future Farmers of America
Future Homemakers of America
Girl Scouts
Hiking clubs
Hospital auxiliaries
Junior Red Cross

Safety clubs
Safety drives
School farms

School forests
Sports (individual, intramural
team, and intermural team)

A well-balanced program of such activities should be offered by every secondary school. Moreover (see p. 49), every extra-class activity—as well as all other school activities—should be productive of a safe and healthful environment. This is an important and often difficult part of the school's responsibilities.

We have also seen (Principle 6) why the high school should have its students make a direct study of the problems of making a living. Schools can furnish direct learnings of a vocational nature through such extra-class activities as:

Arts and crafts clubs
Career assemblies
Career days or weeks
Departmental clubs in agriculture, art, business education, home economics, industrial education, music, and science
Excursions and field trips
FDA
FFA
FHA
4-H Club

FTA
Hospital auxiliaries
Journalism clubs
Library clubs
Radio clubs
Religious education groups
School farms
School forests
School publications
Skilled performance groups in music
TV clubs

Direct learnings related to the improvement of family living should also be afforded by the extra-class activity program through social activities in which wholesome boy-girl relationships are consciously established and maintained, such as:

Arts and crafts clubs
Departmental clubs in art, home economics, hygiene, industrial arts, and science

4-H Club
FFA
FHA
Individual and chamber music activities

The high school should also enable its students to make a direct study of the problems related to society's physical security (Principle 6)—the management of natural resources, national defense, and the like (see also Chapter 4). Every high school student should acquire important direct learnings regarding these necessities for survival through one or more extra-class activities such as the following:

Conservation clubs	International relations clubs
Departmental clubs in foreign languages, history, science, and other social studies	Nature study organizations
	Travel clubs
	United Nations auxiliaries
Foreign correspondence groups	

Another basic social process which high school students should study directly is that relating to spiritual growth (Principle 6). Again, this part of its necessary task can best be accomplished by the public secondary school if direct learnings relating to spiritual growth are afforded not only by the formal instructional program but also by such extra-class activities as:

Boy Scouts	Hi-Y
Camp Fire Girls	Religious clubs
Girl Scouts	Tri-Y

Providing for aesthetic satisfactions is still another basic social process in which high school students should gain experience (Principle 6). The school should help students develop aesthetic sensitivity through as many as possible of the extra-class activities which it offers. These are provided in great abundance in our better high schools; examples are:

Art and handicraft clubs	Excursions to art galleries and exhibits
Art appreciation groups	Jewelry-making clubs
Art exhibits	Literary societies
Assemblies	Music festivals
Choirs	Opera clubs
Choral speaking groups	Performing groups in music
Choruses	Photography clubs
Dance groups	Poetry clubs
Departmental clubs in art, English, home economics, industrial arts, music, and physical education	Symphony clubs
	Water ballets

The secondary school should also have its students gain experience in recreation (Principle 6). And, again, direct learnings in this respect should be afforded by its extra-class activities. The activities which are useful for this purpose include virtually all that have previously been listed, and dances and parties in addition.

The remaining basic social process relates to social organization and control (Principle 6): students must learn so to organize themselves that all of the other necessary processes will be carried on as effectively as possible. The public secondary school should also provide direct learnings respecting this basic social process through its extra-class activities program:

Assembly committees	Know-your-city clubs
Boys' state	Know-your-state clubs
Class organizations	Student councils
Departmental clubs in civics and history	Student courts and other student government
Girls' state	

Every extra-class activity
should be so conceived and so conducted
that only desirable concomitant learnings will result

Desirable concomitant learnings are learnings which are in harmony with the proper purposes of the American public secondary school. And the proper purposes, of course, were presented in Chapter 4. As a whole, then, the concomitant learnings which are by-products of participation in the extra-class activities of the school should enable students to:

1. Derive values from the past which help them prepare for the future (Principle 2).
2. Think and communicate effectively (Principle 3).
3. Understand, accept, and live the democratic way of life (Principle 4).
4. Understand, appreciate, and apply the principles of safe and healthful living (Principle 5).
5. Prepare themselves for the problems of making a living, strengthening the family, and providing for physical security, spiritual growth, aesthetics, recreation, and social organization and control (Principle 6).
6. Help their school live up to the ideal of equality of educational opportunity (Principle 7).
7. Help their school use what is known about the learning process (Principle 8).
8. Help their parents and other adults understand the purposes and program of the public secondary school and show them its effectiveness (Principle 9).

Now let us comment on these categories of desirable concomitant learnings one by one. No matter what it is—the stamp club, the school newspaper, the junior prom, the student council, the school orchestra, the debate team, the intramural sports program—every extra-class activity draws upon the past, for all knowledge and skills have roots in the past. But this unavoidable utilization of the past may not result in concomitant learnings which will be useful in the future. What the students experience and accept (i.e., what they learn) in any extra-class activity is predominantly determined by the way that activity is conceived and conducted by the school.

Let us consider two hypothetical groups of high school students on the staffs of their respective school newspapers. In both instances, these pupils are helped by their faculty advisors to draw upon the past in discovering and learning the necessary skills of news gathering, news writing, newspaper make-up, etc. These *direct* learnings, obviously, make for more effective living by the students in question. In School *A* the faculty advisor, with full administrative approval, puts the determination of editorial policy up to the student staff and encourages these pupils to base their decisions on considerations of what the relevant proper purposes of the public secondary school are, what best promotes the general welfare of the student body, what constitutes tact, and the like. In School *B* the editorial policy is based on the same considerations, but here its determination is not put up to the student staff at all—the faculty advisor, with the full backing of the school principal, simply announces what the policy is and politely makes it known that he will enforce it.

We can be sure that if both groups of students accept the situation in their respective schools quite different concomitant learnings are being acquired in the two schools, though the direct learnings are similar. In School *A* the pupils on the newspaper staff are concomitantly learning to make discriminating judgments affecting the general welfare of the student body, to use freedom responsibly, and to behave tactfully. The youths in School *B* are not acquiring these learnings so far as their experiences with the determining of editorial policy are concerned. To the contrary, they are concomitantly learning to expect someone else to do their thinking for them, a learning which unfits them to live effectively in a free society. Because the school newspaper undertaking is quite differently conceived and conducted in these two schools, the concomitant learnings acquired through participating in this activity are quite different in the two instances. The group of students in School *A* are being much better oriented to and prepared for the future than are those in School *B*.

Whether the teacher is aware of it or not, concomitant learnings of *some* sort are certain to occur in any extra-class activity. Only if the activity is conceived and conducted in consonance with the basic principles of secondary education can we be assured that these unavoidable by-products of pupil participation will be of a desirable nature.

We have seen (Chapter 4, Principle 3) that teaching students to think and to communicate effectively must be made a top-level priority task of the school if societal strength and individual well-being are best to be ensured. This holds for every extra-class activity as well as for every subject offered by the secondary school. In this chapter we have already noted that the subject matter of such activities as writers' clubs, literary societies, school publications, and departmental clubs of many sorts affords *direct* learnings in this important respect. It must be remembered that participation in every extra-class activity, regardless of its subject matter, inevitably results in *concomitant* learnings which make youths either (a) more skilled in thinking and communicating effectively or (b) less so. Let us see why this is true by noting certain aspects of interscholastic football in two high schools in which this activity is quite differently conceived and conducted.

In School *C* the football coach helps all the boys on the squad see why the offensive plays he is teaching are likely to work in the kinds of situations for which they are designed, and why each player must do his assigned task well if the ball is to be advanced. And when the game is under way he neither calls plays from the bench nor sends in substitutes with special instructions to the quarterback regarding what play or plays to call next. Also, this coach recognizes that he is teaching speech by example every time he utters a word; he sees to it that the example he sets is habitually a good one. In School *D* the football coach concentrates his instruction regarding offensive plays on the quarterback who calls the signals. The other players may not understand the reasons behind the coach's instructions, but he is satisfied if they do what they must to make each play work. The example set by this coach when he speaks leaves much to be desired.

As we have already observed, students learn whatever they experience and accept. If the boys on both football squads accept what their coach does, the two groups are acquiring markedly different concomitant learnings in respect to thinking and communicating. Those in School *C* are directly learning to reason in football situations, and concomitantly learning that it is both pleasurable and profitable to think things out for oneself—a learning quite likely to transfer to other situations. In School *D* the quarterback is directly learning to reason about football situations, but the other players are not. Both the quarterback and his teammates are concomitantly learning that it is proper to leave the "heavy thinking" to someone else—the quarterback because he has learned to expect the coach to do his thinking for him in critical situations by calling the signals from the bench, the other players because decisions come to them from the quarterback.

Most adolescents identify themselves with and model themselves after some adult whom they admire. The football coach is usually such a person to the players on the team. If this is true in both schools, one group of boys will concomitantly learn to communicate more effectively or find their previously acquired skills reinforced by the model which their coach affords; while the other youths will have the efforts of their English teachers nullified by what they concomitantly learn on the football squad.

In School *C* the football coach is honoring the principle that teaching youth to think and communicate effectively is a first-priority responsibility of every faculty member. He so conceives and conducts the extra-class activity for which he is responsible that students who take part in it are concomitantly learning to think and communicate more skillfully. In School *D* the football coach may be unaware of this principle, indifferent to it, or incapable of carrying it out. Much of what the boys on his squad are concomitantly learning subverts one of the proper purposes of the public secondary school.

Again, the way that any extra-class activity is conceived and conducted will determine whether or not the students who take part in it concomitantly learn to think and to communicate more effectively.

Likewise, the way that any extra-class activity is conceived and conducted will determine whether or not students will learn concomitantly to understand, accept, and live the democratic way of life (Principle 4). To make this demonstration, three considerations must be kept in mind. First, as already noted, students learn whatever they experience and accept. Second, since participation in extra-class activities is voluntary, students who take part in them are obviously likely to accept most of what goes on in them. Third, what goes on in any given extra-class activity either is, or is not, predominantly democratic.

In any given extra-class activity, either there is, or there is not, a prevailing respect for the sacredness of human personality. If there is such a prevailing respect, the participating students will concomitantly learn to respect the sacredness of human personality. If no such respect prevails, they will not acquire this concomitant learning in the activity in question. If any practice prevails which denies that all human beings are of supreme and equal moral worth (showing favoritism, employing sarcasm, permitting the cost of participating to be so high as to exclude any student, excluding any student because of race, religion, social status, clothing, etc.), the participating youths will concomitantly learn to regard human beings as of unequal moral worth—a learning subversive to American democracy.

In any extra-class activity, either there is, or there is not, a prevailing insistence upon integrity. If there is, the participating students will concomitantly learn to value integrity. If there is not, this concomitant learning so necessary to societal good health will not be acquired in the activity under consideration. If a climate of poor sportsmanship, deceit, or any other form of cheating prevails in the activity (e.g., if a football coach calls signals from the bench, if a debate coach writes the speeches which the debating students give, if a faculty sponsor writes some of the material which goes into the school newspaper), the students will learn to cheat as a by-product of their participation.

Similarly, in any extra-class activity the participating youths either do or do not concomitantly learn to use freedom wisely, to make wholesome adjustments to the opposite sex, to feel that they belong and are accepted by their fellows, to acquire a merited feeling of self-confidence, to work at self-imposed tasks, to criticize tactfully and to differ peaceably, to tolerate opposed points of view, to help shape the views of the group through persuasion based on reason, to work cooperatively for the common good, to select and follow wise leadership, to lead without dominating, and to govern themselves wisely. Again, unless extra-class activities are properly planned, these important by-products of participation will not be learned; further, the very opposites of these important learnings will concomitantly be acquired if what goes on in an extra-class activity gives students satisfying experiences in respect to these opposites. Since teaching youths to understand, appreciate, and live the democratic way of life is a top-priority task of the public secondary school, each extra-class activity offered by the secondary school should be so conceived and so conducted that democratic values, understandings, and skills will be learned concomitantly by the students who take part in it. This thesis was advanced many years ago by Fretwell,[1] who, more than any other person, has helped us to glimpse the values potential in extra-class activities. He said, "It is the business of the school to organize the whole situation so that there is a favorable opportunity for everyone, teachers as well as pupils, to practice the qualities of the good citizen here and now with results satisfying to the one doing the practicing."

Everything that a student does in any extra-class activity is either conducive to bodily safety or to bodily injury or worse; it is also either hygienic or unhygienic. Obviously, if any activity is conducted under safe, hygienic conditions, the participating students who accept this circumstance as necessary or desirable are concomitantly learning how to live safely and healthfully in respect to the life situation to which this extra-class activity relates (Principle 5). And, of course, if the activity is carried on in an unsafe or unhygienic environment which the participating youths are led to regard as acceptable, quite the opposite concomitant learning will result. The faculty advisor of every extra-class activity must be alert to these alternatives if the school is to discharge its necessary responsibilities.

Almost every extra-class activity affords experiences through which students either will or will not fit themselves to carry on the other basic social processes successfully (Principle 6). Which it will be depends on what experiences the activities provide, and this, of course, is determined by how these undertakings are conceived and conducted. If the students must work hard to succeed in an activity, they will concomitantly acquire good work habits which will fit them to cope successfully with the problem of making a living. If they do not have to work hard, the resultant concomitant learning will make them less fit for the world of work. If students are induced to establish and maintain wholesome boy-girl relations in the pursuit of their extra-class activities, a good basis for a happy marriage will

---

[1] Elbert K. Fretwell, *Extra-Curricular Activities in Secondary Schools,* Houghton Mifflin, Boston, 1931, p. 2.

be built; if they are not, no such concomitant outcome can reasonably be expected. If high school youths are led to establish and maintain self-imposed law and order and to make prudent use of their material resources, the necessary groundwork will concomitantly be laid for securing the nation against internal disorder and the wasteful use of its natural resources. If the school fails to teach good government and physical security, the burden will be placed on adult education to teach it. Spiritual growth, also, can be either nurtured or stunted by the concomitant learnings which extra-class activities afford. Everything that high school students do relates to aesthetics; through their extra-class activities, students either will or will not learn concomitantly to appreciate and create beauty. Participation in extra-class activities can either broaden the students' appreciation of the need for a rounded variety of leisure time pursuits, or it can be so narrow as to handicap them severely in this respect. How the faculty views and carries on its extra-class activities program are again the determining factors. In properly thought-out and supervised extra-class activities students will concomitantly learn much that will help them organize and govern, but in poorly planned and supervised activities they may acquire antidemocratic learnings.

The American public secondary school is obligated to provide equal educational opportunity for all the educable youth of the community (Principle 7). The concomitant learnings afforded by its extra-class activities will serve either to help or to hinder the school in discharging this necessary responsibility. It is inevitable that students who take part in any activity will concomitantly learn either to view their fellows as persons of supreme and equal moral worth or to regard favoritism and special privileges as acceptable, even desirable. Only if all its extra-class activities are so designed and carried on that the former of these two alternatives results, will the school have the enthusiastic support of its students in its efforts to serve equally well all the educable youth in its district.

The school can most capably perform its function only if it capitalizes upon what is known about the learning process (Principle 8). What students can and will learn concomitantly through taking part in a properly conceived and effectively conducted program of extra-class activities will be of enormous help here. We know that the most effective learning will result only if the students see a clear and sensible relationship between what the school asks them to do and something they want for themselves. The right kind of departmental club will arouse students' interests and lead them to a renewed interest in the content of their courses (whether agriculture, art, business education, English, foreign languages, history and the other social studies, home economics, mathematics, physical education, science, or unified studies). The "subject matter" of almost all other extra-class activities relates to one or more of the school's courses. Nearly all extra-class activities can help youths engaged in them to generate the interests and consequent purposes which will make the courses which the school offers mean more to them. As Fretwell [2] phrased it over a quarter of a century ago, "Wherever possible, extra-curricular activities should grow out of curricular activities and return to them to enrich them."

The concomitant learnings which students acquire from taking part in a good program of extra-class activities will also enable the school better to honor the ninth and final basic principle presented in Chapter 4. If there is considerable pupil-teacher planning within the extra-class activities of the school, and if the students are thus encouraged to consider the necessary purposes of the public school, these youths will often be able to help their parents and other adults understand these purposes. These adults will, of course, then be in a better position to support the school in doing what it ought to do. And if students are invited to help plan the activities in which they are engaged, parents and other adults who talk with these young people can gain a better understanding of the technical operation of the school.

Who should take part in extra-class activities?

All the educable youth of the community should be able to take part in any extra-class activity which attracts them and for which they possess the necessary skills and capabilities. If all young people are to be treated as persons of equal moral worth, as our ethic postulates, then they must all have equal access to the good life, at least so far as this is possible within the limits imposed by nature. As we have pointed out before, this means that the school must provide equal educational opportunity and equal encouragement to remain in high school until graduation. Equality of educational opportunity is a rather empty concept if some adolescents are discouraged from taking advantage of it.

[2] Fretwell, *Extra-Curricular Activities*, p. 2.

Young people like to take part in extra-class activities; they usually look forward eagerly to this part of their school life (see p. 101, Chapter 5). All youths must find it equally possible to take part in these activities if they are to be equally encouraged to remain in high school. We should never forget that a sizable majority of the many early school leavers so carefully studied by Dillon and Hecker (see p. 103, Chapter 5) had not taken part in a single extra-class activity.

Since participation in extra-class activities seems to lead youths to remain in school, all pupils should be able to take part in them. But there is another equally compelling reason. Since extra-class activities which are properly conceived and administered help students make themselves competent to carry on the basic social processes upon which our communal and individual well-being depends, the school cannot perform its proper function unless all its students can learn whatever they are capable of learning in any extra-class activity as well as in any regular course.

Thus if the school is to discharge its obligations to society, all educable youth must find it possible to participate in a rounded variety of the extra-class activities as well as to take the courses offered by the school. This assertion can be disputed successfully only if it can be shown that the extra-class activities program affords no learnings necessary or desirable for all youths to acquire which are not afforded by the school's courses. It is the author's considered judgment that this cannot be shown, that all high school students can acquire many such additional learnings through participation in a balanced program of properly conceived and conducted extra-class activities.

What conditions are necessary for an effective program of extra-class activities?

A well-trained and dedicated corps of teachers is needed

Good teachers are needed to sponsor extra-class activities no less than to give instruction in the classroom. The well-trained teacher is fully aware that the school's extra-class activities are an important, and for the students an engrossing, part of the educational program. He realizes that these activities can be justified only if they benefit the pupils. He knows what direct and concomitant learnings can be gained in the activities which he sponsors, and he knows how these activities must be conducted so that students will acquire these learnings. He knows also what other conditions (see below) must be fulfilled in order to provide an effective program of extra-class activities, and he is, of course, ready to do his part in meeting them.

Knowing these things and being ready are imperative; but they are not enough. The teachers who successfully sponsor these activities are necessarily dedicated persons. Under all but the most favorable conditions the sponsoring of extra-class activities is largely financially unrewarded. Ideally, the time and effort required of the teaching staff for all of the desirable tasks are appraised, and the tasks are divided equitably among the teachers, each of whom should have a reasonable total work load. Few indeed are the secondary schools, however, in which the work-load situation even approximates this ideal. Too often the teachers who sponsor extra-class activities are dedicated men and women who voluntarily accept an overload.

Laymen and students should be involved
in shaping the purposes and scope of the program

The unfortunate work-load situation noted in the preceding paragraph can never be remedied by the teachers alone. Instead, only as lay citizens who pay the bills are persuaded of the worth of extra-class activities will sufficient funds be supplied to employ the additional teachers needed to prevent the overloading of any faculty sponsor. No better way of inducing this persuasion has yet been discovered than inviting representative parents and other laymen to consider with teachers and pupils what the educational needs of the youths of the community are and what relevant values a well-rounded program of extra-class activities can yield. In addition, since high school students will soon be voters in the community, representative students should also help shape the policies which govern the extra-class activities program.

There are at least two other good reasons for securing this lay involvement, both expressed in the ninth basic principle in Chapter 4. First, the school is functioning as a public institution in the best sense only if laymen shape its major purposes. Although all operative policies relating to extra-class activities are necessarily approved, tacitly if not formally, by the laymen who constitute the board of education, these policies do not typically originate at the hands of these or other lay citizens, but rather they are nearly always formulated by one or more persons on the school faculty. This deficiency will be remedied when representative lay citizens, on the invitation of the school board, serve on a lay advisory group, one of whose functions is to advise in respect to these activities.

And second, the school faculty has an obligation to make clear to the citizens of the community why the procedures it employs are believed to be effective. This understanding will increase as representative laymen cooperate with teachers and student leaders in improving their school's extra-class activities program.

There is a sound pedagogical reason for involving students, too, in these deliberations. The public school in a free society is obligated to teach its students the processes of self-government. Students who share in planning their own extra-class activities are gaining experience in self-government which can be exceedingly valuable to them.

Knowledge of the learning process should be applied

Only well-trained teachers can meet this condition; only they can make extra-class activities an effective part of the whole educational program. Let us observe some of the things which such a teacher will do in order to make his extra-class activity beneficial to the students who are participating in it.

First and foremost, the well-trained teacher knows that he who does the doing acquires the learning: whoever does the planning learns to plan, whoever carries out the plan learns to do the work which the plan requires, and whoever evaluates the results of the work learns to evaluate. Because he is determined to apply these truths, the well-trained teacher is less concerned with product than he is with process. For instance, if he is the faculty sponsor of the school newspaper, he is more interested in the educational experiences which his students undergo in publishing the paper and the educational experiences which the other students who read it have than he is in winning a prize for his school's paper in competition with other schools. He knows that the prize is more likely to be won if he, the sponsor, does all the really important work—plans each issue, decides editorial policies, writes the news stories, makes up the pages, etc. But he also knows that if he does these things, he and not the students will acquire the learning which these processes afford.

Here the well-trained sponsor of an extra-class activity likens himself, as it were, to the wise teacher of mathematics. If the primary aim of teaching mathematics were to solve the problems with the least expenditure of time and effort, the teacher would solve them himself and give the students something else to do. He might let them adjust the window shades or erase the blackboards, but he would not let them work on the problems; for if they did, some of them would undoubtedly come out with the wrong answers and this would be a waste of time. The wise teacher knows, however, that the primary purpose of a course in mathematics is that students learn mathematics, and he knows that if students are to learn mathematics they must grapple with mathematics problems. They must do this even though they proceed awkwardly, take a long time, and make many mistakes. This is how they learn, and what his students are *learning* is always the chief concern of the wise teacher of any subject—or the wise sponsor of any extra-class activity. Neither, of course, can afford to be indifferent to the products which their students create, but their chief concern is with what is learned through carrying on the processes by which these products are created.

The well-trained sponsor knows that the students in his activity must understand and value what the activity offers if they are to give their best efforts to it and so benefit from taking part in it. For this reason, and also because he wants them to learn to plan wisely, the sponsor involves his young people as fully as possible in planning the activities of the group. Here he proceeds cautiously and with a sharp eye to the readiness of the students. He realizes that if he involves his students too little they will think, rightly, that they are being treated childishly or tyrannically; they will withdraw, probably without waiting to see whether he changes his tactics. On the other hand, he knows that if he plunges them into planning activities which are beyond their capacities, they will fail and as a consequence will acquire (i.e., learn) a feeling of distaste for planning and a desire to depend upon him even more than they did before. Hence the wise sponsor attempts to devise steps which will be big enough to challenge his students but small enough to assure a fair degree of success for their efforts. He knows that what students experience with satisfaction they are apt to repeat, hence apt to learn better.

To be interesting, an activity must be meaningfully structured; this generally means that it must be centered on a problem. Students in a given extra-class activity, for instance, may set themselves the task of publishing a handbook for the student body. The problem is to produce an interesting handbook which will not cost more than any student can afford to pay. Such a problem satisfies the requirements of meaningfulness: the students can understand its structure. Not only will each step be meaningful, but the result will probably win the applause of the group.

The wise sponsor knows that the purposes of his students will determine what they learn. For this reason he is skeptical of extrinsic rewards—pins, keys, numerals, letters, and the like—and he uses them sparingly. He realizes that these things have some value as inducements to achievement; he may even think of them as bribes. But he knows that if the student's purpose is to win a coveted numeral by playing softball, then what the student learns is to win a numeral by playing softball, not to like the game of softball. He knows that the student is not likely to continue to play softball in out-of-school life unless he again finds it linked to some appealing extrinsic reward. The well-trained sponsor wants his students to take part in his activity for its own sake, for the intrinsic satisfactions which it affords. He believes, with John Dewey, that the test of the continuity of experience should be applied. If the student continues the activity on his own, the activity has met the test. If he does not, the activity has failed.

These are by no means all the things known about learning which are used by the well-trained sponsor of an extra-class activity. But they are the things which beginning teachers, in their laudable desire to make a good showing in the activities which they undertake to sponsor, are apt to overlook, and this is why we have discussed them here.

Every extra-class organization
should be chartered and held accountable

There is no such thing as full student government of a public high school, nor should there be. But if the high school is to do what it should to help its students make themselves competent members of a free society, there must be extensive and responsible student participation in the governing of the school. Let us first chart an ideal governing arrangement in a secondary school. Then let us observe some of the steps by which a school should approach this ideal.

Some sort of representative school-wide student governing body should be established, composed of students who are both nominated and elected by their fellow students. This organization should be supervised by a faculty member who (a) possesses a scholarly knowledge of the principles of representative government and its operation, (b) recognizes and sympathizes with the need for students to acquire both the direct and concomitant learnings which participation in self-government can yield, and (c) is skilled in working informally with adolescents and is generally respected and liked by them. All but perhaps one or two of the student representatives on this governing board—most schools would probably call it the Student Council—should be delegates from one of the primary (face-to-face) groups into which the school is divided and in which time is given to the discussion of student affairs. Every student in most high schools is a member of such a group, the group being usually known as a homeroom (in some schools as a division meeting). One or more of the highest officers of the governing board should be chosen in school-wide elections.

This governing board should function under a charter granted by the administration of the school. The charter should stipulate the aspects of school life over which the administration delegates to the student governing board its authority to govern. The charter should specify the objectives for which the governing board will be held accountable and the criteria by which its performance will be judged. The charter should also state that the principal of the school has no choice but to revoke any delegation of authority which the students show they are unable or unwilling to exercise acceptably. Finally, the charter should provide for its own amendment whenever the school administration thinks this is desirable.

This charter should be worked out by the principal or his representative, the teacher who is to sponsor and supervise the student governing board, and representative student leaders. A school should probably begin in a small way; that is, it should include in the charter at first only the activities for which most of the students are obviously capable of assuming a good measure of responsibility. The charter might state, for instance, that the students will be responsible for no more than welcoming visitors to the school, conducting pep rallies, and perhaps controlling pupil conduct in the halls. As the students gain experience in governing themselves, as graduating students pass along their experience in responsibility to entering students, they probably will want to take on a larger share of responsibility for the operation of the school. When this happens the principal, acting upon the advice of the faculty advisor to the governing board, should amend the charter to include whatever new responsibilities it is believed that the students will prove themselves capable of learning to undertake successfully. In time, this could include all or virtually all the extra-class organizations and activities in the school.

The student governing board should in turn charter each of the extra-class activities which have been entrusted to it. Each of these charters should state the major objectives of the activity in question and the criteria by which the performance of the students engaged in the activity will be judged. It should stipulate that appropriate records must be kept, that the performance of those engaged in the activity will be evaluated from time to time by the student governing board, and that the group's charter will be revoked and the activity discontinued whenever there is continuing evidence that the objectives of the activity are not being achieved.

Until this chartering of student councils is a much more common practice than it is at present, there will continue to be, from the students' point of view, a good deal of sham in the student governing activities of our secondary schools. Students do not see that the head of the school is legally responsible for the good administration of his school and that he is obliged by law to intervene when he sees things going badly in activities over which the students mistakenly believe they have, or should have, full jurisdiction. A charter which satisfies the specifications we have noted, if it is faithfully followed, will remedy this unfortunate situation for students and administrators alike.

Readers of this book can probably recall from their own days in high school a number of extra-class activities whose purposes were vague and in which there was much dawdling. Some activities exist in little more than name—they are merely activities which students join in order to increase their listings in the school yearbook. Such activities are evils which should have been eliminated from our school systems long ago. If each extra-class activity were chartered, as we have suggested, and the charters were faithfully enforced, our schools would quickly rid themselves of these superfluous "activities."

Students' interests should be surveyed from time to time as one basis for determining what extra-class activities are to be offered

Notice that we have said *one* basis, not *the* basis. We have already stated that the purposes of extra-class activities, like the purposes of all else that goes on in the public secondary school, are dictated by what the school should help its students to learn. High school youths should be helped to learn whatever will help them carry on the basic social processes on which the strength of our country and the individual well-being of its citizens depend (see pp. 22, 33-34). But there is no single road to learning. Any extra-class activity can yield an enormous variety of concomitant learnings. This makes it desirable for the high school to offer a much greater variety of extra-class activities than the average high school now does.

The proportion of young people who go to high school has vastly increased in the past several decades, and now many students bring to their schooling interests which were formerly unrepresented among the high school population. In addition, our world is changing so rapidly that everyone's interests, particularly young people's, are constantly expanding and shifting. Moreover, participation in extra-class activities is voluntary, which means that students will probably avoid activities that do not appeal to them.

No secondary school should assume that its particular program of extra-class activities suits the interests of its students. It should survey these interests from time to time—perhaps every three or four years—and rearrange its program of extra-class activities in accordance with the results of the surveys. This practice, unfortunately, is quite rare. Too many schools perpetuate their established extra-class activities far beyond the time when some have ceased to serve the needs of the students. Many extra-class programs are composed primarily of activities which the teachers themselves happen to want to sponsor. No good program is likely to result from such practices.

Since young people are of equal moral worth and should be equally well served by the public school, every student should be able to find at least one extra-class activity in his school which appeals to him. The fact that some of our better schools modify their extra-class programs to take account of the full range of the socially desirable interests of young people suggests that the teachers and principals in these schools believe in this precept.

Students should be kept informed of the extra-class activities offered

No elective system can work well unless those who do the electing know what the offerings are among which they may choose. A surprising number of schools pay little attention to the orientation of students to the extra-class program, and as a consequence the students are ignorant of the activities which might appeal to them.

To choose wisely among various activities, the student must know more than their names. He must know what the principal purposes of each activity are, what the participants are expected to do, what special abilities, if any, are required, what other eligibility requirements there may be, how much time each activity is likely to take, and what financial cost, if any, each activity entails. If he decides to enroll in an activity, he should also know how to register and where to report.

In an increasing number of high schools this information is publicized sytematically through group guidance, homeroom programs, handbooks, school newspapers, and assemblies. Counselors advise students about extra-class activities as carefully as about course selections. These schools recognize that extra-class activities constitute an important part of the total educational program. Only when this recognition is universal will many of the benefits to students which are potential in these activities be realized.

No student should be barred from any extra-class activity by financial costs

A sufficient case against expensive activities can be made from the fact that learning is denied to students who cannot afford to participate. But there are other important considerations, too. To make the accessibility of any desirable learning contingent upon the pupil's economic status is, of course, to violate Principle 7. If all human beings are to be treated as persons of supreme and equal moral worth, the public school must serve all educable youths equally well. But a youth's educability has nothing to do with the size of his family's purse. To bar him from any extra-class activity offered by a public school simply because he can't pay the required fee is to deny him opportunities to which he has just as much right as anyone else.

Another consideration may be even more important. Since every experience results in learning, the student who is excluded on financial grounds acquires concomitant learnings from the experience of exclusion itself, learnings which are utterly contrary to the purposes of the public school system and to the basic concepts of our society. In other words, the experience of being excluded produces not only the negative effects of deprivation but the positive effects of what we might call contamination. It should surprise no one if the pupil who is excluded from participation in an extra-class activity because he cannot pay its costs interprets his experience as the school's avowal of his inferiority to the pupils who can afford these extra expenses. Such a pupil will be learning concomitantly that his school does not regard all students as equally worthy, but on the contrary values those with money above those without. If he accepts this experience, he learns to regard himself as inferior, as a second-class citizen of the school. He sees, furthermore, that his school is providing unequal educational opportunities for him and his more fortunate fellows, and if he accepts the situation, he is learning to regard this practice as proper and perhaps inevitable. But however he reacts to his experience—whether he accepts it or rejects it—he is quite certainly learning to view the school as a humbug when its spokesmen assert their dedication to the democratic ideal of equal educational opportunity.

The students who *can* afford to participate when some or many of their schoolmates cannot are likewise acquiring undesirable concomitant learnings. If they recognize the inequality of treatment and accept it, they are concomitantly learning both to regard themselves as superior to some or many of their fellows and to regard as proper the practice of discriminating on the basis of wealth. And whether they accept or reject the situation, they too are learning that their school is a humbug when those in charge say that it is dedicated to the ideal of equal educational opportunity.

We saw in Chapter 5 that the costs of taking part in extra-class activities have been found to be of a magnitude sufficient to discourage if not to prohibit a sizable number of students from the lower socioeconomic levels from participating in them. These students are thus often prevented from taking part in a variety of extra-class activities. We saw also that students from poor families participate in far fewer extra-class activities than students from middle-income or well-to-do families. Finally, we saw that more than two thirds of the young people who drop out of high school have never taken part in any extra-class activity and that these early school leavers are predominantly students from families in the lower socioeconomic groups.

If educational opportunity is to be equal, extra-class activities must be either free to pupils or so inexpensive that no pupil in the community is prevented from taking part in a variety of these activities. The Board of Education in Bloomington, Illinois, at the suggestion of the superintendent of schools, a few years ago decided that all extra-class activities in Bloomington Senior High School should be made free to all students. Three years later, it was found that the holding power of this school, already much better than average, had increased by about 16 per cent. Like a good many other high schools, this one is fortunate in having dedicated teachers who in the interim did many other things to make their school fulfill the needs of its students; consequently, the increase in holding power cannot be attributed to any single factor. But no one in the Bloomington school system doubts that eliminating the costs of extra-class activities had a good deal to do with the school's improved holding power. Many schools sell students an activity book which entitles them to participate in most extra-class activities. The cost of the activity book varies, but in many cases it is far too high, even though it is much less than students once paid to participate in the various activities individually.

Every student should find it possible
to take part in a variety of extra-class activities

We noted in Chapter 4 that ninth-grade pupils may vary by as much as eleven years in their mental ages. Even in chronological age they range from as young as eleven years to as old as fifteen. In physical stature they may be as small as an average fourth-grade child or as fully developed as most high school graduates.[3] These variances signify great differences in social as well as mental and physical de-

[3] Illinois Curriculum Program, *The Nature of the School Population in Illinois*, Springfield, Office of Superintendent of Public Instruction, 1955, p. 19.

velopment. The result is that pupils differ greatly in their interests and capabilities respecting extra-class activities.

If the high school's extra-class activities are to be well suited to its student body, then, the program must include activities which are graduated with respect to both level of capability required and maturity of interest presupposed. Furthermore, if the program is to be so suited, and if it is to have a broad enough scope, there must be at least one activity relating to each of the basic social processes which appeals to the interests and is geared to the capabilities of each student.

All students who have the required interest and ability should be admitted to these activities. To determine eligibility on any other grounds is intolerable in the public schools of a free society, for this practice presupposes that students are of unequal innate worth. It is as reprehensible to admit pupils to an extra-class activity on the basis of social position, wealth, clothes, clique, or personal liking as it would be to do so in respect to an art, English, foreign language, mathematics, science, business, or any other course offered by the school.

Secondary schools generally require a student to be doing passing work in his school subjects in order to be eligible to take part in any extra-class activity. This may be defensible for activities in which interscholastic competitions are held. But the rule itself cannot be squared with the purposes of the public secondary school unless it can be demonstrated that no extra-class activity affords anything that should be learned during adolescence respecting the basic social processes which could not better be learned through taking the courses which the school offers. This has never been demonstrated, and the author believes, as stated earlier in this chapter, that it would be impossible to demonstrate it. To the contrary, many of the important learnings which our youths must acquire if the public school is to fulfill its proper purpose can better be acquired through participation in extra-class activities. It is as indefensible to exclude a youngster from any extra-class activity because of poor performance in school subjects as it would be to exclude him from all of his English, history, music, and physical education classes if his performance were poor in algebra.

Whatever the strength of our country and the individual well-being of its citizens require be learned during adolescence the public high school should see that its students learn. *What is to be learned* and *where this learning best takes place* should be the determining factors. If these determinants are rigorously applied, and if the school regards its extra-class activities as part of its educational program, the passing-marks requirements cannot be justified. If, however, the school mistakenly regards its extra-class activities simply as play-things for its students and does not conduct them properly, it can perhaps justify this requirement. It could far better justify the com-plete abolition of its extra-class activities, for the school is by defini-tion an educational and not a recreational institution. It is keeping faith with the supporting public only when everything that it is doing is educational.

Participation in extra-class activities should be controlled through guidance

Mechanical devices for the controlling of extra-class activity partici-pation (of which the point system and the method of limiting by permitting pupils to engage in some maximum number of "major" and "minor" activities are but two examples) are based on the erroneous assumption that all students are essentially alike. They presuppose that the same number of extra-class activities is suitable for all high school pupils. This presupposition is absurd, for young-sters in the same high school grade differ in chronological and in mental age by as much as five and eleven years respectively—and these differences are even greater when the four high school grades are considered collectively.

As the authors [4] of an excellent treatise on extra-class activities have said, "It is as much the function of a guidance program to assist the student in the planning of [his] activities as it is to aid him in the election of classes." Obviously, only when all that is pertinent about a student is taken into account can a school decide which and how many extra-class activities he should take part in at a time. Equipped with a good cumulative record for the student in question, the guidance counselor is quite capable of helping the youth make sensible decisions in these respects. Even if adequate records of the pupil's extra-class activity participations are lacking, as they too

[4] Edgar G. Johnston and Roland C. Faunce, *Student Activities in Secondary Schools*, The Ronald Press Company, New York, 1952, p. 321.

frequently are, the counselor is probably still the person who is best equipped to help the student arrive at these important decisions.

Every extra-class organization
should be required to keep a record of its undertakings
and of the accomplishments of its members

If we were to discover that the classroom teachers in a given school kept no records of their classroom activities or the achievements of their students, we would say that their negligence was preposterous. If what students learn is worth learning, it is worth recording. Records must be kept if one is to know whether or not a teacher is successful in teaching what he is supposed to teach, and the school must know whether he is successful if it is to justify the spending of public funds—to say nothing of the students' time and effort—on the teacher's subject. If there are no cumulative records of student achievement, how can counselors guide students intelligently in their further educational development?

As we pointed out near the beginning of this chapter, the extra-class activities sponsored or even permitted by a school are a part of its educational program because students learn from every experience they undergo. Therefore, records of each student's accomplishments in extra-class activities are just as necessary as records of his accomplishments in English, science, mathematics, or any other subject.

Every extra-class activity should have a place
on a well-planned school calendar

Every secondary school should have a carefully planned calendar which, among many other things, indicates the regular meeting time and place of all extra-class activities, and the time and place of all special extra-class events. If such a calendar is designed, undesirable conflicts will be held to a minimum. A well-planned school calendar also takes account of all the known community events in which the high school pupils and their parents and teachers are apt to be involved, thus avoiding or at least minimizing all conflicts between the dates of school and community undertakings. Failure to exercise this care not only injures the extra-class activity program of the school, but also may result in the quite needless straining of school-community relations.

Every extra-class activity should adhere strictly to a budgeting, requisitioning, and accounting system

Students may easily learn lax financial practices if they are permitted to handle either funds or property without controls which are applied before any laxness or wrongdoing can occur. If students are to learn good money management practices, every extra-class activity must have a budget within which it must be operated. If pupils are to learn to be accountable for materials and other property, they must operate their extra-class activities under a requisitioning and accounting system in which wastefulness or dishonesty is prevented if possible, and penalized promptly if not. If good business practices are to be acquired by those who take part in extra-class activities, careful financial records must be kept and all books must be competently audited at stated intervals.

Summary

Every extra-class activity of the school is a part of its educational program. To make this part of its program fulfill the proper purposes of the public secondary school, activities should be provided which collectively afford *direct* learnings respecting all of the basic social processes on which societal strength and individual well-being depend. Every extra-class activity should be so conceived and conducted that the concomitant learnings which result from them will be desirable, that is, in accord with the basic principles presented in Chapter 4.

It is necessary to the proper purposes of the public school that all students find it equally possible to take part in any extra-class activity which interests them and for which they have the requisite capabilities. Certain conditions must be provided if students are to benefit as much as possible from the extra-class activities of the secondary school: first, and most crucial, the sponsors of these student undertakings must be well-trained and dedicated teachers; second, laymen and students as well as teachers must be involved in the shaping of the purposes and scope of the program; third, knowledge of the learning process must be used in conducting these activities.

Other requirements are that each extra-class activity be chartered and that all who participate in it be held accountable for the achieving of its stated purposes; that students' interests be surveyed from time to time as one basis for determining what activities are to be offered; that the orientation program of the school ensure that every student is well informed about its extra-class activity offerings; that every activity either be free or cost so little that no student will be prevented from participating in a well-rounded variety of these enterprises; that the only eligibility requirements be the student's interest in participating and his ability to learn to do so; that the extent of students' participation be controlled through guidance; that records be kept of what is undertaken in each activity and of the accomplishments of each student involved; that every extra-class activity be given a place on a well-planned school calendar; and that there be strict adherence to a defensible budgeting, requisitioning, and accounting system.

PROVIDING FOR

THE EFFECTIVE GUIDANCE OF YOUTH

If one were to visit a random selection of the secondary schools in this country, he would encounter sharply differing points of view on the guidance of youth. This situation is quite puzzling unless one knows something about the evolution of the organized guidance movement since its beginning late in the first decade of this century.[1]

Schools hold differing views on guidance because they are at different stages in this evolution. Let us now sketch this illuminating part of the history of secondary education. We shall try to show why the guidance practices found in schools at the most advanced stage of this evolution are those which are most in accord with the basic principles of secondary education.

Guidance theorists have largely devoted themselves to answering two questions:

1. What should be the aim of secondary school guidance?

2. Who should carry it out?

[1] Good teachers, including Plato, Aristotle, and Quintilian, have always been concerned with the guidance of their students, but as a school-wide movement which involved an analysis of the process and systematic attempts to make more adequate provisions for it, the organized guidance movement had its beginnings in American schools in the early 1900's.

Secondary schools have greatly extended
the scope of their guidance services to youth

Under the stimulation of Frank Parsons and Eli Weaver, the persons in charge of many leading secondary schools realized, by about 1910, that students who went directly from high school into the labor market needed more help in making the many choices which confronted them in selecting an occupation, securing appropriate training, finding a suitable job, and making whatever adjustments on the job were necessary in order for them to make good. The term "vocational guidance" was coined to denote this important service, and increasing numbers of secondary schools began to provide it.

During the early 1920's, however, William M. Proctor pointed out in an influential book that most high school youths need more than vocational guidance.[2] Proctor said among other things that they need help in choosing school subjects, extra-class activities, and colleges or vocational schools, that their needs extend far beyond occupational considerations. Even though its adherents argued that "vocational guidance," if properly interpreted, included all of these things, the expanded concept of "educational and vocational guidance" was well on its way to general acceptance by 1930.

Once this line of reasoning had been opened by Proctor, others pursued it further. Koos and Kefauver argued in a book published in the early 1930's[3] that secondary education had four principal purposes and that each of them required a species of guidance appropriate to it. They held that the high school aims to help youth learn to function competently in four main areas of endeavor—healthful living, and social-civic, leisure-time, and vocational activities. This led to the use of the terms "health guidance," "social-civic guidance," and "recreational guidance," as well as "vocational guidance" to describe the kinds of help needed by high school youth.[4]

Very shortly after the Koos and Kefauver volume appeared, John M. Brewer published a book entitled *Education as Guidance* in which he argued convincingly that all instruction bears on the

[2] William M. Proctor, *Educational and Vocational Guidance*, Houghton Mifflin Co., Boston, 1925.

[3] Leonard V. Koos and Grayson N. Kefauver, *Guidance in Secondary Schools*, The Macmillan Company, New York, 1932.

[4] Grayson N. Kefauver and Harold C. Hand, *Appraising Guidance in Secondary Schools*, The Macmillan Company, New York, 1941, pp. 16-37.

choices which pupils are called upon to make.[5] Many readers of Professor Brewer's book drew the unwarranted inference that all education is guidance, and several understandably began to wonder what good purpose could be served by continuing to employ the term "guidance" if this were true.

This is the confused state of mind which is found among the officials of some secondary schools at the present time. An increasing number, however, recognize that the term "education" means the processes by which persistent changes are induced in the behavior of the student, and that its principal components are instruction and guidance. Instruction is that part of the educational process which results in the acquisition of attitudes, beliefs, allegiances, and mental and physical skills; it teaches "what, how, and why," but it does not necessarily result in intelligent self-direction. These educators feel that it is incumbent upon the public schools of a free society to do whatever needs to be done to help youth to become intelligently self-directive. They also feel that only those young people who have acquired the discipline of choice—those who can command the principles and skills which they must learn in order to choose wisely—are capable of intelligent self-direction, that regardless of how limited guidance may have been in scope, one of its central concerns has always been the teaching of the discipline of choice, and that guidance must continue to be a part of the educational program if the schools are to turn out young citizens capable of ordering their lives intelligently.

If, as many schools believe, the proper business of schools is to help youth become intelligently self-directive in nearly all that they do, guidance—as the teaching of the discipline of choice—should extend to a great many decisions, both big and little, with which youths are confronted. These schools recognize that all young people face a variety of adjustment problems in the normal process of growing up; that these problems go well beyond those which relate to an occupational choice, healthful living, social-civic and recreational pursuits, and the choosing of school subjects and extra-class activities; and that it is with virtually all of this full range of problems that students should be helped to learn to make wise choices.

The additional adjustment problems of youths include making

[5] John M. Brewer, *Education as Guidance*, The Macmillan Company, New York, 1932.

friends and getting along well with others, acquiring social skills, improving their personal appearance, avoiding embarrassment by knowing what to say and do in different situations, acquiring grown-up emotional control, securing spending money and making it go around, finding time to get things done, improving study skills and acquiring better work habits, gaining independence from their family, resolving problems of military service, developing a philosophy of life, deciding questions of right and wrong, building self-confidence, and becoming a person of consequence. These, like all other adjustment problems, require the secondary school student to make choices—choices which, we now know, he often cannot make wisely without help.

Students need—and this is a point to which we shall return later—specific kinds of help. They do not need to have their problems solved for them, but they definitely do need wise counsel in their attempts to work out their problems for themselves. If a student's problems are resolved for him, he is denied the kind of experience through which he may learn the principles and skills of intelligent self-direction; only those who repeatedly attempt to make wise decisions can possibly learn the discipline of choice. If making wise choices in a variety of situations has been a satisfying experience for the student, he will probably transfer what he has learned to out-of-school situations—that is, he will be more likely to exercise intelligent self-direction in his everyday affairs after his high school days are over. We know from the findings of psychological research that the "identity of elements" influences transfer; that is, the more closely one situation—e.g., the out-of-school situation—resembles another situation—e.g., a school situation—the greater the likelihood that transfer will take place. This, of course, is one of the reasons it is desirable for students to have satisfying experiences in intelligent self-direction by solving as many as possible of the problems which arise while they are in school: the greater this range of problems, the greater the likelihood that, when they have left school, an "identity of elements" will occur which will allow them to apply throughout later life the principles of critical thinking which they learned in school.

We have seen how the conception of guidance has grown from a concern for teaching the discipline of choice in matters relating to making a living to the present concern in the better secondary schools for teaching the discipline of choice in respect to almost all of the daily activities encountered in the life of a student. This development represents closer adherence to the fourth basic principle presented in Chapter 4. As we pointed out in our elaboration of this principle, freedom to choose is one of the most valued privileges of our way of life, and a wise choice requires intelligent self-direction. The founders of the guidance movement recognized this; they stressed the importance of helping American youth learn how to exercise the freedom to work at an occupation of one's own choosing. By increasing the scope of its guidance program over the years, the secondary school has progressively taught the discipline of choice in respect to an ever-increasing number of decisions—decisions which the citizens of a free society are expected to make. Thus the schools have increasingly honored an important part of our fourth basic principle.

We said earlier that teaching the discipline of choice has always been *one* of the main purposes of guidance. There is a second important purpose which has likewise been increasingly in evidence throughout the history of the guidance movement in this country. Guidance has become more and more concerned with creating and maintaining the conditions under which optimum learning will take place in all that the school teaches. Later in this chapter we shall see how extensively those who guide youth effectively capitalize upon what is known about the learning process. By so doing, of course, they have honored the eighth basic principle presented in Chapter 4.

Classroom teachers should guide as they instruct

As we have already suggested, another result of the evolution which we briefly described above has been a changed view as to who should be responsible for the guidance of youth. This has resulted from a changed conception of the proper relationship between guidance and instruction.

From its beginning as a systematic undertaking in the first decade of this century, guidance was regarded as an adjunct service supplementary to the instructional program of the secondary school. The business of the teachers was to instruct; guidance was to be left to specially trained counselors. This separatist philosophy of guidance was initially based on the grounds that the vocational guidance of youth required specialized knowledge and skill which classroom teachers did not possess. As the scope of guidance was enlarged to include educational, health, social-civic, and recreational as well as vocational choices, the belief persisted that specialized knowledge and skill beyond that possessed by classroom teachers was required. Consequently, the separatist point of view continued to prevail. This separatist philosophy of guidance still exists in a substantial number of our secondary schools today.

In a sizable and growing number of secondary schools, however, the separatist philosophy of guidance has been abandoned. It has been replaced by the belief that all instruction should be guidance-centered, that every classroom teacher should guide as he instructs, and that the principal functions of the specialized guidance counselors should be (a) to help the teachers make themselves competent guides, (b) to deal directly only with those pupils who are referred to them by the teachers as students whose problems are difficult enough to require the help of specialists, and (c) to provide certain services which will be described later in this chapter. These schools, as well as those in which the separatist philosophy prevails, believe that there should indeed be an organized guidance program, but its primary function, according to the newer point of view, should be to provide classroom teachers with all the available resources for guidance and to help the teachers use these resources.[6]

We shall note why so many secondary schools are now finding it desirable to give up the separatist position, and we shall see that the basic explanation lies in their attempt to honor more fully some of the principles elaborated in Chapter 4.

To make our analysis we must first consider the practices which are likely to ensue in schools which adhere to the separatist point of view. When guidance is regarded as an adjunct service supplementary to the instructional program of the school, the guidance counselors have two principal functions to perform: the distributive function and the adjustive function.

In carrying on the distributive function, the counselor seeks to aid the pupil in formulating the goals which he should set for himself in vocational, social-civic, recreational, and other pursuits. To do this, he must first help the student acquire the knowledge of self and of the world which the student must possess before he can formulate reasonable goals. Then, through counseling, he must help

---

[6] Camilla M. Low, ed., *Guidance in the Curriculum,* Yearbook of the Association for Curriculum Development, National Education Association, 1955.

the youth integrate these two categories of knowledge and shape his goals accordingly. The counselor's next responsibility is to help the student select and enter the high school courses and extra-class activities—and later, if need be, the college or trade school—in which he can find the preparation necessary to the achieving of his goals. To do this, he must help the youth to acquaint himself with the purposes and requirements of the school's subjects and extra-class activities, and later if need be with the offerings and requirements of colleges and trade schools. Then he must help the student match these against his purposes and capabilities and choose those which are both suitable for him and desired by him and his parents. When these choices have been made and acted upon, the counselor has discharged the distributive function of guidance.

In practice, the attempt to work out the distributive function of guidance has violated some of the basic principles of American public secondary education. If the schools could provide one full-time counselor for each one hundred pupils and if this counselor could meet with these students in a group situation for an average of four or five hours each week, the various aspects of the distributive function might be performed adequately. In other words, under such favorable conditions the counselor might be able to do all the things he is supposed to do: he might administer the necessary tests and give the necessary inventories, interpret the results of these tests and inventories, present the necessary information on vocational, social-civic, and recreational pursuits, assure himself that each student's self-knowledge is sufficient to direct him toward a reasonable choice of goals in these vocational, social-civic, and recreational pursuits, explain the purposes and requirements of the school's courses and extra-class activities, and offer the necessary counseling to assure that each student's choice of courses and activities is wisely made. But it is a rare high school indeed in which each full-time counselor is assigned fewer than five hundred students, and almost nowhere are counselors who work under the separatist philosophy of guidance in touch with each of their advisees as much as one hour per month, to say nothing of five hours per week.

Nor is this all that must be said about the distributive function under the separatist philosophy. In schools which accept this philosophy the responsibility for seeing that each student "fits" the courses in which he enrolls rests with the counselors, not with the teachers. Under this philosophy, the subjects are quite fixed and only those students for whom they are suitable—i.e., those who will benefit from them and who are capable of doing the required work— are supposed to enter them. If, as very frequently happens, no suitable combination of school subjects can be found for a student, the counselor has no authority to bring about necessary modifications in the subjects—for guidance and not instruction is his business, just as instruction and not the guidance of pupils is the business of the teachers. True, the counselor can suggest that instruction be made more flexible or that more suitable new courses be added, but these changes take considerable time to accomplish and hence the problems of the present advisees are not solved. If these pupils remain in school, all the counselor can do is to help them choose the subjects for which they are least ill-suited.

This brings us to the second of the two principal functions of guidance under the separatist philosophy—the adjustive function. The counselor helps maladjusted pupils to adjust. Sometimes the counselor succeeds, but frequently he does not. If the student's difficulty stems from an inappropriate goal, this can often be remedied by skillful counseling. But if, as is very often the case, the maladjustment results from the fact that school subjects suited to the purposes and especially to the capabilities of the student cannot be found, both he and the counselor are frustrated.

The reader has probably already recognized the basic principles which these separatist practices violate. Any school in which these practices are in vogue fails to serve equally well all the youths of the community. It violates also certain of the basic commitments of the American people: we must have citizens who are capable of intelligent self-direction if several of these principles are to be carried out, but the discipline of choice cannot be taught adequately through any such practice as we have just described. In addition, a school which engages in such practices does not make full use of what is known about the learning process (Principle 8).

Each of these basic principles is honored by the schools which have rejected the separatist philosophy in favor of the teacher-centered approach to guidance described in an earlier paragraph. In such a school the teachers are responsible for helping their pupils learn to choose in almost everything they do; the discipline of choice is taught respecting nearly all decisions the student makes rather than only a few. Such a method not only satisfies a condition for effective learning, but vastly increases the chance of producing young citizens who will exercise intelligent self-direction in their daily activities. When teachers guide as well as instruct, they are responsible for shaping their instruction to fit the capabilities and needs of their students; thus the courses of instruction are more likely to be adapted to the educationally significant characteristics of the youth of the community and the school is more likely to serve all students equally well. These basic principles are honored when counselors have time to help students who have extraordinarily difficult problems, problems which require the skill and knowledge of a specialist. It is no wonder, then, that guidance in our secondary schools is evolving toward an enlargement of its scope and a more and more resolute rejection of the separatist point of view.

Let us summarize this introductory section. The purpose of guidance has always been to provide optimum conditions for learning and to help youths become skilled in intelligent self-direction: guidance has always taught the discipline of choice. Schools have become more and more aware of the needs of youth; the scope of guidance in the secondary schools has been enlarged as a consequence. The separatist viewpoint has resulted in inadequate assistance to students who are trying to learn the skills of intelligent self-direction; the growing recognition of the defects inherent in this position has led to its gradual abandonment in many secondary schools. A growing number of schools are recognizing that the aims of guidance are best realized when each teacher guides as he instructs, when specialized guidance counselors help teachers to become competent guides, and when schools organize systematic guidance programs which will provide the teachers with all the available resources for guidance. The fact that the many developments in the philosophy and practice of guidance have evolved over a comparatively long period of time and at an uneven rate explains why schools are currently in different phases of this evolution and why what is done under the name "guidance" differs so much from school to school.

In the rest of this chapter we will offer help designed for anyone who wishes to guide as well as to instruct the youth in his charge. First, we shall point out what good teachers do in order to integrate guidance with instruction. Then we shall sketch the principal services which a well-organized guidance program provides. In these sketches we shall describe the means good teachers use to contribute to the effectiveness of these services, and we shall note how each service helps them guide as well as instruct the students in their classes.

How a teacher guides as he instructs

The teacher knows what a student must be able to do in order to be intelligently self-directive

Since the main purpose of guidance is to help students to become intelligently self-directive, the teacher who guides as he instructs must know the behavior which students need to learn in order to be capable of such self-direction. He knows that intelligent self-direction involves wise planning of socially desirable activities, wise executing of the plan, and wise evaluation of its results.

He knows that wise planning of socially desirable activities can result only from intelligent selection among socially desirable goals which the students themselves both desire and can attain. He knows that the outcome is successful only when the plan is faithfully and vigorously executed and that to do this the purpose must be in the minds of the doers all the time. He knows that the outcome has been evaluated only when the purpose of the undertaking has been compared to its results.

Not only does the teacher who successfully guides as he instructs know that the components of intelligent self-direction are wise planning, wise executing, and wise evaluating, but also he realizes that it is not the teacher but the students who must learn to plan, execute, and evaluate wisely if they are to become capable of intelligent self-direction. What does this mean in practice?

The teacher involves his students in teacher-pupil planning

He recognizes and utilizes that very important principle of psychology mentioned before: whoever does the doing acquires the learning.

What this means, of course, is that only students who have a part in planning, executing, and evaluating what they do will learn to plan wisely, execute wisely, and evaluate wisely. Since these are its components, intelligent self-direction can be learned by students only as they plan and evaluate as well as execute.

Because teachers realize this, they encourage their students to share in planning and evaluating their instruction. Since this participation provides one of the conditions necessary for effective learning, and since it enables youths to acquire the skill in intelligent self-direction which the basic commitments of the American people require for their fulfillment, these teachers particularly honor two of the basic principles of secondary education which were elaborated in Chapter 4.

The teacher adapts his instruction to his students' individual needs, capabilities, and interests

Students are greatly helped in their efforts to become intelligently self-directive when a teacher adapts his instruction to their individual needs, capabilities, and interests.

The bright student must be challenged by tasks worthy of his talents if he is to exercise and hence learn the kind of self-direction which is socially desirable. If what he is expected, asked, or permitted to do does not challenge him, he will not be interested or profitably employed. He will be bored, and he cannot be expected to endure boredom for very long. To make things interesting for himself, the bright pupil will indeed become self-directive, but usually in ways that are not socially desirable. He will direct himself into excessive daydreaming or into aggressive activities which will distort his personal development and disturb the classroom. Only when they are engaged in tasks worthy of their mental abilities can exceptionally capable students be expected to practice, enjoy, and hence learn the skills of wholesome self-direction.

No less than his brilliant schoolmate, the pupil of meager talents needs to acquire the skills of intelligent self-direction. But no one is apt to devote himself to the practice of skills relating to tasks which are consistently beyond his capacity to perform. That way lies only frustration—frustration from which the pupil will seek to escape through self-directed activities which are neither permanently beneficial to him nor conducive to good order in the classroom. Thus he will indeed give himself to the assiduous practice of self-direction, but his goals will scarcely coincide with any of the legitimate purposes of the public school. Only when the tasks which are set before him are reasonably well suited to his capacities can such a pupil be expected to practice with satisfaction, and hence to learn, socially desirable self-direction.

Not only gifted and dull-normal youth, but all students, regardless of their capabilities for learning, are more likely to acquire skills of effective self-direction when the instruction provided for them is geared to their capabilities.

But simply adapting the work to the capabilities of the pupils will not suffice. It is no less necessary that what they are expected or asked to do should be meaningful to them—i.e., adapted to their varying needs and interests. Bright or slow, high school pupils will not willingly be self-directive in endeavors which have no appeal for them. But if what the classroom teacher would have his students do captures their interest, there is almost no limit to the opportunities which are presented to him to engage his pupils in the satisfying practice of the skills of socially desirable self-direction. No other member of the school staff has such abundant opportunities to help pupils achieve this central purpose of guidance.

All this relates to one of the basic principles of secondary education: the teacher who effectively guides as he instructs adapts his teaching to the educationally significant characteristics of his students—what they are able to learn, what they need to learn, and what they are ready to learn. And in so doing he also necessarily honors Principle 7, which implies that the worth of each student should be respected at all times and that each student should be helped to develop to the full limit of his abilities.

The teacher relates his instruction to the personal problems of his students

The teacher who integrates guidance and instruction recognizes two important truths concerning the personal problems which confront students. First, the discipline of choice cannot be inculcated in students merely by telling them that to choose wisely is a good thing and that to do so they must wisely plan, execute, and evaluate; students must have repeated satisfying experiences in making wise decisions if they are to acquire and use the skills of intelligent self-direction. Their immediate personal problems afford excellent opportunities for them to learn to do so. Consequently, the teacher capitalizes on these opportunities by relating the content of his instruction to the immediate problems that confront his students, though of course he is careful not to make himself or his subject appear ridiculous by stretching this relationship too far.

Second, students' immediate personal problems usually must be resolved before the students will pay much attention to the subject matter presented to them. A student's failure to resolve his problems will often create a deep-rooted feeling of inadequacy which may prevent the student from trying to learn or lead him to give up too easily if he attempts the work and finds it difficult.

By way of illustration, the girl who is anxiously awaiting an invitation to a school dance from a favorite boy or the boy who is worried lest he be turned down by a favorite girl will understandably find schoolwork rather dull and unimportant until this more pressing problem is resolved. The perceptive teacher knows that a failure to resolve any similar personal problem may lead to mental truancy in his class. He knows that such problems—problems of acceptance or group status, problems of dress and personal appearance, ill health, friendlessness, lack of adequate spending money, family difficulties, inadequate social skills, desire for athletic prowess, conflicts with others, lack of recognition, lack of purpose, conflicting ideas of right and wrong, guilt feelings, inadequate rest, faulty vision or hearing, arrested physical development, impending military service, and so on—are brought by students into every secondary school classroom. A teacher cannot keep them out.

The teacher who guides as he instructs tries to incorporate treatments of these problems into his classroom teaching. He recognizes that the problems of his pupils can become a rich source of motivation for learning the behavior which the school is trying to teach. The social studies teacher, for example, can turn a concern about military service among his students from an impediment into an asset. Even before the outbreak of the war in Korea made it necessary for young men to be drafted in large numbers for the armed forces, the one among some 330 problems of youth which was the most frequently checked by about 3500 senior boys in 57 Illinois high schools was concern about military service.[7] This concern takes many forms; in a recent study [8] involving nearly 3000 junior and senior boys in a sampling of 56 secondary schools in 30 states, slightly more than 270 problems relating to military service were discovered to be of concern. For example, many of the students wanted to know what they owed their country that required them

[7] Harold C. Hand, *Principal Findings of the 1947-48 Basic Studies, Circular Series A, No. 51,* Illinois Secondary School Curriculum Program Bulletin No. 2, Office of the Superintendent of Public Instruction, Springfield, Ill., 1949, p. 69.

[8] Oliver L. Rapp, *Military Problems Facing High School Boys,* unpublished dissertation, College of Education, University of Illinois, 1956.

to serve in its armed forces. Many said they couldn't understand why our country needed a large military force. Even larger numbers indicated that they couldn't see any reason for working hard in their high school courses when this wouldn't count in the armed services; and they wondered if they shouldn't "eat, drink, and be merry," since they might later be killed in battle. No teacher can present his subject convincingly to such young men until he has begun to help them resolve these personal problems. Moreover, any program of social studies instruction can legitimately concern itself with the problems raised by these students; indeed, such problems cannot be solved except by bringing into action some of the concepts which should derive from the factual content of courses in social studies.

A teacher who takes account of his pupils' problems both enhances his teaching of subject matter and helps his pupils solve their problems. By so doing he places his students in situations in which they are strongly motivated to learn to plan, to execute, and to evaluate wisely—in short, to become proficient in the necessary skills of intelligent self-direction. Further, such a teacher helps his students build confidence in themselves, so that they will face future problems with more assurance. The students, in turn, will apply themselves more diligently to the tasks of learning. The benefits to the students from a well-integrated program of instruction and guidance multiply as the teacher deals with the students' concerns to which his subject matter sensibly relates.

To help students resolve their pressing personal problems is to provide one of the conditions necessary for effective learning. Teachers who do so, then, are honoring one of the basic principles of secondary education. No less important, they are contributing to the fulfillment of the principle which implies that the school should muster all the resources at its command to promote the advancement of human well-being and happiness.

The teacher who successfully guides as he instructs helps his students to formulate and achieve desirable goals respecting the social processes of thinking and communicating, making a living, managing a home and strengthening the family, living healthfully and safely, providing for other aspects of physical security, spending leisure time wholesomely and enjoyably, satisfying the hunger for aesthetic experience, acquiring spiritual growth, and maintaining and safeguarding the nation's basic social institutions. Each subject, obviously, pertains more immediately to some of these processes than to others.

We have already seen (Chapters 3 and 4) that our society can be made and kept strong only if all these basic social processes are effectively carried out, that this can be done only if our people are adequately educated to do so, and that the responsibility of the secondary schools is to assist in teaching the nation's youth whatever in this respect the well-being of our society requires that adolescents be taught. To learn most effectively (Chapter 4), a student must perceive a relationship between something he wants and that which he is expected to learn; i.e., a student must be motivated by a goal which demands for its fulfillment the student's successful mastery of the lesson he is expected to learn. Thus we see that the schools can preserve the strength of society only if the students themselves are impelled by specific and important goals in respect to each of the basic social processes.

Good teachers combine guidance and instruction, first by helping their students formulate and strengthen purposes which pertain to the basic social processes to which their subject matter relates, and then by helping their students pursue these purposes through the instruction which they provide.

To become the kind of teacher who can effectively integrate guidance and instruction in this way, one must understand how a teacher helps his students to formulate worthy and appropriate goals within the context of our basic social processes. To begin with, the experienced teacher knows that virtually all the desires which his students bring to the first meeting of his class relate in one way or another to one or more—usually to several—of these processes. This relationship between process and course material is generally not fully understood by the student. Every normal youth, for example, wants to be respected and admired by others, but few perceive that this basic hunger actually relates to almost all the basic social processes. With the help of a good teacher, however, most students can be brought to realize that respect and admiration have their price; they can be made to understand that a student who wishes to win widespread respect and admiration must treat his fellows democratically, communicate effectively, think clearly, learn how to spend his leisure time in socially approved ways, be reasonably healthy and vigorous, look well-groomed, support his school loyally, get along well with his family, command a wide range of information about everyday activities, and be willing to work for the spending money that is necessary for a place of respect in the school community. These requirements are related to nearly all of the basic social processes.

Under the stimulation of good teachers most high school students understand that they will as adults continue to desire the respect and admiration of others and that to win and keep this social approval they must get and hold a good job; treat their fellow men decently; live healthfully and safely; spend their leisure time wisely as well as enjoyably; be patriotic citizens who take a constructive part in civic affairs; be good husbands or wives, capable home managers, and wise parents; develop good tastes; and that to do these things capably they must be able to think and communicate effectively, and use our civilization's funded "know-how" as well as other elements of the cultural heritage.

One of the tragedies of the present day is that too many youths do not come under the influence of such teachers. Youths who are not so influenced hunger for the admiration and respect of their fellows just as much as those who do. If not guided by wise teachers, a distressing number of youths attempt to satisfy this hunger through attention-getting misbehavior of many kinds, perhaps even through vandalism and gang warfare. Unguided—more often misguided—they do not sense the long-range relationships which are involved.

By the process of pointing out relationships, good teachers help students understand why, if they are to realize their legitimate desires, they must particularize their goals in all of life's principal activities. Goal building, like everything else we would have the students undertake, must make sense to them if they are to devote themselves willingly—to say nothing of enthusiastically—to it.

Once he feels that goal building makes sense to his students, the good teacher proceeds to help them shape specific purposes in those areas of life's endeavors to which his subject is primarily related—purposes which bear a reasonable relationship to the respective capacities of his students, which take account of their interests, and which appear to be attainable in terms of financial, familial, and similar considerations. Here the wise classroom teacher makes extensive use of his students' cumulative records and, if need be, of the specialized counseling services provided by the school's guidance program (see below). Then, as his students attain more distinct conceptions of their purposes, he shapes and reshapes his instruction, revising and reordering the content and the manner of what he does in order to bring it close to his students' primary concerns. He provides, in other words, a necessary condition for effective learning, and by doing so he not only makes his subject more interesting, but also makes himself, so to speak, the pursued instead of the pursuer— a state of affairs which all good teachers devoutly desire.

The teacher cooperates with other teachers in identifying and meeting the needs of his students

Good teachers know their students well. They are aware not only of the students' needs and problems pertaining to their own subject matter, but also of many more which are closely related to one or more of their colleagues' fields. These guidance-oriented teachers take steps to see that something is done about the students' needs and problems with which their fellow teachers are most competent to deal. By one device or another, they call the attention of these other teachers to what they have discovered, talk with them about the students concerned, and thus attempt to see that the help which the students need will be given to them. The guidance-oriented teacher is equally assiduous in learning from other teachers whatever he can about his students, and he especially welcomes whatever additional light his colleagues can shed on the specific needs and problems of his students to which his own teaching field is particularly related.

When they reciprocate in this way, teachers are honoring the basic principle which implies that the educationally significant characteristics of youth must be taken into account if students are to be educated most effectively. They are also attesting their belief that each student is a person of supreme moral worth whose development must be facilitated.

As we shall note a little later in this chapter, by contributing to and making extensive use of their students' cumulative records teachers can learn a great deal about the students in their school. The development and maintenance of these cumulative records (see pp. 212-13) is one of the important services which the specialized counselor provides for classroom teachers—a service which enables the teachers to know far better than they would otherwise the many different students in their classes. Even so, no teacher can know well as many as, say, one hundred and fifty students in any school term.

Good schools frequently offer unified or core courses, which usually meet for two class periods per day, a practice which cuts in half the number of different students the teacher faces during the two periods under the traditional method of dealing with each subject separately.

The teacher recognizes his limitations
and refers to specialists the students whose problems
are too difficult for him to help resolve unaided

Good teachers so far as possible relate their instruction to the important personal problems of their students (see pp. 202-04). These teachers recognize, however, that neither their subject matter nor their teaching procedures, nor those of their fellow classroom teachers, can be sufficiently modified to give adequate attention to some students' personal problems. They are aware that some students have problems which require a specialized competence which classroom teachers do not possess. Consequently, as they discover students with these exceptionally difficult problems, good teachers bring them to the attention of specially trained persons who can give the needed help.

The teacher who is concerned with the guidance as well as the instruction of the students in his classes faces several types of problems which lie outside the scope of his or his colleagues' subject matter, or which call for a specialized competence which neither he nor they possess. Students who appear with a rash, or in a feverish condition, or who persistently lack energy, or who give any other indication of serious illness or poor health, he refers to the school nurse or the school doctor. Similar referrals are made of those who give evidence of a hearing loss or a visual disability. Students with a persistent and handicapping speech difficulty he will call to the attention of the speech correctionist. Those who have particularly serious disabilities in reading he will refer to the reading clinic. Students who give continued evidence of emotional disturbances will be referred to the school psychologist for diagnosis and arrangements for therapy. The good teacher recognizes that his students should be referred to specialized counselors for the interpretation of certain kinds of test results. He directs his students to counselors in order to secure specialized knowledge—information about an occupation or college or trade school or industry, for example. The good teacher also calls the attention of counselors to any youth who badly needs eye glasses, a hearing aid, textbooks or other instructional materials, clothing, part-time employment, or other special assistance.

When a teacher refers a student to a specialist, he is acting in accordance with Principle 8. He deals with more of the educationally significant characteristics of youth. He honors this principle still further by following whatever recommendations the specialist may make in each case.

Important services provided
by a well-organized guidance program

Seven important services are provided by a well-organized program of guidance. These complement or supplement the primary work of guidance, the work performed by sympathetic and competent classroom teachers who combine guidance and instruction in the ways already described. Although these seven additional services are either directed or performed by specialists, none can be effective without the active participation of classroom teachers.

It is generally believed that there should be one full-time counselor for every 250 students in a school. A large school, therefore, should have a corps of such counselors. In high schools which have enrollments of less than 250 the most usual, but by no means ideal, practice is to provide a part-time counselor—frequently a classroom teacher who has had some (but seldom enough) specialized training in the field of guidance and who may devote from a fourth to a half of his time to this work.

Orienting new students

The student who is new to the school must adapt himself to a great many things before he can become an effective member of the student body or benefit from the services of his new school. He must know where things are—the bicycle racks or parking lot, his classrooms, his locker, the library, the lunchroom, the toilets, the offices of the school officials with whom he is expected to deal. More difficult, he must know the usual procedures involved in making a class schedule, in getting books and other materials, in selecting extra-class activities, in passing between classes, in using the library, in patronizing the cafeteria, in using the school's health service, in availing himself of counseling aids, in being readmitted after an absence, in participating in school assemblies, in attending school games, parties, and dances, in making a success of his courses, in winning new friends—in adjusting himself, in short, to the traditions, expectations, and requirements of his new school.

Classroom teachers should take part by helping new pupils at every turn. In many schools, most of this orientation will be provided through a "homeroom" period—a period in each day or in certain days of the week when a teacher presides over an assigned group of pupils for whom he is expected to provide guidance throughout the year or, in some schools, throughout the entire academic period of three or four years. The homeroom teacher is not without help in deciding what to do and what materials to use in the orientation of new students. Under the leadership of the guidance staff, orientation aids are commonly developed through the joint efforts of counselors, classroom teachers, supervisors, school administrators, and upper-class students. But it is the teacher who works directly with newly-enrolled students and who puts these orientation aids to work.

In other schools, students are oriented through core or common learnings courses. These are classes in which the work is organized around important social and personal problems. Since the need for orientation is related to an important cluster of personal problems, it would be strange if they were not dealt with in such courses.

Some schools set aside one or more days before the opening of school for the orientation of new students. Here the neophytes meet their new teachers, the other school officials, and the student leaders, and are conducted—frequently by their new homeroom teachers or by older students who are their "big brothers" or "big sisters" or members of the welcoming committee of the Student Council—on a guided tour of the school during which they visit their classrooms, the library, the cafeteria, the auditorium, the gymnasium and playing fields, and other facilities of the school.

Other schools provide such guided tours during a special visiting day held during the late spring prior to the matriculation of the new pupils. Again, the classroom teachers must play a prominent role if the visiting day is to be a success.

Actually, effective orientation is a process, as are all other aspects of guidance, not simply an event. It must go on during much if not all of the pupil's first year in his new school. And classroom teachers must participate at nearly every turn if this function is to be well performed.

Discovering educationally significant facts about students

Teachers who integrate guidance and instruction are always on the alert to discover all that they can about their students. The many things which perceptive teachers can learn about their students during their long period of association constitute much of what must be known if the school is to serve the students well. But not all; certain kinds of information can be obtained only through tests and inventories made and interpreted by experts.

Such information is needed about the physical condition and health of the students. Only doctors, dentists, and registered nurses are competent to test visual and auditory acuity and to make dental and general health examinations. In good schools these important examinations are made at regular intervals. But between examinations students may develop faulty vision or hearing, or suffer from other impairments of health. As we have already pointed out, teachers who are oriented toward guidance will make immediate use of medical service when they encounter a student who for any reason seems to need treatment. All teachers are constantly on the alert for signs of physical disability among their students; good teachers will welcome the recommendations which come to them from the school doctor, dentist, or nurse.

Good schools concern themselves with the emotional as well as the physical health of students. In cases of emotional disturbance, often only the clinician who is highly trained in psychology—sometimes only the fully licensed psychotherapist—is competent to make a diagnosis. Therapy in such cases may require modifications in instructional materials, teaching methods, and other aspects of classroom procedure. Teachers who are dedicated to the welfare of their students will seek and carry out the recommendations of the school psychiatrist.

Aptitude testing, another element of any good educational program, also requires the services of specially trained personnel. Psychometrics is a highly specialized field; much damage has been done by inadequately trained persons who have attempted to interpret test data. The good teacher always looks to properly qualified counselors for the interpretations of aptitude tests which his students have taken.

A well-organized guidance program includes provisions for comprehensive achievement testing, systematically performed under the supervision of competently trained persons.

The inventorying of students' interests is another important specialized service which a good guidance program includes. The results obtained from such inventories should be assessed with the kind and degree of caution which only a counselor who is well trained in psychology is likely to exercise consistently. These interpretations are very useful to teachers who are intelligently alert to the classroom aspects of a guidance program.

Collecting and recording important information about students and making this available to teachers

If teachers' observations of students, and their exchange of such information, occur only casually, in random conversation or in response to an immediate and specific need, much useful information will never be exchanged at all and the information which comes to a teacher is apt to be incomplete and poorly organized. Guidance and instruction cannot be effectively integrated on the basis of such partial knowledge. The teacher should have at his command virtually all the pertinent known data about each of his students.

One of the aims of any well-organized guidance program is to satisfy this need for all pertinent known data by maintaining a cumulative record for each student in the school. The records should be kept up to date, and teachers should be instructed in their use. As its name suggests, the cumulative record of each student increases in size as he progresses from grade to grade; ideally, it is begun when he enters nursery school or kindergarten and is passed on with him through all the years of his schooling. Each student's record should contain everything about him that is educationally significant which teachers or specialized counselors will find helpful in their work: his health record, his home background, his scholastic and extra-class activity achievements, his educational and vocational preferences or plans, the summaries of his aptitude tests, his interest and attitude inventories, and whatever scales he has completed, his out-of-school work, play, and travel experiences, and anecdotal reports of significant instances of his behavior at different periods.

Gathering, recording, and keeping up to date this wealth of necessary information about each student and giving teachers whatever assistance they require in using it are not easy jobs, but they are services which the trained counselors in any well-organized guidance program will provide.

Good teachers not only use the cumulative record but also contribute to it. Some of the attendance records, all school marks, and most records of extra-class participations derive, of course, from the reports of classroom teachers. So do most of the significant anecdotal reports which are incorporated into the cumulative record. Teachers are also frequently in a position to contribute significant items bearing on a student's home background, his out-of-school work, play, and travel experiences, and his educational and vocational plans or preferences.

Helping students acquire educational and vocational information

Aside from a student's biological inheritance, all that he is he has learned (see Chapter 3). What kind of education the high school youth acquires will help determine the kind of adult he will become. To be intelligently self-directive about the kind of adult he is to become, the high school student must first become intelligently self-directive about his education. He must acquire no small amount of information about school courses, extra-class activities, colleges, vocational schools, and the like. This is why every good guidance program sees to it that students are provided with adequate educational information.

Every good guidance program emphasizes the need for adequate vocational information for a similar reason. A person's vocation largely determines many things in his life—his income, his associates, his usefulness to the community, to name but three. Intelligent self-direction must, therefore, include the wise choice of an occupation. This is possible only if one has first acquired adequate information which will make one aware of possible occupations, their nature, the social worth of the services they render, the preparation they require, the salaries they pay, the relationship between the supply of workers and the demand for them, and so on.

Neither educational nor vocational information can be provided adequately for high school youth unless all classroom teachers make their important contributions. Each is a specialist in one or more fields, and each knows the educational requirements necessary for achievement in the field or fields of his specialty. Each of these areas of knowledge is also related to some family of occupations, and hence each teacher knows much about the requirements for entering some of these occupations. There probably will be serious gaps in the knowledge of high school students about educational and vocational opportunities unless classroom teachers impart such information in the course of their regular teaching program. It is a legitimate though incidental part of their regular subject matter.

Classroom teachers may also be involved in the educational and vocational aspects of the formal guidance program. Vocational and educational information is commonly dispensed through homeroom programs, and in many schools all or nearly all teachers are assigned a homeroom. The problem of choosing a vocation and learning to embark on it interests students greatly, and most teachers, as homeroom sponsors, should treat this subject in detail. Most will need the help of their guidance counselors in order to do so as effectively as possible.

Providing counseling services for youth

High school students face many important problems which require wise counseling. And counseling is wise if it helps students to become more wisely self-directive about the problems they confront. Hence counseling is not simply telling a student what to do. A wise counselor helps the student combine (a) information about the object of his thought (what subjects to take, what occupation to choose, what college to attend, and so on), (b) his basic values, and (c) information about himself (his capabilities, preferences, limitations, and so on). The next step is to help him to base his decision intelligently on these three categories of information. When the counseling function is viewed in these terms, it is easy to see why counseling should be as nondirective as possible, i.e., why the pupil and not the counselor should do the deciding. Only by making decisions can students learn to decide wisely, to guide themselves intelligently. The counselor can be most helpful by limiting himself to asking questions which will make the student aware of the factors involved in the decision. But the decision itself should rest with the student.

A good guidance program provides trained counselors skilled in these arts of counseling. In good secondary schools these specialists consider themselves teachers of teachers as well as counselors of students. They realize that most of the counseling should be done by the classroom teachers, and so they make themselves responsible for helping the teachers become more skilled in the art of wise counseling. They also help the instructional staff become more proficient in recognizing the symptoms of those problems of youth which can be resolved only with the aid of some specially trained person, and they encourage and assist the teachers to make all such needed referrals properly and promptly. The hope of these guidance counselors is that, aside from channeling pupils to other specialists, it will be necessary for them to deal directly only with those students whose problems require expert attention. As we have pointed out in the opening section of this chapter, and as experienced counselors know only too well, adequate guidance can be provided only if teachers willingly accept and discharge their responsibilities for counseling regarding the many problems which they are competent to help their students resolve wisely, thus making it possible for staff specialists to devote their time to the complicated problems with which they ought to deal.

Helping students place themselves successfully when school days are ended

The purpose of education, and hence of the school, is to induct children and young people into their nation's culture, to help them become effective members of society. From high school young Americans either attend a college or other institution for post-high-school training, enter an occupation, or become homemakers. The really effective secondary school attempts, therefore, to enable each graduate to do one or the other of three things, depending upon his or her preferences. Some it helps to place in an appropriate college or other institution for adult education. It helps those who plan to continue their formal education to select an appropriate college or other institution, to apply for admittance, and to learn what they can of its traditions, requirements, housing arrangements, and the like.

The good high school also makes a systematic attempt to help students find appropriate vocations for themselves. Long before the senior year, the school seeks to assist each such pupil to make at least a tentative choice of occupation, so that he may direct the rest of his secondary school program toward helping himself as much as possible with his future work. The school also helps those who plan to enter an occupation as soon as they graduate to learn how to apply for jobs and to get in touch with employment agencies or employers.

It tries to prepare all its pupils for worthy home membership, but seeks especially to help those who plan to marry soon to acquire the knowledge and skills which are needed for homemaking. The school does not, of course, maintain a matrimonial agency, though it does deliberately provide the instruction and the wholesome environment which lead to the wise choice of a marriage partner.

If these guidance tasks are to be performed capably, classroom teachers must contribute to them in many ways. Although a special vocational counselor will ordinarily be assigned to help students find jobs, classroom teachers should help, too. Teachers, through their contacts in the community, often learn of vacation or part-time jobs which may give students valuable experience, and they should, of course, transmit this information at once to the proper school official. Teachers often must write letters of recommendation and have interviews with employment officials. And most important, they can help pupils acquire not only the vocational competence, but also the social skills and work habits which make for success in business and industry.

The success of the school's college placement officer will vary directly with the quality of the product which the classroom teachers make available to him. Every high school teacher has an intimate knowledge of at least one college or university. This information, consolidated and made available to pupils, will be very useful to college-bound students.

Keeping in touch with graduates

The only really valid measure of the worth of a school is the behavioral test: how capably do its graduates perform? To appraise its effectiveness in helping its pupils acquire vocational competence, the school must study its graduates while they are working. To appraise its college-preparatory program, the school must study the records its graduates are making in college. Similarly, the school must look to the performance of its graduates to determine how well it has helped its students prepare themselves to manage a home, spend leisure time wholesomely, take an effective part in civic affairs, or carry on any of the other basic social functions upon which both individual and societal well-being depend.

These behavioral tests not only reveal how capably the high school is performing its functions; they also diagnose weaknesses in the school program. The strong or faulty performances of the graduates on the job, in college, and in the community at large reveal some of the strong or weak points of the high school. Armed with such information, the faculty of a school is in a good position to revise its program.

But it is not only to appraise and strengthen its program that good high schools study the performance of their graduates. Beginning job-holders and college students can frequently be helped by counselors who know them well to make adjustments which will turn possible failures into successes. To a more limited extent, similar help can also be given to recent graduates who need assistance in other life activities. One of the important purposes of the follow-up service which good guidance programs provide, then, is to help recent graduates who need it.

The follow-up service is usually made the responsibility of a specially trained person. Certain of the potential benefits in the follow-up service, however, can be realized only with the cooperation of classroom teachers. Unless teachers are concerned about the welfare of youth they will be unmoved by any data obtained from graduates which suggest that improvements in the instructional program are needed. And if such changes are to be made, teachers must be willing to experiment, to try new approaches, taking such data into account. Fortunately, all but a very few public secondary school teachers are keenly interested in young people; they welcome factual evidence and are eager to make improvements in their schools once they realize the need for them.

Summary

A brief review of the history of the guidance movement in this country has revealed why our better secondary schools have rejected the separatist philosophy of guidance—a philosophy which regards guidance as an adjunct to the instructional program, which holds that the business of teachers is to instruct but not to guide, which asserts that the guidance of youth should be performed chiefly, if not exclusively, by specialized personnel. Our better schools now believe that every teacher should combine guidance and instruction, that teachers should be supported by an organized program of guidance services which will enable them to offer better guidance as part of their classroom work, and that specialized personnel should deal directly, for the most part, only with those students whose problems are too difficult for classroom teachers to approach without aid.

Regardless of the scope of the guidance service, its primary purposes have always been the same: to help young people to become intelligently self-directive, and to help provide the conditions under which optimum learning will take place in all that the school teaches.

Teachers have several ways of helping students become more intelligently self-directive under a program of integrated guidance and instruction. A teacher who guides as he instructs knows how a student can become intelligently self-directive. A teaching method is needed which requires the students to help plan and evaluate, as well as execute, the projects undertaken by the class. Guidance and instruction can be effectively integrated only if the teacher adapts his instruction to the individual needs, capacities, and interests of his students. The instruction should be related as far as possible to the personal problems of the students, who will thereby take a livelier interest in the subjects which they study and become more intelligently self-directive. The teacher should help his students to formulate their goals—that is, socially desirable goals related to the basic social processes of our society—within the context provided by his own subject matter. It is extremely necessary for guidance-oriented teachers to cooperate in identifying and meeting the needs of their students. Finally, teachers who successfully guide as they instruct recognize their own limitations and refer to specialists those students whose problems are too difficult for the teachers to help resolve without aid.

A well-organized guidance program provides important services in a number of areas—the orientation of new students, the discovery of educationally significant facts about high school students, the maintenance of records which will supply teachers with important information about their students, the provision of necessary vocational and educational information to students, the maintenance of counseling services for students, the offering of advice and assistance to graduates as they begin their post-high school activities, and the administration of a system to report on progress made by graduates. Teachers must take a responsible part in each service if it is to succeed. In addition, one of the chief purposes of each service is to enable teachers to serve their students more capably by combining effective guidance with their instruction.

chapter 10

APPRAISING AND REPORTING

PUPIL ACHIEVEMENT

The purpose of this chapter is to show what the basic principles of
secondary education imply for the appraising and reporting of pupil
achievement. But first we shall distinguish between measurement
and appraisal.

Measurement and appraisal

The results of a measurement (a pupil's score on a test, for example)
do not indicate whether an appraisal (the pupil's mark) should be
high or low. Suppose that two high school boys, Dick and Bob,
want to find out how much they weigh. Each steps on the scales.
This is measurement, and it is objective: everyone who reads the
scales correctly will obtain the same result. Independent of any
value judgment, the scales will say that each boy weighs so many
pounds and so many ounces.

Let us say that Bob weighs 185 pounds and Dick only 95 pounds.
This is an objective measurement: any two or more persons who
can read the figures on the scale accurately will agree that Bob and
Dick weigh 185 and 95 pounds, respectively. The figures themselves
constitute no appraisal of either boy.

Appraisal, which always involves judgment, is always made in
accordance with some purpose or goal. Suppose, in this instance,
that both boys want to enter the Marine Corps. In the light of this
purpose, we would judge, i.e., estimate, that, so far as their weights

220

are concerned, Bob is an excellent prospect but Dick will certainly be rejected. This is appraisal. If we assign a single letter mark to each boy, we might give Bob an A and Dick an F.

But let us suppose that, instead of wanting to enlist in the Marines, both boys want to become jockeys. A race horse that carried a rider weighing 185 pounds would be under an impossible handicap, whereas a 95-pound rider would be about as light a human burden as could be found. Hence, if we were assigning single letter marks with this purpose in mind, we would reverse our former judgments and give an A to Dick, an F to Bob.

An appraisal, then, is not based solely on measurement. An appraisal is always relative to a purpose; the same measurement, as we have seen, can lead to a high or a low appraisal, depending on the purpose.

This is equally true of the measurement and appraisal of pupils' achievements in English, science, mathematics, music, physical education, or any other school subject or activity. Suppose, for instance, that John and Harry are classmates in a high school science course. Suppose, furthermore, that John makes a score of 110 and Harry a score of 130 on a test for which the highest possible score is 150. If the purpose of the person who judges these test scores—i.e., if the basis upon which the performances of the two boys are appraised—is to show who excels whom, and if the appraisals are to be recorded in terms of single letter marks, then Harry will receive a higher letter mark than John. But if the purpose of the person doing the appraising is to show how close each boy came to learning as much in science as he is deemed capable, and if John is a dull student and Harry a boy of exceptionally high aptitude, then their performances on the science test will be appraised quite differently. If John has achieved as much as a person of his native capacity could be expected to achieve, while Harry's higher score indicates only a mediocre level of achievement for a pupil of his high academic aptitude, then John will deserve a higher letter mark than Harry, thus reversing the marks even though they are based on the same test scores as before.

Let us take a different case. Suppose that the goal in the mind of a teacher is to prepare his pupils for the demands which will be made on them in daily life after they have graduated from high school. Sam intends to go to work in a factory, but Jim plans to enter college and study to become an engineer. On a 160-point test in mathematics, Sam and Jim make identical scores of 95. The teacher knows that this level of attainment is more than adequate for the factory work which Sam will do, but is inadequate for the mathematics courses required by the college of engineering which Jim plans to attend. In this case, if the teacher sticks to his criterion, he will give Jim a lower letter mark than Sam, in spite of the fact that the two boys made identical test scores. Again, measurement alone does not determine appraisal.

Suppose that a business education teacher who uses a single-letter marking system (A, B, C, D, and F for failure) gives a final examination in a course in business machines, which has a perfect score of 200, and obtains the distribution of test scores shown in Table 6.

TABLE **6**   **Hypothetical distribution of test scores in a class in business machines**

SCORE	NUMBER OF PUPILS	SCORE	NUMBER OF PUPILS
200	0	110–119	5
190–199	0	100–109	7
180–189	0	90–99	6
170–179	0	80–89	4
160–169	0	70–79	2
150–159	0	60–69	2
140–149	1	50–59	0
130–139	2	Below 50	1
120–129	3		

It is clear that nothing here indicates to the teacher how many, if any, of his pupils should receive A's, B's, or any of the other letter marks. The results of his measurements (test scores), in other words, yield no appraisal by themselves. If the test measures what pupils know about business machines, if the purpose of the course is to prepare students for employment in business firms which demand a knowledge of such machines, and if these firms will employ no one who makes a score of less than 170 on the test, then clearly every pupil in the class should receive a failing mark. In this case, all pupils would receive the same letter mark, regardless of their relative position in the test scores. Suppose, on the other hand, that the critical score is 80; no firm will employ a student whose score is lower than this. All but five of the 33 students scored 80 or higher. How many, if any, of these 28 passing students should receive an A, a B, and so on? Because he made the highest score, should the student whose score fell in the 140-149 interval be assigned an A? His score still represents a knowledge of less than three-fourths of all the questions about business machines which were asked on the test. Is this enough for an A? Again, measurement alone can yield no appraisal. To appraise, one must cast the measurements against criteria which are independent of the measurements themselves.

But suppose the test scores shown above were derived from a test given in an English class, where no exact criterion of success or failure is furnished by sources outside the school. How the English teacher will assign single letter marks on the basis of his distribution of test scores will depend in every instance upon the criterion he follows; he must make a judgment in every case. If his criterion is simply relative excellence of performance, perhaps he will give A's to the one, the three, or even the six students whose scores are the highest in the total distribution. But whether he assigns one, three, or six A's is determined by a judgment (an appraisal) which he himself must make, not by the test scores alone (the results of measurement). If, however, the test was intended to measure the understanding of the students in terms of the entire content of the course, and if the teacher's criterion is absolute rather than relative achievement, then this teacher would quite certainly not assign an A to anyone, since the highest score indicates a knowledge of only three-fourths of the content of the course. No one would receive an A, and perhaps none might be thought worthy of a B. On the other hand, the teacher's criterion might be each student's relative achievement in terms of his own capacity to learn. In this case, the brilliant pupil who made the highest score and the dull pupil whose score was the lowest would both receive a mark of A if in the teacher's judgment each had achieved as much as it was possible for him to achieve.

In each of these illustrations the measurement alone did not determine the appraisal, and this is true for every conceivable act of judgment. The measurement is simply a datum. In every case the criterion employed by the appraiser determines whether this datum will yield a high or low appraisal.

The best measurements attainable should be used to appraise pupil achievement

Any appraisal not based on valid measurement is partly guesswork, and since guesses are often inaccurate, such appraisals are very likely to be unfair. Our dedication to the democratic ideal forbids unfairness, and nowhere more than in our educational system. When a teacher reports an inaccurate, and hence a misleading, appraisal to a pupil, to his parents, to employers, or to college admission officials, he is offering an undependable basis for judgment. Only when appraisal is based on valid and reliable measurements can a dependable basis for judgment be obtained.

The chief types of measurement available to teachers are observations of pupil behavior in relevant and reasonably stable situations, work samples, and tests. All three kinds of measurement must be used if the operation of chance is to be kept to a minimum.

We have already noted earlier in this book that the business of education is to bring about changes in behavior. The only proof of learning is changed behavior; a pupil who continues to behave, overtly and covertly, as he always has has not learned anything. Therefore observation of pupil behavior is the best kind of measurement.

To measure behavioral change, the teacher must do four things. First, he must know precisely what changes in behavior he is trying to bring about. Second, he must find or create situations in which the pupil may manifest this changed behavior. Third, he must repeatedly observe the pupil in these situations to see to what degree the pupil reveals the changes in behavior which the teacher has attempted to facilitate. Fourth, he must record his observations; each record should be dated, anecdotal (i.e., it should tell what the student did and under what circumstances), and part of a cumulative documentation. None of these four steps contains an appraisal.

Suppose that Mr. Edwards, a physical education teacher, is trying to teach the boys in his class to be good sportsmen. One of the boys had a problem of behavior in respect to his relationship with umpires. When the term began, Mr. Edwards observed that this boy, whom we will call Larry, consistently complained if the umpire's close decisions went against him. During the term, as Mr. Edwards worked at the problem of helping Larry improve this aspect of his sportsmanship, he observed the boy as he participated in competitive games. In September he observed and recorded the fact that Larry became angry and created a disturbance when he was called out trying to steal second in a softball game. In October he observed and recorded the fact that Larry looked angry but said nothing when his team was penalized for being offside in a touch football match. In December Mr. Edwards was obliged to record a regression; Larry had slammed the ball on the floor, complained loudly, and sulked when the referee called him for a double dribble in a basketball game. In January and February the record showed that Larry had held his tongue and only grimaced when he was penalized for other fouls. In March Mr. Edwards was able to record that Larry had held up his hand to indicate to the scorer that he was the one being penalized for a body contact foul and that he seemed composed and in no way resentful. Entries recorded by Mr. Edwards during the baseball season in the spring showed that with one minor exception Larry had taken with good grace the four close decisions which had been called against him. The important point to note here is that the making and recording of these observations by Mr. Edwards were acts solely of measurement, not of appraisal. Only when Mr. Edwards applies the criterion of good sportsmanship to these accumulated data will he arrive at an appraisal.

Second, suppose that Miss Jones, a teacher of high school English, is trying to help pupils learn to enjoy better literature. In her conferences with individual pupils, held soon after the beginning of the fall semester, she quickly discovered that Kenneth read practically nothing but comic books when he was left to his own devices. As a part of her program to encourage the use of better reading materials, Miss Jones set aside occasional days when the pupils were invited to spend the class period reading what they pleased, either in the classroom or in the school library. Through October and November her anecdotal records showed that Kenneth was observed to be reading nothing but comic books during these free reading periods and that he did not use the school library. In December she observed that, although Kenneth still read the comics, he also spent a little time reading *Popular Mechanics* and *Air Facts*. The school librarian reported just before Christmas that Kenneth had asked for two occupational information books which contained chapters on aviation. In late January Miss Jones discovered that Kenneth had taken Lindbergh's *The Spirit of St. Louis* from the school library, and her anecdotal record for February showed that he had made an interesting report on it to the class. In March Miss Jones observed Kenneth in the library reading one of Langewiesche's articles on flying in *Harper's Magazine*. By the end of the year the anecdotal record kept by Miss Jones revealed that Kenneth occasionally spent part of the free reading periods reading articles in *Harper's Magazine* and *The Atlantic Monthly*, although two of his favorite comic books were still in evidence. Again, Miss Jones has measured, not appraised. These recorded observations are the measurements from which Miss Jones will, of course, eventually derive an appraisal, but only when she applies her criterion to these observations will appraisal result.

Now let us consider work samples, our second type of measurement. Mr. Andrews, let us say, is a teacher who believes that the precepts taught in his art course should be applied to nearly every aspect of daily living: to the clothes we wear, the flowers in our gardens, the furnishings in our homes, the highways on which we drive, and so on. He encourages each pupil to undertake some project in self-improvement as a part of the work in his course.

Sarah, who took that course as a junior, chose to improve her room at home. When she described it to Mr. Andrews and made a diagram for him soon after the fall semester began, he concluded that her small room was in fact very much in need of improvement. The colors of the drapes, the rug, and the chair covering clashed violently; the rug's large pattern made the little room seem even smaller; the disproportionately high ceiling was a light color, thus creating the illusion of even greater height; the furniture in the room was old, dark, and awkwardly arranged, the blue wallpaper made these large old pieces seem too prominent; there were too many pictures on the walls, and they were poorly hung; and the top of Sarah's dresser was anything but pleasing to a sensitive eye.

Sarah attempted to apply in her room the principles she learned in Mr. Andrews' art class, principles relating to line, mass, color, repetition, emphasis, rhythm, proportion, and balance. Thus her room became a work sample, and in late May, when she reported to Mr. Andrews what she had done, he was able to see that her work sample was proof that she had learned well. The unpleasant clash of colors was gone from her room; the large figured rug had been exchanged for a small plain one; the ceiling, now a darker color, seemed lower, giving the room a more intimate appearance; warm-hued wall colorings provided an integrated background for the old furniture, which was now arranged in good order; several of the pictures had disappeared and those that remained were well hung; and Sarah could demonstrate that the top of her dresser now presented an orderly and attractive appearance. Obviously Sarah had changed her behavior. Her perceptions had changed, her sense of values had changed, and her conduct, as revealed in her efforts to rearrange her room and persuade her father to have the walls and ceiling redecorated, had changed.

Work samples which give concrete evidence of learning can supplement any high school instruction, and they afford the teacher a valuable means for gathering objective data.

Tests are the third principal way of measuring pupil achievement. To be useful, a test must be both *valid* and *reliable*. A test is valid if it measures what it purports to measure. For example, a teacher of English whose primary objective in a certain course is to teach literary appreciation knows that a test concerned chiefly with the birth and death dates of great authors and the publication dates of their works is not a valid test for him to use. He is trying to teach appreciation; and a knowledge of dates, though perhaps important in other contexts, does not contribute very much to an appreciation of literature. Hence a test of the pupils' knowledge of dates simply does not measure what the teacher is teaching. It is an *invalid* test. A teacher who used such a test to secure measurements on which to base an appraisal of his pupils' achievements in literary appreciation would be providing himself with a false basis for judgment.

A test is *reliable* if whatever it measures is measured consistently. To measure consistently, a test must, of course, measure accurately. If the same test is given to a mathematics class today and again two weeks from today, and if the pupils who score high on the test today score low two weeks from today, this test, other things being equal, is unreliable: it does not measure consistently. It is like a rubber band, and no right-minded person would claim that one can measure consistently or accurately with a rubber band. We practice a kind of deception if we base our appraisals of pupil achievement on rubber-band tests.

The construction of a valid and reliable test requires more specialized technical skill than many teachers possess. In order to construct a proper test the least one needs is the training provided by university courses in testing and educational statistics, and all students of education should certainly enroll in such courses before they go out to teach.

This technical training would not be so necessary if the many carefully constructed, standardized tests now available really fit the particular courses which teachers are called upon to teach and the particular circumstances in which these courses must be taught. These tests are almost without exception very reliable; they provide accurate and consistent measurements. But their validity *for a particular course* should always be questioned. Only if the teacher's objectives coincide with the testmaker's objectives will the test be valid for the course. Reliability can be built into a test by a skillful testmaker, but validity cannot. If a particular test does not measure what a particular teacher is attempting to teach, it is not valid for that teacher's course, though of course it may still be valid for other courses.

The more a teacher adapts his teaching to the individual differences of youth and to the particular needs of his community—i.e., the more scrupulously he follows the known practices of good teaching—the less likelihood there is that any standardized test will fill his particular requirements, that it will be valid for his course. This will impel the teacher to construct his own tests. But unless he possesses the necessary technical training, his tests are almost certain to lack both validity and reliability. The utmost care should be exercised in the construction of individual tests at all times. The teacher who, for purposes of appraising and reporting the achievements of his pupils, uses tests which are seriously deficient in either validity or reliability will be misleading (perhaps unwittingly) his pupils, their parents, and employers or college admission officials.

**All learned behavior
with which the school is properly concerned
should be measured and appraised**

The generalization expressed in this heading is a correlate of Principle 1 (Chapter 4): the high school is obligated to assist in providing the education for youth which will enable them to carry on the basic social processes.

One of these basic social processes (see pp. 43-45) is concerned with providing "social cement" with which to bind together the huge community of Americans, the cement being our whole amalgam of commonly held values, beliefs, aspirations, and modes of conduct. In Chapter 4 we described these values, beliefs, aspirations, and modes of conduct. They can all be learned; indeed the public secondary school is obligated to help its students learn them. The scope of the school's program of measurement and appraisal will correspond to the full range of the school's responsibilities only if all of these learnings are measured and appraised. The school should measure and appraise the extent to which its pupils adhere to the following directives:

1. Value human life, happiness, and well-being above all material things.

2. Regard all persons as of equal moral worth: Respect them accordingly; regard justice and equality of educational opportunity as their birthrights; reject and combat snobbery and racial and religious prejudices; be sensitive to the needs, desires, and rights of others; be tactful.

3. Understand why the American social faith is valid; know its historical sanctions.

4. Have faith in human intelligence: Understand why human happiness and well-being can best be advanced only if there is an unrestricted play of intelligence upon all subjects of inquiry; formulate independent judgments; secure consent by persuasion based on rational argument; dissent peaceably and intelligently.

5. Regard all persons as moral creatures living in a moral order, in which distinctions are made between good and evil: Value the good and abhor the evil; suffer in conscience from doing evil and treasure the inner satisfactions which come from doing good; accept the consequences of personal actions.

6. Understand, exercise, and defend the rights of the individual: Defend the constitutional guarantees of freedom of thought, belief, speech, assembly, and press; recognize the

limits and responsibilities of personal freedom; appraise all social arrangements by their effects on each person; protect all legally constituted minorities in their Constitutional right to attempt to persuade the majority to their opinion through reason.

7. Have faith in democracy: Act upon the principle of the greatest good for the greatest number; participate in the government of the group; help establish and maintain democratically instituted law and order; recognize, support, and follow wise leadership, or, if chosen to lead, lead wisely; conversely, recognize and repudiate unwise leadership.

Of the three methods of measurement which we have discussed, the method of direct observation is by far the most fruitful for purposes of appraising the accomplishments of students in the respects just noted. Work samples, it is true, can be secured in some instances; virtually no useful tests are available. Teachers must rely mainly upon direct observation.

Finally, if the pupil's behavior in every facet of school life is to be measured and appraised, his progress in each of the other seven basic social processes must be measured and appraised. In other words, the school should measure and appraise the extent to which each pupil is learning to:

—Think and communicate.
—Earn his livelihood.
—Provide for his and others' physical security, i.e., manage their natural resources, strengthen their bodies, safeguard themselves against accidents, disease, and external enemies.
—Strengthen the family.
—Provide for his aesthetic satisfactions and spiritual needs.
—Provide for his leisure time.
—Regulate human conduct through social organization based on authority.

Here again, direct observations of pupil behavior offer the best means available for measuring pupil achievement. But far more in the way of work samples is possible here, and most of our standard achievement tests relate in some way to one or another of these basic processes.

Schools should never report finer distinctions than measurements permit

The generalization expressed in this heading is violated by every school which uses the percentage system of marking and reporting. If Mary's report card, for instance, says that she earned a 94 in English, a 97 in Spanish I, an 89 in General Science, and an 81 in Home Economics I, she and her parents are being misled by her school. The fact is that, whether they are based on direct observation of pupil behavior, work samples, or tests, no existing measures of achievement enable us to say with even reasonable accuracy that Mary deserved a 94 but Harry only a 93 in English, mathematics, or any other subject. Analogously, no grocer whose scales weigh only in pounds and ounces has the right to put up a bag of flour and then print on the label that the contents of the bag weigh so many pounds, ounces, and grains. If he did so, we would know that beyond the level of pounds and ounces his measurement was mere guesswork, and we would quite properly resent his attempt to disguise a guess as a verified fact.

Unfortunately, most parents know very little about educational measurements and hence are ignorant of the deceptions embodied in the percentage system of marking. And, of course, the teachers who still use this method—a decreasing number—do not mean to be misleading. They report in percentages either because they are obliged to do so by their schools or because they themselves don't know enough about educational measurements to realize the fallacies inherent in the percentage system.

Actually, teachers can distinguish with only a fair degree of reliability among as many as five levels of pupil achievement, to say nothing of the one hundred levels demanded by the percentage system. Even when the distinctions demanded of the teacher are as coarse as those involved in the five-level method, the results, as research studies have shown, are likely to be disquieting, to say the least. These studies have described cases in which an examination paper of the essay type judged good or excellent by one teacher was pronounced very poor or a failure by another teacher. We have all heard the story about the model examination paper, worked out by an expert examiner to serve as a key, which fell into the hands of another examiner and was marked as a failure; the story is by no means fanciful.

Any marking and reporting system which attempts to make distinctions among more than five levels of pupil achievement is of very doubtful value. But by being careful and conscientious, teachers using the five-level system can achieve reasonable accuracy.

Reports of achievement should be accurately labeled

This is a matter of simple truthfulness. Suppose our grocer sold us a package which he had labeled "sugar" but which, when we arrived at home, we discovered to contain a mixture of sugar, flour, salt and white sand. Does this differ in principle from the practice of reporting an appraisal labeled "English I" which in reality is based on a vague combination of achievements in the subject matter of English I and in dependability, cooperation, school citizenship, effort, and the like? In either case the person who reads the label is being deceived.

If two or more aspects of a pupil's achievement are to be appraised, each should be treated separately

This is an extension of the point which we discussed in the last paragraph. Let us suppose that a certain high school uses a five-letter (A, B, C, D, and F) marking and reporting system, that it bases its appraisals of its pupils on an equally weighted combination of (a) achievement in subject matter and (b) achievement in other important modes of behavior such as work habits, cooperation, punctuality, dependability, good citizenship, and so on, and that all these bases are lumped together in determining, say, Maud's, Fred's, and Barbara's marks of B in English I.

No one except the person or persons who made these appraisals can tell what these three marks in English I really mean. Maud's mark of B was given to her because her achievement in English and her development in respect to the other qualities considered were both judged to be of B quality. Fred's mark of B in the same subject was given because his achievement in English was judged to be worth an A but his development in the other respects was thought to be worth only a C; since the two aspects of his achievement are equally weighted, his resultant mark was a B in English I. Barbara, who also earned a B in English I, was given this mark because her achievement in English was worth a C while her development in respect to the other qualities was worth an A, thus producing a B when the two equally-weighted appraisals were combined. Here we have three appraisals of B, all labeled English I; yet the achievement of the three students in the subject studied ranged from excellent to mediocre, and so did their achievements in the other areas of behavior which were included in the reports. It seems fair to call this the "scrambled eggs" type of reporting: no one but the cook really knows what the ingredients are or what proportions exist among them.

If reports are to be labeled accurately and are to help those who receive them, each quality of the pupil's achievement which enters into the report of his progress must be appraised and reported separately. An appraisal labeled "English I" will be based on achievement in the subject matter of English I, and on nothing else. Each principal component of achievement in English I will be labeled and reported separately.[1] Similarly, each of the other important qualities, or combinations of qualities, which are considered pertinent to achievement in the given course will be appropriately labeled and separately reported. If this had been done in the high school which appraised the achievements of Maud, Fred, and Barbara, they would have received a B, an A, and a C, respectively, under the label "English I," with further distinctions indicated among their achievements in each of the principal instructional elements of the course. And the other important types of development which were scrambled together in our illustrations would also have been separately reported under appropriately descriptive labels. If these things had been done, there would be far less likelihood that Maud, Fred, Barbara, their parents, and the employers or college admission officials who receive their records will be misled.

If two or more bases for appraisal are used, each resultant appraisal should be reported separately

This is an important point which deals with a knotty problem. To help our readers perceive how knotty it really is, we invite them to respond to the following "birdland inventory."

---

[1] This is done in far too few high schools. The University High School, University of Illinois, is one of the few schools in which the principal components of achievement in each subject are named in the report form and the pupil's achievement in respect to each of these components is separately appraised and reported.

An inventory designed to call attention
to certain difficult issues
in appraising and reporting pupil achievement

Let us suppose that in a certain country the fledgling birds, instead of the children, are required by law to go to school. All the schools in this country offer courses in flying. But just as the children of America differ greatly in their capacities to learn the subject matter they are required to learn, so all the bird pupils in our imaginary country differ greatly in their capacities to learn to fly. Some are equipped by nature to learn to fly swiftly; others are not.

What are the really difficult problems of marking faced by the schools of this imaginary country? We shall present two situations and a number of questions about each. We shall ask our readers to check the answers they think appropriate.

SITUATION A

Sam Sparrow and Sid Swallow [2] were both below the legal school leaving age, and both were enrolled in the same course in flying. The sole purpose of this course was to teach the pupils to fly as swiftly as possible. When the course began, Sam could fly twenty miles per hour, but Sid could do forty. Both were conscientious pupils, and both studied as hard as they could. Each learned everything that it was possible for him to learn in the course. But because nature had endowed them differently, Sam Sparrow could fly only forty miles per hour when he finished the course, whereas Sid Swallow managed fifty miles per hour on his final examination.

The first question: How would you appraise and mark Sam and Sid in respect to their achievements in learning to fly rapidly? (Check one answer.)

___ 1. Sid Swallow should be given a higher mark than Sam because he was able to fly faster than Sam at the end of the course.

___ 2. Sam and Sid should be given the same mark because they both studied as hard as they could and learned as much as they were capable of learning.

___ 3. Sam Sparrow should be given a higher mark because he improved his flying speed by 100 per cent while Sid improved his by only 25 per cent.

The second question: What are the probable consequences in each instance? (Check every probable outcome.)

1. *If Sid Swallow is given a higher mark than Sam Sparrow:*

___ a. Sam Sparrow will feel that the school is unfair because it stigmatizes him as a second-class student no matter how hard he studies.

---

[2] Sparrows and swallows, of course, are not the same species of bird; we do not mean to imply that our children belong to two different species, but simply that they differ greatly in their capacities to learn.

—— b. Sam Sparrow's parents will feel either that the school is unfair because it stigmatizes their child as a second-class student no matter how hard he tries, or that they should goad their child to do the impossible (i.e., to fly as fast as Sid).

—— c. Sam Sparrow will become discouraged and give up studying when he discovers that no matter how hard he tries he cannot succeed.

—— d. Sam Sparrow will be more likely than Sid to quit school before he receives the best possible preparation for living a happy and successful life.

—— e. Sid Swallow will be tempted to give less than his best efforts to his studies when he learns that he can always fly faster than the Sams in his class without really trying and that he will always receive higher marks than they receive as long as he continues to excel them.

2. *If Sam Sparrow is given a higher mark than Sid, or if both are given the same mark:*

—— a. Sam Sparrow's parents will be led mistakenly to believe that their son is as good a flier as Sid is.

—— b. Sid Swallow's parents will either be led mistakenly to believe that their son can fly no faster than Sam Sparrow, or they will feel that the school is unfair because it awards Sam Sparrow a mark as high as or higher than their son received, even though their son can fly faster.

—— c. The Director of Admissions at Bird College will be led mistakenly to believe that Sam can fly as fast as or faster than Sid, and hence he will conclude that Sam is as likely to succeed in college as Sid.

—— d. Sam Sparrow will be led to believe that, relative to the swallows, he is a better flier than he actually is.

—— e. Sid Swallow will either be led to believe that, relative to the sparrows, he is a much poorer flier than he really is, or he will feel that the school is unfair because it awarded Sam, the slower flier, a mark as high as or higher than it gave him.

—— f. Mr. Eagle, Personnel Director of the Rapid Message Delivery Service, Inc., will be led erroneously to believe that Sam Sparrow is as good a flier as Sid, and consequently he will conclude that Sam will be able to relay messages as rapidly as Sid.

The third question: In the light of these considerations, how should Sam and Sid be marked? (Check one answer.)

—— 1. Sid Swallow should be given a higher mark than Sam because he was able to fly faster than Sam could at the end of the course.

—— 2. Sam and Sid should be given the same mark because they both studied as hard as they could and learned everything that they were capable of learning.

—— 3. Sam Sparrow should be given the higher mark because he improved his flying speed by 100 per cent while Sid improved his by only 25 per cent.

___ 4. None of these three ways of marking is acceptable. They are unfair or misleading for the two students and for any other persons who expect to be guided by the marks the students receive. No teacher of good conscience would be willing to mark these students in any of these three ways. It must be possible to devise a system which will remove these difficulties.

SITUATION B

Sadie Sparrow and Sally Swallow were also below the legal school leaving age, and both were also enrolled in the same course in flying. When the course began, Sadie Sparrow could fly fifteen miles per hour, whereas Sally could attain forty-five miles per hour. Sadie Sparrow studied as hard as she possibly could and doubled her speed by the time the course ended; she achieved thirty miles per hour on her final examination. Sally Swallow dawdled through the course and didn't study at all; on her final examination she flew forty-five miles per hour, the same speed she attained before the course began.

The fourth question: How should Sadie and Sally be marked? (Check one answer.)

___ 1. Sally Swallow should be given a higher mark than Sadie because she flew much faster than Sadie did at the end of the course.

___ 2. Sadie Sparrow should be given a higher mark than Sally because she improved her flying speed by 100 per cent while Sally made no improvement at all.

___ 3. Sadie and Sally should be given the same mark, Sadie because she worked hard and learned as much as she could, Sally because even without studying she could fly fast.

The fifth question: What are the probable consequences in each case? (Check every probable outcome.)

   1. *If Sally Swallow is given a higher mark than Sadie Sparrow:*

___ a. Sadie Sparrow will feel that the school is unfair because, even though Sally did no studying and did not improve her flying speed, Sally received the higher mark, while she, who worked hard and learned a good deal, earned very little for her efforts.

___ b. Sadie Sparrow's parents will either feel that the school is unfair because it awarded the higher mark to a pupil who dawdled and did not improve at all, while their own daughter's effort and improvement were unrecognized, or they will exert pressure on Sadie to make her do what she cannot do (i.e., learn to fly as swiftly as Sally).

___ c. Sadie Sparrow will become discouraged and give up studying as hard as she is able to when she discovers that her best efforts only bring her an inferior mark.

___ d. Sadie Sparrow will be much more likely than Sally to leave school before she has acquired the best possible preparation for living a happy and successful life.

__ e. Sally Swallow will probably finish her schooling with the mistaken conviction that a person can succeed without trying if he has a lot of innate ability.

__ f. The Director of Admissions at Bird College will be led mistakenly to believe that because her marks are good, Sally has developed the study habits which are required for success in college.

__ g. Mr. Eagle, Personnel Director of the Rapid Message Delivery Service, Inc., will be led mistakenly to believe that because Sally's marks are good she has acquired the good work habits which the employees of his firm must possess if they are to succeed in its employ.

2. *If Sadie Sparrow is given a higher mark than Sally, or if both are given the same mark:*

__ a. Sadie Sparrow's parents will be led mistakenly to believe that their daughter is as good a flier as Sally is.

__ b. Sally Swallow's parents will either be led mistakenly to believe that their daughter can fly no faster than Sadie Sparrow can, or they will feel that the school is unfair because the slower-flying Sadie was given a higher mark than their Sally.

__ c. Sadie Sparrow will be led to believe that, relative to the swallows, she is a much better flier than she really is.

__ d. Sally Swallow will either be led to believe that, relative to the sparrows, she is a much poorer flier than she really is, or she will feel that the school is unfair because it gave the slower-flying Sadie a mark as high as or higher than it gave her.

__ e. The Director of Admissions at Bird College will be led mistakenly to believe that Sadie can fly as fast as or faster than Sally can, and hence he will conclude that Sadie is at least as likely to succeed in college as Sally.

__ f. Mr. Eagle, Personnel Director of the Rapid Message Delivery Service, Inc., will be led mistakenly to believe that Sadie can fly as fast as or faster than Sally can, and hence he will conclude that she could deliver messages as fast as or faster than Sally could.

The sixth question: What do these foregoing considerations lead one to conclude about the way Sadie and Sally should be marked? (Check one answer.)

__ 1. Sally Swallow should be given a higher mark than Sadie because she was able to fly faster than Sadie could at the end of the course.

__ 2. Sadie Sparrow should be given a higher mark than Sally because she improved her flying speed by 100 per cent while Sally made no improvement at all.

__ 3. Sadie and Sally should be given the same mark; Sadie because she worked hard and learned a good deal, Sally because even without studying she could fly fast.

__ 4. No teacher of good conscience would willingly mark these two students in any of these three ways, for each would be unfair or misleading for the pupils, parents and others concerned. Any marking system which forces a teacher into this distressing position is radically wrong. The marking system commonly found in our secondary schools gives rise to precisely the same frustrating perplexities that one encounters in responding to this birdland inventory. It must be possible to devise a better system.

The author feels that something is radically wrong with such a marking system and that it is possible to devise a better one.

Let us examine two suggestions made by some of our students, neither of which is satisfactory. One suggestion is that pupils should be sorted into two, three, or more groups according to their capacity to learn, that they should then be appraised solely on the basis of comparative achievement, with the pupil's ability group as his comparison group. But this would lead us into a distressing difficulty. Suppose that Edgar is in the most intelligent group and that his relative achievement there is the greatest; he would be assigned a mark of A. Keith is the top-ranking pupil in the least intelligent group; he also would be given an A, although his achievement is far below Edgar's and represents only about the D level of performance in Edgar's group. One can see clearly how misleading such a marking system would be for anyone who used the school records without understanding it.

A refinement of this suggestion is that subnumerals be assigned to each ability group except the highest. In this case, Arnold's A in the second level group would be reported as A_2, and Keith's would be written as A_3, assuming that there were only three ability groups. But this would fool nobody, except perhaps the persons who invented it. The pupils in the middle and lowest ability groups would quickly sense that their marks were inferior and that they were being deceived by an appearance of equality which did not exist.

We hasten to interject here the qualification that these comments are in no way meant to condemn the double-track or triple-track solution to the problem of individual differences among pupils; this solution involves real adjustments in the instructional program of the school—adjustments suited to the different capacities and needs of the students. When this teaching method is used properly, appropriately descriptive designations are given to the courses at the different levels, courses which, as we have said, differ in content as well as in name. But even when the pupils' assignment to groups is based on their ability to handle the subject matter of their groups, a considerable range of aptitudes exists among the pupils in each group. Hence the problems of appraising and reporting pupil achievement which we have been considering would still remain.

A second suggestion for an improved marking system proposes that a "mixed mark" be used. Thus the impasse illustrated by the hypothetical situations of Sam and Sadie Sparrow and Sid and Sally Swallow would be resolved by giving the pupils a mixed mark based on both their improvement and their comparative standing. But this is reminiscent of the scrambled-eggs mark which no one can explain but the cook, the person who made the appraisal. For example, suppose Bill made by far the highest score in his class on a pre-test given before taking a mathematics course. He also made the highest score on an equivalent test given at the end of the course, but his second score was only a little higher than his first. If the five-letter marking system were used, his superior level of performance at the end of the course would give him an A on the basis of comparative standings. But he had increased his knowledge of mathematics so little during the course that he deserved no more than a C on the basis of improvement. His mixed mark, therefore, would be a B. John, on the other hand, made one of the lowest scores on the pre-test, but he worked to the limit of his capabilities during the course, and his post-test results made it clear to his teacher that he had increased his mathematical knowledge as much as he possibly could. This would obviously entitle him to an A on the basis of growth. However, his final test score placed him still slightly below the middle of his grade group, giving him a C on the basis of comparative standings. Hence, as in Bill's case, his mixed mark would be a B. But although these two marks of B appear the same on the school record, they mean two quite different things, and to anyone who does not know how they were determined they are dangerously deceptive. This variant of the scrambled eggs system is no more acceptable than the other solutions to the problem. It is only less unfair, less misleading, than appraisals based solely on one or the other of the two measurements are.

A marking system should appraise and report *separately* the pupil's achievement in *each area of learning* (each subject, each area of development). And each of these achievements should be appraised and reported, again separately, on the basis of as many as possible of three criteria:

1. The *criterion of estimated possible growth:* How does the pupil's accomplishment compare with his probable capacity for learning?

2. The *criterion of comparative standing:* How does the pupil's accomplishment compare with that of other pupils?

3. The *life-activity criterion:* How does the pupil's accomplishment compare with the degree of accomplishment which is required for success in out-of-school life?

The school should use these three criteria whenever they are feasible—always separately. It is not difficult to understand why. Educational opportunity is not equal unless all young people are equally encouraged to attend school (see Chapter 4). To encourage them equally, the school must report pupil achievement separately in accordance with the criterion of estimated possible growth, because, if this is not done, the pupils of lower intellectual aptitude will find that no matter how hard they work they always receive inferior marks. Any marking system which assigns a permanently inferior status to such pupils will, of course, discourage them from remaining in school.

The criterion of estimated possible growth is equally desirable in reporting—always provided that the growth reports are separated from other reports in the same area of learning—the achievement of the more gifted students. Gifted students should make the most of their greater capabilities; they should be urged to work diligently in high school. A school which relies solely on the criterion of comparative standing allows its bright pupils to earn high marks without exerting themselves and hence without developing themselves to the limit of their capacities. But if the school issues one report of their achievements judged by the criterion of estimated possible growth, and another judged by the criterion of comparative standing, these bright pupils will discover that laziness will bring them low marks in respect to the first of these criteria and that they must use their capabilities to the greatest extent in order to earn consistently high marks.

Schools which maintain an Honor Roll should fix their standards for honor students solely in terms of marks which have been separately determined by the use of the criterion of estimated possible growth. Only this system gives an equal chance to every student, since each student's standard of excellence is established in terms of his own capacities. Such an Honor Roll stimulates all pupils to exert themselves and encourages the less capable as well as the gifted pupils to remain in school.

But the criterion of comparative standing is important, too. Our individual and societal well-being depend upon the use of the criterion of comparative standing in our schools, because both kinds of well-being demand that all our citizens be as intelligently self-directive as possible. Accurate knowledge of oneself is a necessary prerequisite to intelligent self-direction. A pupil should know how his capabilities and achievements compare with those of others, particularly others in his own age group. A free society is a competitive society, and the individual competes primarily against the others who are more or less his own age. The separate use of the criterion of comparative standing in the appraising and reporting of a pupil's achievement helps him compare his own capacities and achievements with those of the other youths in his age group.

Furthermore, as illustrated in the "birdland inventory," personnel officers in business and industry and college admission officials need reliable information concerning the relative "strengths" of the high school graduates with whom they deal. Neither the scrambled eggs system of marking nor the separate use of marks based on the criterion of estimated possible growth alone can afford this information; business and college officials need data derived from school records which report marks based solely on the criterion of comparative standing. Since our individual as well as our societal well-being is enhanced when our high school graduates are well located in business, industry, or college, the criterion of comparative standing, when it is employed separately to appraise and report the achievement of high school pupils, is an important contribution to education.

At the same time, of course, personnel officers and college admission officials can use marks based solely on the criterion of estimated possible growth. These marks can tell the official whether or not the candidate he is considering has acquired effective work habits during his high school days. The student whose achievement in high school has been consistently near the limit of his capacity to learn, i.e., the student who has worked hard, is likely to continue to be a conscientious worker in college or on the job; and this, of course, is one of the ingredients of success.

The usefulness of the life-activity criterion follows from Principle 1, Chapter 4. Reports based on the life-activity criterion afford the high school an important kind of self-appraisal; they tell the high school how well it is performing its fundamental task, how well it is preparing the country's youths to take an effective part in life's activities.

The criterion of estimated possible growth is derived from the teacher's judgment of his pupils' capabilities, so this criterion is not difficult to apply. But the criterion of estimated possible growth is not always used wisely; sometimes a teacher does not make an accurate estimate of the capacities of a pupil in his class. If the school does not have an adequate testing program, if no cumulative record can be consulted, the teacher will not have much to go on except his shrewdness in estimating a pupil's capacity. In a school which employs a well-developed program of achievement, intelligence, and other aptitude tests and which keeps thorough cumulative records for each pupil, the experienced teacher can form a reasonably satisfactory estimate of each pupil's innate capacity to learn in the particular course in question.

Similarly, the criterion of comparative standing can be applied in every secondary school. The better the measurement the more capably the teacher can determine the comparative standings of his pupils; appraisals based on measurements which are invalid or seriously unreliable are no better than guesses. Teachers should exercise great care in selecting or constructing and in administering tests. If valid and reliable measures are used, the criterion of comparative standing can be applied quite accurately by any competent teacher.

But the life-activity criterion is not so easy to apply. If the businessmen of the community require of their typists a speed of fifty words per minute, or if a stipulated level of accomplishment on a standard test in a particular branch of mathematics is required for admission to colleges of engineering, then the life-activity criterion should constitute one of the three bases for separately appraising and reporting the achievements of pupils in the appropriate courses. But for most of the courses which are taught in our high schools no one knows exactly what the related life-activity criteria are. And the author doubts the validity of teachers' judgments in this respect.

In one large high school, for example, teachers were asked, department by department, to outline the minimum content of their respective teaching fields which they believed would be required of a person who wished to function at the level of minimum effectiveness in the daily nonspecialized life of his community. Their answers were organized into a test which was administered to all the teachers in the school; none among them correctly answered more than one-third of the questions. One must conclude either that no member of this faculty, all of whom were college graduates, was competent to carry on the daily nonspecialized activities which are required of the average citizen, or that the teachers had a vastly inflated idea of what pupils must learn from them in order to function as citizens at the minimum level of adequacy. Under the circumstances, the latter conclusion seems more reasonable, and hence one is left with a profound lack of confidence in the ability of these teachers to determine what is required from their students. But what other group or individual could give a more accurate judgment? Probably none. Even our institutions of higher learning have been extremely vague in their estimates of the competence required for college work. A partial exception is the University of Illinois, which has published a bulletin in which the mathematical competencies a student must possess in order to do successful work in the College of Engineering are set forth.[3] More such life-activity criteria are sorely needed, and the day may come when we shall have them. But we have them for very few subjects at the present time.

The fact that teachers cannot usually apply the life-activity criterion accurately (because they usually do not know what the out-of-school requirements for competence in their subjects are) does not imply that schools should be satisfied to produce graduates who are capable only of a minimum level of performance in the life-activities of the average citizen. The inference we should make is that no pupil should be branded a failure on the basis of the life-activity criterion if his teachers signally overestimate the requirements of the minimum level of performance. If the level below which failure occurs is unknown, no one can say when a pupil's performance is successful or unsuccessful.

[3] Kenneth B. Henderson and others, *Mathematical Needs of Prospective Students in the College of Engineering of the University of Illinois,* University of Illinois Bulletin, Vol. 89, No. 9, September 1951.

Pupils should help appraise their educational achievements

This generalization is a correlative of Principle 2: the public schools in a democracy should help young citizens acquire the skills of intelligent self-direction. Our reasoning here can be put quite simply. Skill in appraising one's own academic achievement is prerequisite to the intelligent self-direction of one's present or future schooling, and this skill can be acquired only through guided practice. Hence students should be encouraged to participate in the appraisal of their own academic achievement.

A teacher whose pupils participate in defining the purposes of his course, and in planning the classroom activities and other learning experiences by means of which these purposes are to be achieved, will probably encounter little difficulty in enlisting the co-operation of his pupils in appraising their own educational achievements. Pupils should not, of course, assign their own marks; the teacher and the pupil together should review the purposes of the units of work for which the pupil is being marked, note the criteria by which the pupil's work is judged, and examine together the evidence which reveals the pupil's accomplishments.

Symbols used in the appraising and reporting system should be uniform at all the school levels of the community

A uniform marking system avoids confusion. In one city school system three different methods of marking are used; one in the elementary schools, a second in the junior high schools, and a third in the senior high schools. The elementary schools employ a simple two-level distinction between passing and failing, much to the dissatisfaction of many of the parents. The junior high schools use a five-level scale, ranging downward from E for excellent. In the senior high school the letter E means failure. In the senior high school a single mark is given in what, without definition, is labeled "citizenship." The junior high school, on the other hand, includes on its report forms a rather lengthy list of desirable qualities which the teachers are trying to inculcate in their pupils, but no appraisal of any sort is recorded unless the individual pupil is thought to be developing unsatisfactorily. It should not be difficult to visualize the trouble one would encounter in trying to interpret the pupils' cumulative records in this community. These cumulative records are seldom consulted by the teachers, and the parents are unable to learn how well their children are doing. In this city as everywhere, uniformity in the appraising and reporting systems of all the schools would be a considerable help to everyone concerned.

The appraising and reporting system should be understood and accepted by teachers, pupils, parents, and other citizens of the community

The laymen's confusion and error caused by an incomprehensible marking system may destroy their confidence in the schools of the community. If either the teachers, the pupils, or the laymen do not accept the school's marking practices, conflict is certain and nearly all of the aims of appraising and reporting are being subverted. The participation of everyone concerned is often the key to understanding and approval.

The community's other educational agencies should help appraise and report pupils' educational accomplishments

The public high school is only one of the community's educational agencies (see Chapter 4). The school's responsibility is to work with these other agencies in the education of our youths. Laymen from the community should help shape the broad purposes of the school and should have a voice in appraising the school's products.

The question is not whether the people of the community will appraise the educational achievements of the pupils and announce their conclusions. Such appraisals by parents, newspaper editors, clergymen, radio and television commentators, employers, college professors, and other citizens are going on all the time and will probably continue. The question is whether or not these appraisals will be made *jointly* with the school. Most now are not, and one of the chief unresolved problems of the public high school is how to change this situation.

Although some of these appraisals by citizens are valid, most are not—usually because they are based on the observation of only one, or at most a very few, of the pupils. They are appraisals which usually begin with "I know a boy who . . . ." Most citizens, however, unaware of the reliability of their data, continue to speak their minds confidently on the school's performance. Since the failures among students are usually more dramatic than the successes, the public high school receives many an unwarranted criticism. This will continue until teachers and school administrators bring about joint appraisals by the school and its public.

The Illinois Curriculum Program, a statewide enterprise conducted under the auspices of the Office of the Superintendent of Public Instruction in Illinois, has devised a means of bringing about such joint appraisals. The plan calls for more than twenty individual projects, which are known as Local Area Consensus Studies. Each project is devoted to a major subject or service area of the high school program, e.g., to science, mathematics, guidance, safety education, and so on. In each of these "local" projects all the teachers in the school,[4] representative student leaders, and a large cross section of parents and other citizens convene to define the purposes of the subject studied, to appraise the school's efforts to fulfill these purposes, and to plan improvements. Any community which undertakes this score of local action projects, and which rotates the membership of its panel of lay citizens, will involve a great many laymen in a joint appraisal of the work of the school.

Another device, one much more widely used, for securing lay participation is the citizen's advisory council. These councils have been created under the auspices of a good many boards of education throughout the country. Usually one of their functions is to study the current practices of the school and interpret them to the other citizens of the community. Among the other aspects of the school program with which they deal are the systems of appraising and reporting pupil achievement.

A third type of lay involvement has been undertaken in a city of medium size in the Midwest. The schools in this community were suffering from a mild, general dissatisfaction with the system of appraising and reporting pupil achievement. A three-step project was set up to remedy the situation. The first step was to decide, on the basis of community-wide consensus, what specifications the marking and reporting system should meet. The second was to see whether or not current practices met these specifications. The third step was to retain the practices which met these specifications, to abandon those which did not, and to devise substitute practices

---

[4] In small and medium-sized schools only. In large institutions teacher-representatives from each department are chosen.

which would bring the whole system into conformity with the community's desires.

The first step was accomplished by asking all teachers, all parents who could be reached, all members of the citizen's advisory council, and a fairly large number of student leaders to list (a) the things they wanted their appraising and reporting system to do, and (b) the things they did not want it to do. The consensus, somewhat rephrased, was that the appraising and reporting system should

1. Indicate how the pupil's scholastic achievement compares with his estimated potential achievement; that is, the pupil who works as hard as he can should receive a high mark.

2. Indicate how the pupil's scholastic achievement compares with the achievement of other pupils; that is, a pupil whose achievement is superior to others' should receive a high mark.

3. Indicate the extent to which the pupil has developed good work habits, desirable attitudes, the ability to get along well with others, and other qualities of good citizenship.

4. Indicate the reason for any pupil's lack of progress.

5. Be fair to each pupil.

6. Encourage pupils, the more capable as well as the less capable, to exert their best efforts.

7. Provide intelligible and accurate information to pupils, parents, employers, and college admission officials.

8. Be uniform, as far as possible, throughout the entire school system.

The second step was carried out by a group of parents and teachers, including administrators, from all school levels. They found that most of the current practices in their school system either violated or ignored these eight specifications. Unable to salvage more than a few of their current practices, this group of parents and teachers devised a tentative system (the third step) which met all eight specifications. They solicited criticism of it from about thirty other lay citizens—parents, employers, and college admissions officials, and thus incorporated several constructive suggestions into the tentative system.

This tentative system is in harmony, not only with the specifications which were worked out in this particular city, but also with most of the generalizations which have been discussed in this chapter. It was specified that two kinds of pupil achievement be appraised and reported, namely, scholastic achievement and the development of qualities of good citizenship; these encompass the "learned behavior with which the school is properly concerned." Two other generalizations presented in this chapter state that "reports of achievement should be accurately labeled" and that "if two or more aspects of a pupil's achievement are to be appraised, each should be treated separately." The special planning group accomplished these ends by recommending that scholastic achievement and the development of certain specified qualities of good citizenship should be separately appraised, separately labeled, and separately reported.

The first and second specifications stipulate that scholastic achievement should be appraised on two bases: one, in terms of what it is reasonable to expect the pupil to achieve; second, in terms of how well his achievement compares with that of other pupils. On this point, one of our generalizations states that "if two or more bases for appraisal are used, each resultant appraisal should be reported separately." The planning group proposed that two separate appraisals of scholastic achievement determined by the two bases above be reported for each subject of study. Development in specified qualities of good citizenship was to be judged by comparing a pupil's achievement with "what it is reasonable to expect from a pupil of his age," except at the senior high school level, where the life-activity criterion was used.

Another of our generalizations states that "schools should never report finer distinctions than measurements permit." As we have already observed, teachers who are careful and intelligent can distinguish among five levels of achievement with a reasonable degree of accuracy; the planning group recommended and described three five-level scales. Still another of our generalizations avers that "symbols used in the appraising and reporting system should be uniform at all the school levels of the community." The planning group included this point among its recommendations.

The planning group also included the seventh generalization, that the appraising and reporting system should be understood by teachers, pupils, parents, and other citizens of the community. They recommended that the tentative system which they had devised should be carefully studied during the ensuing year by teachers, parents, and (at the middle and upper grades) pupils in each of the schools in the city. Furthermore, they recommended that all the resulting suggestions for modifications of the tentative appraising and reporting system should be communicated to a central steering committee comprised of representative teachers and parents from each school in the community, and that this steering committee should choose the suggested modifications to be embodied in the final system. The special planning group believed that their tentative system should be put into effect, in other words, only after it had been studied, interpreted, modified, and accepted on a city-wide basis through this machinery of representative committees.

This still leaves several of our generalizations which the planning group did not deal with explicitly. The group was well aware that "the best measurements attainable should be used to report pupil achievement." But the group chose to begin its work with the assumption that the best attainable measurements were already being made—an assumption which, though not fully merited, has foundation. The group also was aware that "pupils should have a part in appraising their own educational achievements" and that "the community's other educational agencies should help appraise and report pupils' educational accomplishments," but no systematic way of realizing either of these very desirable ends was proposed. The first of these latter two is an intrinsic part of good teaching and probably can never be reduced to any merely systematic procedure. The question of whether or not the certificate of attendance should be considered was not raised (see below).

To involve the community in the school's work of appraisal, however, the planning group might have recommended that a two-way communication system be established between the school and the parents, so that parents could appraise and report the principal kinds of pupil achievement reflected in what children commonly do at home. Or they might have suggested that systematic follow-up studies of former students be conducted among employers and college officials, or (this had been done in a limited way several years earlier) that the senior school question former students to obtain their opinions of the preparations the school gave them for the various principal functions of daily life—wage-earning, studying in college, managing personal finances, making a home, rearing children, taking part in civic affairs, and so forth. These, of course, are the ultimate criteria by which any community should judge the work of its educational system, and hence these are the criteria by which the actual achievements of pupils should be appraised and reported.

As this book was being written, the revised system of appraising and reporting described here had been in use in the city where it was developed for a little less than two years. The important part of the report card which is now used at the senior high school level in this city is reproduced in Table 7.

What is done at graduation time should conform to the principle of equality of educational opportunity

The awarding of a high school diploma is a way of reporting that the student has graduated from school. Some people argue that the diploma should be given only to students who have done well in their studies and that the rest should receive merely a certificate of high school attendance. Some go further and insist that the diploma should be given only to students whose level of achievement in the usual college-preparatory subjects qualifies them for successful college work.

Should the diploma be reserved for students well prepared for college?

This proposal arises from the assumption that the only commendable aim of the public secondary school is to prepare students for college. A stigma would be attached to the certificate of attendance: the certificate would certify merely that a student had gone to high school, not that he had graduated. A student who went to high school not to prepare himself for college but to fit himself for immediate entry into the worlds of business, industry, or agriculture would be stigmatized regardless of the quality of his noncollege-preparatory work. His high school would not recognize that he had successfully fulfilled a worthy educational aim.

In addition, the proposal presupposes that the public secondary school should encourage the attendance, not of all the educable children, but only of the top half, whose academic aptitudes are average or better. Good college-preparatory work is work which qualifies one to succeed in the courses which colleges offer to their entering students. The typical college or university makes no pre-

TABLE 7   *Report card illustrating the revised system of appraising and reporting*

SUBJECT	Comparative achievement grade *						Personal achievement grade †						Citizenship ‡			
	1st report	2nd report	3rd report	4th report	Exam-ination	Year average	1st report	2nd report	3rd report	4th report	Exam-ination	Year average	1st report	2nd report	3rd report	4th report

* Comparative achievement grade indicates the teacher's judgment of the pupil's mastery of the subject materials offered in the course. It is determined by teacher observation, teacher tests, state and national test. A = excellent, B = good, C = average, D = poor but passing, F = failing, I = incomplete.

† Personal achievement indicates the teacher's judgment of the pupil's achievement in terms of his apparent individual ability. A = excellent, B = good, C = average, D = poor, F = failing.

‡ The Citizenship grade is based on the pupil's general conduct, cooperation, dependability, initiative, work habits, and social attitudes.

tense of offering courses which are suited to the full range of intellectual aptitude of the whole population. Most college courses require of the student at least an average academic aptitude, and this is beyond the capacities of half or more of the college-age youths. Good college-preparatory work in high school, which some would make the prerequisite for a diploma, can be done only by students who are at least average in academic aptitude. If the diploma were reserved for those who had done good work in the college-preparatory subjects, about half of our youths would be stigmatized at commencement time. This is no light matter. The prospect of being publicly stigmatized at the time of graduation would be exceedingly distressing to these young people, distressing enough, in many cases, to cause them to drop out of school well before the twelfth grade is completed.

And finally, the proposal would tend to stigmatize the teachers of all noncollege-preparatory subjects. Because these teachers would be teaching subjects unworthy of credit toward a diploma their prestige would decline.

Most of the people who support this proposal are college or university professors. They would be astonished by the suggestion that the B.A. or B.S. degree should be granted only to students whose college work is of the level of achievement required for admission to the graduate school and that all the rest of the students (over half) should be given only a certificate of attendance at the commencement exercises. Yet this suggestion is no more preposterous than the proposal that high schools should award their diplomas, their official signs of approval, only to students who have successfully qualified for college work.

Should the diploma be reserved for students who have done well in whatever courses they took?

So far as we know, no one has yet offered to define what "done well" really means. All we have heard is that the diploma should be reserved exclusively for students who have "really learned something in high school," and that the others should receive only a certificate of attendance.

As we have already noted in this chapter, three criteria can be used to decide who has "done well," who has "really learned something": the criterion of comparative standing, the criterion of estimated possible growth, and the life-activity criterion.

If the *criterion of comparative standing* is used as a basis for deciding who should and who should not receive the diploma, where should the line be drawn? Has a student satisfied this criterion if his level of accomplishment equals or excels that of half the comparison group? If he equals or excels a third, a fourth, a fifth, a tenth, or perhaps a twentieth of the comparison group? Obviously, some critical point must be set below which the student cannot fall.

But wherever this critical point is set, the use of the criterion of comparative standing to determine who should be denied the diploma violates our democratic ethic. Our American heritage enjoins us to believe in the supreme and equal moral worth of all human beings. All our youths should have equal access to the good life, and we should grant them equal educational opportunity. We do not have equal educational opportunity unless we have equal encouragement to attend high school. The use of the criterion of comparative standing presupposes that only a certain proportion of our youth should be encouraged to attend high school. If a student must equal or excel the average in order to be deemed worthy of the diploma, the school has decided in advance that only half of its students are to receive the diploma; if the dividing line is at the 5 per cent level, one student in twenty has no chance of getting a diploma. Long before their junior year most students would be able to judge whether or not they were likely to be included in the certificate group. Those who believed that they would, and that they could therefore expect nothing but public stigma for their efforts, would undoubtedly try to make their escape, that is, to quit school, long before the end of the twelfth grade. Consequently, the school would be encouraging the attendance of only some of its students. No matter where on the scale the critical point is set, a school following this practice is failing to offer equal encouragement to attend high school.

The use of the criterion of comparative standing to discriminate against certain students in this way makes the individual student's intelligence quotient the factor which principally determines whether or not he will escape the public stigma of the certificate of attendance. Consider, for instance, the plight of the appreciable minority of high school youngsters whose intelligence quotients fall below 90. No matter where the critical point has been set, even as low as the 5 per cent level, some of these students will be publicly stigmatized at the commencement exercises, even though they have worked as hard as they can and have learned as much as they are innately capable of learning.

No public high school faculty which has carefully considered the criterion of comparative standing will give its consent to the use of this method of determining which students shall receive the diploma. Any faculty which does so because it has been misled by specious arguments will reduce the holding power of its school, foment resentment among students and parents alike, and be continually at odds with its community.

The second of the three criteria which a school might use is the *criterion of estimated possible growth.* How well does a student measure up to what he is thought to be capable of achieving? In order to apply this criterion for the purpose of deciding which students should receive a diploma and which should receive a certificate of attendance, one should do two things. First, one should secure a reliable estimate of the student's innate abilities; and second, one should decide how fully a student's actual accomplishments must measure up to his potential before he can be considered worthy of a diploma. Let us examine these two requirements.

The present state of our knowledge would, under certain conditions, permit the teacher who is experienced in working with youth to make gross estimates of most students' capacities to learn in his particular subject field. If the teacher knows, from the scores on standardized tests and teachers' marks, the past performance of a pupil in the teacher's subject field, if he knows the pupil's standing on two or more group intelligence tests, and if he is well acquainted with the pupil's physical and emotional condition, the teacher can usually tell whether the pupil is learning at a rate which approaches his full capacity, at a rate which is markedly below his potential capacity, or at a rate which falls somewhere in between.

Most people would probably agree that if the certificate of attendance is to be given to anyone, it should be given only to those students whose levels of accomplishment have fallen markedly below their estimated potentials, as judged by a significant number of their teachers. Before the stigma of the certificate is inflicted upon any student, however, well-trained teachers of good conscience would be satisfied in their own minds, and be able and willing to demonstrate to the youth and his parents or guardians, that the subjects in which he is or was enrolled are of sufficient value to him and to society to warrant the application of his full abilities.

There should be sufficient proof, including recorded test scores, that other students of approximately the same potential capacity had been able to achieve at the level expected of the student in question. Whenever possible the student should be given standardized achievement tests in his various subjects, and his performances on these tests should be judged in the light of scores made by other students of comparable chronological and mental age. The school doctor and the school psychologist should participate in the final decision in order to make certain that the student's physical or mental health was not an extenuating factor in his failure to achieve as much as should be expected from a person of his capacities. The student's parents or guardians should be a party to the decision-making conference, and the teachers would certainly have held a number of prior conferences with everyone concerned in an effort to encourage the student to put forth his best efforts.

If all these conditions are reasonably well satisfied, the criterion of estimated possible growth can justifiably be used for the purpose of distinguishing between those who will and those who will not be given the diploma. But very few of our high schools can satisfy all of these conditions at the present time. And in the few schools which can satisfy these conditions, the problem is not likely to arise; all of the unacceptable students have been either helped to become acceptably productive long before commencement time, counseled (in rare instances) to enter employment of some kind, or, if incorrigible, committed to a nonschool custodial agency.

There is another difficulty to be faced in applying the criterion of estimated possible growth. Should the diploma be denied youths of high IQ whose achievement is at about the average for the total class? Such a performance would be, of course, markedly below these more able youngsters' potentials. Proponents of the certificate of attendance commonly argue that the criterion of comparative achievement, not that of estimated possible growth, should be employed in the case of gifted pupils; if it were, these pupils would receive the diploma even though the difference between their possible and their actual level of achievement was at least as great as that of the dull student who would receive and be stigmatized by the certificate of attendance.

This double standard rigs the situation in favor of the more capable students. Regardless of their capacities, all pupils have an equal chance to perform well when judged by the criterion of estimated possible growth. Yet this proposal would hold the dull but not the bright student to this standard, for, unlike his less fortunate classmate, the latter can do work of average quality even though the discrepancy between his performance and his capacity is very great. This proposal would provide an easy escape from the standard for the bright student, but would hold the dull pupil to it. The proposal, then, would provide quite unequal encouragement to attend high school.

This suggests that these proponents either have not thought the matter through, or that they are indifferent to the obligation of the public school to provide equal encouragement to attend school. Or they shrug their shoulders, say that it wouldn't do to withhold the diploma from any student whose achievement is as high as the average for the class, and seem disposed to drop the matter—thus suggesting that they believe it is chiefly the less capable youths who should be candidates for the certificate, or that these less fortunate youngsters should not be in high school anyhow.

Finally, we come to the third criterion which might be used to determine which students are to receive the diploma, the *life-activity criterion*. This criterion asks whether the student's level of accomplishment satisfies the requirements of the out-of-school activities to which his schoolwork is related. Theoretically, perhaps, the life-activity criterion could be defended as a useful means of separating the successful students from their less industrious schoolmates. But it presents one fatal defect: no one knows with any degree of certainty what the student must achieve in most of his school subjects in order to perform well in the nonspecialized activities of everyday life which are related to these subjects (see pp. 242-43). Hence any school which used this criterion in deciding to whom its diplomas should be awarded would be basing its decisions on nothing better than guesswork, and no conscientious high school faculty would be willing to stigmatize any of its students on that basis.

Summary

The system of appraisal and reporting is extremely important in the work of any high school. Measurement and appraisal are not the same thing: measurement alone yields no appraisal; appraisal always involves a criterion, and different criteria can yield different appraisals from the same measurements. Three criteria for appraisal are

1. The *criterion of estimated possible growth:* How does the pupil's accomplishment compare with his probable capacity for learning?
2. The *criterion of comparative standing:* How does the pupil's accomplishment compare with that of other pupils?
3. The *life-activity criterion:* How does the pupil's accomplishment compare with the degree of accomplishment which is required for success in out-of-school life?

Each of the following postulates describes an important characteristic of a defensible appraising and reporting system.

—The best measurement attainable should be used to report pupil achievement.

—All learned behavior with which the school is properly concerned should be measured and appraised.

—Schools should never report finer distinctions than measurements permit.

—Reports of achievement should be accurately labeled.

—If two or more aspects of a pupil's achievement are to be appraised, each should be treated separately.

—If two or more bases for appraisal are used, each resultant appraisal should be reported separately.

—Pupils should help appraise their educational achievements.

—Symbols used in the appraising and reporting system should be uniform at all the school levels of the community.

—The appraising and reporting system should be understood and accepted by teachers, pupils, parents, and other citizens of the community.

—The community's other educational agencies should be invited to help appraise and report pupils' educational accomplishments.

—What is done at graduation time should conform to the principle of equality of educational opportunity.

chapter 11

THE TEACHER'S ROLE

IN IMPROVING THE CURRICULUM

Three things must be done in order to present an adequate discussion of the teacher's role in improving the curriculum of his school. First, we must define "curriculum." Second, we must point out what the chief operations are which comprise curriculum improvement. And, third, we must describe how teachers help perform these operations.

What is the "curriculum"?

In the past most people, including professional educators, have used the term "curriculum" to denote only the school's formal program of studies, i.e., the subjects of instruction such as art, English, mathematics, science, and so on. Today, most laymen still use the term in this way.

Most professional educators, however, have adopted a broader definition of the term. There is good reason to believe that every experience results in some learning, whether it is studying the binomial theorem in a mathematics class, planning the photographs for a school yearbook in a meeting of a camera club, discussing a choice of vocation in a counselor's office, reading an eye chart in the school's health center, finding a book in the school library, asking a girl for a date on the way to the school cafeteria, remaining at home on the evening of a school dance because of inability to pay the price of admission, or any of the thousands of other things that can happen to a student in connection with his school life. As a consequence of each experience, the student either acquires new information (or misinformation), or he fixes more firmly in his mind information (or misinformation) he has already acquired; he either gains some new understanding (or misunderstanding), or he reinforces an understanding (or misunderstanding) he has gained previously; he either learns a new skill or he sharpens or dulls a skill he has learned before. The word "curriculum" shall mean here *all the experiences which students have under the auspices of the school.*

Improving the curriculum of the public secondary school, then, means improving any experience which any student has while under the control of the school. The criteria for determining what constitutes an improvement are derived from the basic principles presented in Chapter 4.

What are the chief components of curriculum improvement?

According to the basic principles set forth in Chapter 4, the public high school must provide a program which takes what is best from the past but be oriented toward the future; the school's first responsibilities must be to teach all educable youths to think and communicate, to understand, appreciate, and practice the democratic way of life, and to understand and apply the principles of safe and healthful living; and in order to discharge these chief responsibilities most capably, the school must also engage its students in a direct study of the basic social processes of making a living, maintaining a family, and providing for spiritual growth, aesthetic satisfactions, recreation, and social organization and control. These principles are the criteria for measuring the accomplishment of any given public high school. Whenever teachers help their school perform any of these tasks more effectively, they are helping to improve the curriculum.

Certain conditions facilitate learning (see Chapter 4). What the school teaches must be suited to what each individual is capable of learning, what he has already learned, and what he is ready to learn. Students learn most effectively when they see a clear and sensible relationship between what they are asked to do and some purpose or goal which they accept; when their needs and motives are taken into account; when they share in planning their educational goals, the means by which these goals will be reached, and the criteria by which their progress will be judged; when personal satisfaction in their accomplishments is reinforced by social approval; when what they learn serves some ongoing purpose; when what is taught satisfies their desire for new experience; when they use more than one of their senses; when verbal activities are supplemented by other direct experience; when they are given material which is meaningfully structured; and when transfer of training is deliberately sought. A teacher who does anything to fulfill any of these conditions is, of course, improving the curriculum of his school.

Chapters 5 through 10 applied the basic principles of education to questions of the school's holding power, its public relations, its discipline, its extra-class activities, its guidance program, and the appraising and reporting of its pupils' achievements. All of these things are related very closely to the school's curriculum.

Improving the school's holding power improves its curriculum

Chapter 5 described eleven things which the secondary school must do in order to improve its holding power. As the school increases its holding power it improves its curriculum since it extends the benefits of schooling to a larger number of adolescent boys and girls. To increase the faculty's dedication to the principle of universal secondary education, to discover and publicize the facts concerning the holding power of the school, to study and publicize the school's hidden tuition costs and the extent of student participation in extra-class activities, to make better provisions in the instructional program for individual differences among students, to solicit and make known the judgments of former students of the value of the school's instructional program to them, to enable teachers to know their students better, to provide more adequate educational and vocational information, to improve and make better use of students' cumulative records, to identify the students who are likely to drop out of school, to help parents value the education of their children —these are the things which the school must do to increase its holding power. Whenever a teacher assists his school to achieve any of these ends, he is not only helping all students then in the school, but also increasing the likelihood that more students will avail themselves of the benefits offered by the school. This is what every well-conceived program of curriculum development is designed to do.

Improving the school's relations with the community improves its curriculum

Chapter 6 described how the school can win the community's approval and support. Any improvement in the relationship between the school and the community is likely to make possible improvements in the school's curriculum, simply because all durable changes in the school derive their support from the community. Consequently, teachers are in all likelihood helping to improve the curriculum when they help parents and other laymen perceive that students are being treated considerately, that teachers are setting desirable examples, and that the educational program is a good one.

Improving the school's discipline improves its curriculum

When teachers establish good discipline by following the precepts in Chapter 7, they are improving the student's experiences at school, hence the curriculum. The precepts discussed in Chapter 7 included the following: inviting students to assist in planning their classwork, integrating guidance and instruction, using relatively long units of instruction, making the classroom environment as attractive as possible, inducing the students to accept the teacher, inviting pupils to help solve problems of individual and group conduct, providing classroom routines which afford students a sense of security without making them feel that they are being treated like children, and, when necessary, punishing students sparingly to teach them the limits of permissibility.

Improving the school's extra-class activities program improves its curriculum

Extra-class activities are a part of the school curriculum (see Chapter 8). Teachers are improving the curriculum, therefore, whenever they improve the extra-class activities program. We repeat here ways of improving it: designing and administering each extra-class activity in such a way that all potential desirable learnings, both direct and concomitant, are as fully realized as possible; providing a variety of extra-class activities which together offer direct learnings regarding all the basic social processes; securing well-trained and dedicated teachers to sponsor extra-class activities; involving lay adults and students as well as teachers in shaping the purposes and scope of the extra-class program; applying what is known about the learning process to all extra-class activities; chartering each extra-class activity in such a way that its aims are specified and its existence continued only as long as these aims are faithfully served; surveying students' interests as one basis for determining whether or not modifications should be made in the existing extra-class program; keeping students reasonably well informed about the activities which are offered; reducing the cost of participation in all extra-class activities to a point which will allow all students to participate in them without financial discomposure; making available to each student a balanced variety of activities which are appropriate to his needs; keeping records of individual and group accomplishments in each activity; controlling student participation in extra-class activities by guidance, not by the use of mechanical devices; including all extra-class activities in a well-planned school calendar; applying to each activity some strict but reasonable system of budgeting, requisitioning, and accounting; and making sure that all the students in the school may participate in any activity in which they are interested and of which they are capable.

Improving the school's guidance program improves its curriculum

In much the same way, everything that students experience in their contacts with the school's guidance program is also part of their curriculum. It is a very important part; for, as we saw in Chapter 9, the chief purposes of guidance are, first, to teach students the discipline of choice, thus fitting them to practice intelligent self-direction, and second, to make conditions throughout the school as conducive to effective learning as possible. Teachers are improving the curriculum, then, when they incorporate guidance in their instruction, i.e., involve their pupils in student-teacher planning, help their students formulate and achieve desirable goals pertaining to those of the basic social processes to which the subject matter being taught sensibly relates, relate their instruction to the personal problems of pressing concern to their pupils, and adapt their instruction to the individual capabilities of their students. Teachers also help to improve the curriculum when they cooperate with their fellows in identifying and meeting the educational needs of the youths in their school; refer students with especially difficult problems to the guidance counselors; help plan and carry out more effective orientation activities, improved arrangements for testing, and strengthened programs of educational and vocational information and of placement and follow up; and make more contributions to and more use of the students' cumulative records.

Improving the school's appraising and reporting system improves its curriculum

Finally, in Chapter 10 we saw that, briefly, the appraising and reporting system of the school bears in an important way upon the student's attitudes toward the school and affects his continuing experience in school. Fair grades can greatly expedite a student's learning experience; a system which assigns unfair grades can only lead to undesirable concomitant learnings, such as feelings of frustration and resentment. The curriculum is directly improved when teachers replace guesswork, so far as possible, with valid and reliable measurement; report separately the resultant appraisal for every basis used; and involve students in evaluating their own accomplishments. The curriculum is also improved, though less directly, when teachers appraise pupil accomplishments in terms of the basic social processes to which their subject matter relates; involve parents and other laymen in evaluating the performance of the student; help make the reporting and appraising system uniform throughout the district schools; and help the community understand and accept this system.

Summary

Chapters 4 through 10 are all devoted to improving the curriculum of the public secondary school. These chapters have described what its students must experience if the school's instructional program, its holding power, its public relations, its discipline, its extra-class activities, its guidance program, and its appraising and reporting system are to be ideal. Taken all together these experiences which students have constitute the curriculum of the school. Not only when they are helping to improve their school's instructional program, then, but also when they are helping to improve its holding power, its public relations, its discipline, its extra-class activities, its guidance program, and its appraising and reporting system, teachers are helping to improve the curriculum of their school.

What is being done to involve teachers in curriculum improvement?

Here we shall turn our attention to the practices more or less typical of good public secondary schools throughout the coutnry. The better the school, the more certain it is that the principal, not someone from a higher echelon, will make the improvement of the educational program his primary concern. Furthermore, in good schools the principal tries his best to involve not only teachers but also pupils and patrons in curriculum development. He knows that the durability of change in school programs depends upon the extent of "ownership" felt by the teachers, pupils, and patrons of the school. He also knows that they feel this sense of ownership more when they have helped discover the need for, plan, and carry out the improvements which should be made.

If teachers are to help make durable improvements in their school, they must first understand what the school should be doing. Second, they must recognize the discrepancies between what the school should be doing and what it is actually doing. Third, they must be competent to help bring about the improvements which these discrepancies show are necessary. Incidentally, the first and second of these requirements must also be met by pupils and patrons if they are to help in making durable improvements in the school program. But the actual making of these improvements usually requires technical skills which laymen do not possess; therefore, they need to be assured that what is to be done will be done by competent professionals, usually teachers.

Everything that the good high school principal does to involve his teachers in improving the curriculum is directed toward satisfying one or more of the three requirements noted above. Now let us consider the many ways in which high school teachers are thus involved.

The prevailing climate in a good high school is one of continuous self-appraisal

To bring about and to sustain this climate is one of the most important things that the good high school principal does. Teachers are far more likely to prove themselves superior if they are self-critical than if they are not; for it is altogether unlikely that self-critical teachers will ever let themselves get into a rut. As long as they teach they will continue to grow professionally in their awareness of the educational needs they should be meeting, in their knowledge of the young people they are serving, in their grasp of the subject matter they teach, and in their command of the learning processes which they mediate. The better a high school is, the more problems its teachers see and the more busily they make improvements. The first requirement for improvement is an atmosphere in which self-criticism is the normal attitude, and in most schools the creation of such an atmosphere is chiefly the responsibility of the principal.

Teachers are encouraged to engage in vacation work and educational travel

Since the teacher's job is to induct young people into the culture which will form their milieu for the rest of their lives, the teacher ought to know as much as he can about the world which his students are entering. Teachers whose practical knowledge of the office, the factory, or the farm is limited are not well equipped to induct students into the world of work. Consequently, teachers are often encouraged to spend at least part of their vacations working in business, industry, or agriculture.

Various studies have shown that a great many teachers have never been more than a few hundred miles away from their homes. Their knowledge and understanding of other national groups is almost wholly academic and obviously not very satisfactory for their work in teaching young people how to get along in our rapidly shrinking world. Educational travel helps, sometimes a great deal, to remedy such deficiencies. This is why the Travel Division of the National Education Association is so active in arranging vacation travel for teachers every year—travel to all parts of the world. Many colleges and universities, associated in the National Council for Educational Travel, also conduct travel-study tours for teachers.

Teachers are encouraged to participate in professional organizations

We know from our ordinary observations in many fields of professional endeavor that the worker who reads professional journals and takes part in the meetings of the organizations which publish them is usually stimulated to examine his own concepts and techniques and to adopt better ones. Virtually every subject and service area in the high school program is represented by some state or national professional organization whose main purpose is to improve that part of the curriculum. Some national professional organizations, such as the National Education Association (NEA) and the Association for Supervision and Curriculum Development (ASCD), serve all teachers, regardless of their particular fields. The *NEA Journal* is one of the best magazines of its kind published in this country; each issue offers many practical suggestions for improving our educational programs. So does *Educational Leadership*, the journal of the ASCD. Both organizations hold national meetings each year, attended by thousands of teachers who come away invariably with many ideas for improving their work. The meetings of the ASCD are concerned almost exclusively with problems which have actually been reported by working teachers who want help.

Moreover, there is a state association open to all teachers in every state. Most of these organizations are both very powerful and very helpful. Their journals and meetings offer much help to teachers who want to improve the curriculum of their schools.

We have noted four kinds of professional organizations—the NEA and ASCD, the state teachers' associations, the national professional organizations in the various special fields, and their counterparts at the state level. Teachers who are active in these organizations and read their journals are being continuously stimulated to think critically of their own work and their own school.

Incidentally, the NEA and many of the state teachers' associations are also actively engaged in safeguarding teacher welfare. They have promoted much of our legislation on the public schools, and they have worked hard to improve teachers' salaries and safeguard tenure. In addition, the Defense Commission of the NEA ably defends public schools and individual teachers against such injuries as unwarranted attacks. A truly professional teacher will feel obligated to join and support the organizations which are working so effectively for his welfare.

Teachers are encouraged to keep up with their professional fields

There are a number of journals published for the teaching profession, in addition to those we have just discussed, which are intended specifically to help teachers improve their work and the programs of their schools; more than thirty such journals are indexed each month in *The Education Index*. In many of our better high schools these journals are furnished to teachers in the teachers' reading room. Among those commonly seen are

Audio-Visual Guide	*National Parent-Teacher*
Clearing House	*Personnel and Guidance*
Educational Digest	*Journal*
Educational Theory	*Review of Educational Re-*
Harvard Educational Review	*search*
Journal of Educational Re-	*School Activities*
search	*School Life*
Journal of Educational Soci-	*School Review*
ology	*Teachers College Record*

Many serious nonprofessional publications frequently offer materials which bear upon public education, and teachers, like intelligent people everywhere, should try to keep abreast of them. One thinks immediately of such magazines as

Atlantic Monthly	*Progressive*
Harper's Magazine	*Reporter*
Nation	*Saturday Review*

New books of professional significance to teachers are published nearly every month. These, too, can be exceedingly helpful to those interested in improving the programs of our public schools. The reading rooms for teachers in our best high schools are well stocked with such materials, and librarians often solicit suggestions from the faculty for new titles that should be added. In some states the system known as the teachers' reading circle has been adopted; collections of professional books, brought up to date each year, are maintained by the state board of education or the state teachers' association and are made available to teachers in schools throughout the state.

In addition to the reading of professional books and magazines, professional study of other kinds can lead toward improvements in the curriculum: the summer school and extension courses offered by many colleges and universities, workshops dealing with professional problems, and teachers' conferences. In many school systems teachers are required to complete a stipulated number of semester or quarter hours of university work during stated intervals in order to become eligible for increases in salary.

During the week preceding the opening of the fall semester, our more advanced school systems often hold preschool conferences primarily devoted to professional study—to planning activities which will improve the program of the school.

Teachers are encouraged to make professional visits

Usually these visits are to outstanding schools in other communities where the visitor has a chance to see what is being done and talk with the teachers of the classes and activities he has observed. In addition, many high school principals encourage intra-city and intra-school visits, especially for young and inexperienced teachers; beginners are asked to observe the work of their more experienced colleagues and obtain whatever advice they can about teaching methods and other curricular problems. Beginning teachers should always seek such opportunities.

Teachers are encouraged to take advantage of the principal's "open door" policy

The office door of a good high school principal, it is often said, is never shut. He is always ready to welcome any teacher who needs help in solving a professional problem or who wishes to offer a suggestion for the improvement of the school. Beginning teachers especially are often in need of wise and sympathetic counsel. The principal knows, of course, that young teachers have many problems when they set out to conduct a class or an extra-class activity, and he welcomes their invitations to visit their classrooms so that he can help to diagnose their difficulties and find the proper remedies. Teachers who use the principal's wisdom in this way are obviously helping to improve the curriculum of their schools.

The good principal welcomes teachers' suggestions for improving the school program; in fact, he asks for them. The principal can inculcate a kind of psychological ownership of the school's whole program among his faculty members if he can involve them in planning it. The teachers themselves show that they are imaginative and inventive when they avail themselves of the principal's open door to make suggestions for improving the school; they show that they are sincere when they assist in securing faculty (and sometimes lay and pupil, as well) consideration of new proposals and when they willingly carry out approved changes.

Teachers are encouraged to participate in the Parent-Teacher Association

The main purpose of the P.T.A., and of most other organizations formed to promote the cooperation of teachers and parents, is to improve the educational program of the school, i.e., its curriculum. Obviously, teachers who are active in such organizations are contributing to curriculum development in their schools.

Teachers are encouraged to participate in other community organizations

Teachers who are active in any community organization—whether it is a church, a historical society, a political action group, a recreational association, or something else altogether—come automatically into close touch with many of their fellow citizens. They develop friendly, informal, and continuing contacts outside their professional group. By doing so they often become aware of flaws in the school—flaws which people outside the school can see more easily than those on the inside. Teachers who become aware of the need for changes then can help bring the changes about, thus improving the school and creating better school-community relations at the same time. As was noted earlier, good school-community relations make it easier to sustain the good work which the school is already doing and to improve its program further.

Teachers are encouraged to use the services of other community youth-serving agencies

Teachers frequently can both learn to know their students better and serve them more intelligently if they use the other agencies which the community offers for the service of youth. Teachers can often help students in eminently practical ways by bringing them into contact with other appropriate agencies. Financial help for needy pupils, for instance, can usually be arranged through such public and private welfare organizations as the Department of Public Welfare, the Aid to Dependent Children, the Family Service, and the Salvation Army. Students in ill health can be helped by a number of different agencies in most communities. Pupils with problems of adjustment can be referred to child guidance and mental health clinics where they can obtain diagnoses and recommendations for therapy. Service clubs, such as Kiwanis, Lions, Optimists, and Rotary, and fraternal organizations, such as the Elks, Knights of Columbus, and Masons, usually maintain standing committees for youth service which can be helpful to the resourceful teacher who wants to find financial aid or counsel for his students. And of course teachers are in a much better position to serve the spiritual needs of their students when they know about the programs of the community's character-building organizations—its churches, its 4-H Clubs, its CYO, YMCA, YWCA, YMHA, YWHA, and so on. Teachers who bring the benefits of any of these agencies to their students are at the same time extending and improving the curriculum of their school.

Teachers are encouraged to take part in making case studies of representative students

This is probably the best single device yet discovered for enabling teachers to discover for themselves the necessity for changing either what they are teaching or the way they are teaching it. When a good case study is made of a student, every significant fact that is known about him is considered in order to estimate what services the school should be providing for him. When, for instance, half a dozen students ranging from high to low in mental ability and socioeconomic backgrounds—to take only two of the possible variables—are examined in terms of their readiness for a school's program, almost invariably deficiencies in the program are exposed, deficiencies in the regular program of instruction, the extra-class program, the health services, and the guidance program. Furthermore, such studies usually reveal a need to improve either the administration or the supervision of the present program, even if no other changes are made in it. Discoveries like these will very quickly destroy the complacency of any conscientious teacher; he will become a partisan for curriculum improvement in his school. It is no wonder that teachers in better schools frequently make such case studies.

Teachers are encouraged to take part in evaluative studies of their schools

The patrons and pupils of a school as well as its teachers must participate in these studies if they are most likely to result in durable improvements. As we stated in Chapter 4, everything done by the public school is determined in the last analysis by public opinion. If lasting improvements are to be made, therefore, the lay citizens of the community must not only know that certain deficiencies exist in their school but must believe that these deficiencies can and should be corrected. The facts which a person discovers for himself are more compelling to him than facts which are discovered by somebody else. The discoverer acquires a sense of psychological ownership of the data and, if improvements are indicated, is much more likely to insist that they be made. This is why lay citizens of the community and high school pupils, as well as all teachers, should be involved in all school self-surveys. Although they all serve the same purpose—to reveal needed improvements in the school's program—evaluative self-surveys take many different forms. Three were mentioned in Chapter 5: holding power, student participation in extra-class activities, and hidden costs of schooling for students.[1] By using the materials of the holding power study, the staff of a high school can find out not only how many of its entering students drop out before graduation, but also what the distinguishing characteristics of these early school leavers are. When one knows what these distinguishing characteristics are, obviously one also knows what kinds of students the high school is not serving effectively and has some way of discovering why they are quitting school. In Chapter 5 we noted in some detail the kinds of improvements which the high school must make if it is to improve its service to these students. A teacher who cooperates in making such a holding power study, a study of participation in extra-class activities, or a study of hidden tuition costs is thus helping to improve the curriculum.

The follow-up study of high school graduates mentioned in Chap-

---

[1] Charles M. Allen, *How to Conduct the Holding Power Study of the Illinois Curriculum Program (Revised)*, Office of the Superintendent of Public Instruction, Springfield, Illinois, 1955.

Harold C. Hand, *How to Conduct the Participation in Extra-class Activities Study*, Office of Superintendent of Public Instruction, Springfield, Illinois, 1949.

Harold C. Hand, *How to Conduct the Hidden Tuition Costs Study*, Office of Superintendent of Public Instruction, Springfield, Illinois, 1949.

ter 10 is another kind of systematic self-appraisal which teachers are often asked to conduct. When the Illinois Curriculum Program materials [2] are used, parents, pupils, and teachers as well as graduates of the high school are involved in the study. The study is organized in terms of fifty-six typical problems which occur in the lives of young adults, problems which fall under a number of headings— making a living, living healthfully and safely, developing an effective personality, managing personal finances wisely, spending leisure time wholesomely and enjoyably, preparing intelligently for marriage and homemaking, using educational opportunities wisely, and taking an effective part in civic affairs. Parents, pupils, and teachers fill out inventories in which they indicate the problems which they believe their school should be treating somewhere in its program. Then a second inventory is given to recent graduates of the school who are asked to tell how much of the help they needed for resolving each of these typical problems they actually received from their high school. A third inventory is given to each teacher, and the teachers are asked to indicate how much of the help the last graduating class needed in preparation for each of the fifty-six problems they believe was given them. All these data are then pooled on a problem-by-problem basis, and the results are made available to parents, pupils, and teachers. The data furnish a focal point for group discussions out of which recommendations will come as to which of the fifty-six problems should be dealt with to a greater extent in the school program. So far as we know, no school has ever conducted this study without concluding that some improvements were needed.

A more common type of follow-up study is limited to finding out how well the high school's program has equipped its students to do work on the college level. Within its limits, such a study can be valuable, especially now that the proportion of high school students who go on to college is increasing. Improvements in the parts of the high school curriculum which are intended to prepare students for college are always beneficial, so long as they do not weaken other parts of the curriculum, and of course this is a matter in which many parents and other laymen are intensely interested.

This suggests another important kind of self-survey which every

[2] Kenneth B. Henderson and John E. Goerwitz, *How to Conduct the Follow-Up Study*, Office of Superintendent of Public Instruction, Springfield, Illinois, 1950.

high school should make. Gifted students are far too often the most neglected students in the school. National security, to say nothing of the school's responsibilities to *all* students, demands that we identify these fortunately endowed boys and girls as early as possible, so that their capabilities may be developed to the fullest extent. A later subsection of this chapter describes a special survey instrument which has been designed for this purpose.

Another local study [3] which many high school teachers have helped to carry out is concerned with the adequacy of the school's guidance services. The materials supplied for this study enable the school to make three kinds of self-appraisal. First, with the use of a check list the school can inventory the personnel, services, procedures, and materials found in its guidance program. The adequacy of the school's program can then be measured against the optimum program which is indicated by the check list. Second, a test which samples the knowledge a person must possess in order to exercise intelligent self-direction is supplied to be administered to seniors about to graduate. In every school where the findings of this test are known to us, the results have shown critical deficiencies in the students' preparation for self-direction. Third, the materials of the study include a student's problem check list, which should be completed by students late in their senior year. Wherever this has been done, the results have shown that students lack much of the training they need in order to face a variety of problems which typically arise in the lives of young people. Very often this lack of training can be attributed directly to inadequacies in the school program.

The local area consensus studies,[4] mentioned earlier in this book, will provide materials for more than twenty separate areas of investigation—that is, study materials will be available for each of the subject fields (art, English, mathematics, etc.) and for each of the service areas (guidance, health, library, etc.) included in a good high school program. The materials for twelve of these subject fields or service areas had been completed and were in use in the schools of Illinois when this book was written. The work of a group composed of the teachers and large groups of representative patrons and pupils

[3] Harry D. Lovelass, *How to Conduct the Study of the Guidance Services of the School,* Office of Superintendent of Public Instruction, Springfield, Illinois, 1949.

[4] Harold C. Hand and Eric H. Johnson, *How to Conduct the Local Area Consensus Studies of the Illinois Curriculum Program,* rev. ed., Office of Superintendent of Public Instruction, Springfield, Illinois, 1956.

involves three tasks, each of which requires that an inventory be taken.

For a subject field, for instance, the first inventory establishes the purposes of the subject's program, asks the respondent to indicate which of these purposes he thinks his school should be trying to achieve, and invites him to estimate how effectively it is doing so. All the teachers in the school (not merely the teachers of the subject), as well as the representative pupils and patrons who are participating in the study, fill out this inventory anonymously at the first meeting of the whole group. Then the data on each purpose are tabulated separately. The results are given to all the participants and are used as the basis for discussions in the small mixed groups into which the participants are divided at subsequent meetings. The aim of these discussions is twofold: first, to create an informed consensus concerning the purposes toward which the high school should strive in this subject; and second, to bring about a mutual realization, based as much as possible on fact, of the extent to which these locally desired purposes are being met by the school's current program in the subject.

When these discussions have been completed, the participants in the study are asked to fill out a second inventory, again anonymously. This second inventory is exactly like the first except that it contains one additional question about each purpose of the program for the subject studied: the respondent is asked to tell which of these desired purposes are not being accomplished. When all the responses to this inventory have been tabulated, those in charge of the study know how the participants feel concerning (1) the purposes that the school's program in the subject studied should be serving, and (2) the improvements that are needed to make the program serve these purposes adequately.

So far, the three groups have accomplished two of their three tasks. The third is to join in recommending to the board of education a specific plan for improvements which most of the participants agree should be made. This plan is prepared by the teachers of the subject being studied, who use a third inventory to remind themselves of everything that the plan should include. This process usually takes several months. Then the proposed plan is taken before the whole study group (all teachers and representative patrons and pupils) where it is explained, discussed, modified if necessary, and finally approved. Once this has been done, the plan is presented to the board of education by the school principal or the superintendent, with the recommendation that it be adopted. When such a plan carries the obvious approval of so many people connected with the school, it will at least be seriously considered, and there is a good chance that it will be adopted.

Opinion polls of various kinds are still another type of survey which schools can use to evaluate their own success, and teachers are occasionally called upon to assist in the process of gathering opinion (see Chapter 6). The improvement of public relations is very often a necessary prelude to any improvement in the school's curriculum, and consequently a teacher who assists in conducting a public opinion poll on questions relating to his school is helping indirectly to pave the way for curricular improvements. He is also helping in a more direct way if the poll contains questions which are directly concerned with the educational program of the school.[5] When, for instance, a poll uncovers a distinctly unfavorable public reaction to specific aspects of the school program, school administrators can take steps to determine whether or not the unfavorable opinion is warranted and improve the unsatisfactory situation if they find that it is.

A great many high schools have conducted self-surveys by using the materials and following the procedures of the Cooperative Study of Secondary School Standards,[6] an enterprise sponsored by all the regional accrediting associations in the United States. The American Council on Education, the National Association of Secondary School Principals, the National Education Association, and the United States Office of Education also assisted in the undertaking. The materials and procedures for self-surveys offered in the *Evaluative Criteria*, 1950 edition, provide a basis for appraising virtually every aspect of the secondary school's function and structure—its subjects, its extra-class activities, its guidance and library services, its administration, its physical plant, and the qualifications of its faculty. However, the designers of this study did not mention the fact that the improvements that may result will be more enduring if lay citizens are involved.

[5] See, for example, the inventories for parents, pupils, and teachers given in the appendices to Harold C. Hand's *What People Think About Their Schools*, World Book Co., Yonkers, New York, 1948, pp. 153-218.
[6] Cooperative Study of Secondary School Standards, *Evaluative Criteria*, Washington, D. C., 1950.

*Teachers are encouraged and helped
to undertake projects for the improvement
of particular aspects of the curriculum*

These projects may take many different forms; they may concern any subject or any of the services offered by the high school. Usually such projects are conducted by leading teachers with the help of consultants from a central supervisory staff, from state departments of education, from nearby colleges or universities, or from other school faculties. Literally thousands of forward-looking high schools in this country are now engaged in projects for the improvement of their instructional programs in agriculture, art, business education, core or unified studies, English and speech, foreign languages, health, mathematics, music, physical education, science, and the social studies. In a great many high schools similar projects have been inaugurated in respect to guidance, health, library, audio-visual aids, and other services.

Curriculum improvement projects involving innovations of emphasis or method in several courses at the same time are also being sponsored by teachers in many of our better secondary schools. National organizations, some created for this purpose and others having expanded their objectives to include it, give valuable help to teachers pursuing these projects. These organizations are of many kinds, and they are interested in many different kinds of educational improvements. The Joint Council on Economic Education, for instance, is staffed by capable economists who help to conduct workshops and conferences for teachers at all school levels. As this book was being written, the Joint Council was affiliated with twenty pilot school systems in which its staff members were helping classroom teachers to plan, carry on, and evaluate projects designed to heighten the economic understanding of pupils in these schools. The expectation is that what is successful in these schools will be adopted by teachers in a great many other schools. Earlier, the Joint Council[7] had assisted teachers in seven cities to plan, conduct, and appraise a program for using new procedures and materials designed to increase pupils' knowledge of our natural resources and the problems involved in using them wisely. This project, known as the Resource-

    [7] Joint Council on Economic Education, "A Brief Report on JCEE's Resource-Use Project," *The Classroom and the Joint Council*, 2 West Forty-sixth Street, New York 36, New York, April, 1956.

Use Project, developed many materials and techniques now available to teachers everywhere. The Joint Council also works with the state councils for economic education active throughout the country.

Conservation education. The Joint Council's Resource-Use Project is an example of what is sometimes called "conservation education." This is also the concern of a number of other organizations which provide useful assistance to teachers: the American Forestry Association; the Isaak Walton League of America; the National Audubon Society; the National Wildlife Federation; the Forest and the Soil Conservation Services of the U.S. Department of Agriculture; the Bureau of Reclamation, the Fish and Wildlife Service, and the National Park Service of the U.S. Department of the Interior; and the U.S. Department of Mines and Geological Survey. Yearbooks on conservation education for the guidance of teachers have been published by the American Association of School Administrators [8] and the Association for Supervision and Curriculum Development.[9] Both of these yearbooks describe successful teaching techniques for use in conservation education, list many textbooks, films, and other useful instructional materials that are available for school programs, and give other kinds of assistance which high school teachers who want to emphasize conservation will find exceedingly helpful.

Home management education. Other projects are possible for those interested in promoting better home management. No small amount of economic understanding is required to manage a home intelligently. This suggests the aim of the curriculum improvement projects which have been assisted by the National Committee for Education in Family Finance (488 Madison Avenue, New York 22, New York). The committee sponsors workshops for high school teachers at many of our principal colleges and universities. For example, one of many such workshops was held at a Midwestern university during a recent summer session. It was attended by high school teachers of business education, home economics, social studies, and vocational agriculture who, in addition to learning a good deal about economics themselves, learned also how to prepare instructional materials for improving the curriculum in their schools.

[8] American Association of School Administrators, *Conservation Education in American Schools,* 1201 Sixteenth Street, N.W., Washington 6, D. C., 1951.

[9] Association for Supervision and Curriculum Development, *Large Was Our Bounty,* 1201 Sixteenth Street, Washington 6, D. C., 1948.

Consumer education.   This is another important aspect of general economic education. In this field the National Association of Secondary School Principals has sponsored the Consumer Education Study. Under the directorship of Thomas H. Briggs, who has long been an outstanding leader in secondary education, the Study has issued a number of publications designed for high school youths. Included are four books—*Consumer Living, Economic Roads for American Democracy, Your Life in the Country,* and *The Buyer's Guide*—as well as eleven teaching-learning units—"The Modern American Consumer," "Learning to Use Advertising," "Time on Your Hands," "Investing in Yourself," "Consumer and the Law," "Using Standards and Labels," "Managing Your Money," "Buying Insurance," "Using Consumer Credit," "Investing in Your Health," and "Effective Shopping." [10] All these materials can be used profitably to improve the curriculum in any high school.

Largely because of the efforts of Briggs, the National Association of Secondary School Principals recently joined with the National Better Business Bureau, Inc., to establish the Council for the Advancement of Secondary Education. In order to secure a reliable guide for its work in economic education, the Council has conducted two ambitious studies to determine the specific objectives of economic education. Teachers of many high school subjects will find that the results of these studies [11] are extremely significant for their own work.

Education for intercultural relations.   One of the kinds of education which is very badly needed throughout the whole world today is education for improved intercultural relations. This is the concern of the Bureau for Intercultural Education (157 West Thirteenth Street, New York 11, New York), another of the national organizations which help teachers to improve the curriculum in their schools. No matter what their fields of specialization may be, secondary school teachers who use *Democracy Demands It,*[12] a resource unit published under the auspices of the Bureau for intercultural education in high schools, can improve their skill in training

[10] These are available from the National Association of Secondary School Principals, 1201 Sixteenth Street, N.W., Washington 6, D. C.

[11] Galen Jones and Baldwin Lee, "Requisites for Economic Literacy," *Bulletin of the National Association of Secondary School Principals,* Vol. 40, No. 217, February 1956, pp. 349-375.

[12] William Van Til *et al., Democracy Demands It,* Harper & Brothers, New York, 1950.

students to respect the dignity of human personality, a task demanded of the teacher by the fourth basic principle presented in Chapter 4. Teachers who consult this valuable instructional aid will also encounter a number of other exceedingly useful publications issued by the Bureau. Each deserves a place in the professional library of every high school.

Education for moral and spiritual values. As we have noted before, our Federal Constitution stipulates that church and state be separated, so sectarian religious doctrines cannot be taught in our public schools. Yet there is a good deal that public school teachers should do in teaching moral and spiritual values to our young people. The Educational Policies Commission, a national organization sponsored jointly by the National Education Association and the American Association of School Administrators, has issued a publication [13] which many teachers will find a valuable source of suggestions.

Safety education. This is another large field in which curriculum improvement projects of concern to teachers of every subject are promoted by a number of national organizations and governmental agencies. Probably the most active of these organizations is the National Safety Council. Others include the American Automobile Association, the American Red Cross, the Metropolitan Life Insurance Company, the National Board of Fire Underwriters, the National Bureau of Casualty and Security Underwriters, the National Conservation Bureau, the National Fire Protection Association, and such agencies of the government as the Bureau of Public Roads of the U.S. Department of Agriculture, the Bureau of Standards, the Civil Aeronautics Administration, the Insurance Department of the U.S. Department of Commerce, and of course the U.S. Public Health Service. The American Association of School Administrators has published a yearbook [14] which describes programs of safety education as they have been conducted in many American schools and also lists courses of study, textbooks, workbooks, films, and tests which are available as instructional aids.

Citizenship education. Whatever his field of specialization, every high school teacher should be interested in improving the teaching

---

[13] Educational Policies Commission, *Moral and Spiritual Values in the Public Schools*, 1201 Sixteenth Street, N.W., Washington 6, D. C.

[14] American Association of School Administrators, *Safety Education*, 1201 Sixteenth Street, N.W., Washington 6, D. C., 1940.

of citizenship in his school. Hundreds of national organizations are trying, by one means or another, to affect the civic training of adolescent students.[15] One is the American Historical Association, specifically its Commission on the Social Studies. The Commission has produced a number of scholarly volumes, including the one just cited by Bessie Louise Pierce, which teachers have found very useful in projects for curriculum improvement. Second, the Educational Policies Commission has published a case book of civic education [16] which contains many outstanding examples of programs for citizenship education, both in the usual subjects of instruction and in extra-class activities; these descriptions of what has been accomplished in many of our better schools have stimulated many teachers to seek means of improving the curriculums in their own schools. A third is the American Association of School Administrators, whose recent yearbook on citizenship education [17] is rich in illustrative practices and in other suggestions for classroom teachers. The fourth organization is the Citizenship Education Project (CEP), sponsored by Teachers College, Columbia University. Strictly speaking, this is not a national organization, but its work is being carried on in so many secondary schools in so many states that we feel justified in including it here. The Project came into being in response to a specific need—the need to teach students to *act* as well as to *know*, to help young people develop the skills of citizenship which life in a democracy requires as well as the understanding of what democracy means in the abstract. The materials devised by the CEP are of two types. One consists of descriptions of a balanced variety of laboratory techniques—citizenship activities for the school and in the community which will afford experience in the functioning of democracy. The other is a card file of annotated references to available materials—books, pamphlets, films, film strips, recordings, and so on—which will help the teacher guide his students to the sources which will give them an excellent understanding of democracy at work. Several thousand high school

[15] Bessie Louise Pierce, *Citizens' Organizations and the Civic Training of Youth*, Charles Scribner's Sons, New York, 1933.
Robert Bruce Raup, *Education and Organized Interests in America*, G. P. Putnam's Sons, New York, 1936.
[16] Educational Policies Commission, *Learning the Ways of Democracy*, 1201 Sixteenth Street, N.W., Washington 6, D. C., 1940.
[17] American Association of School Administrators, *Education for American Citizenship*, 1201 Sixteenth Street, N.W., Washington 6, D. C., 1954.

teachers have used the CEP methods and materials to improve the curriculum in their schools.

Aviation education.   Several national organizations have been established to help teachers with this area of modern experience. What are the aims of aviation education? The development of automotive power has played a major part in the revolution of American life that has taken place since the beginning of this century. New occupations have been created and old ones have died out, methods of warfare have changed sharply, former community controls have vanished, the authority of the home has been weakened, the size and importance of many communities have diminished while others have waxed fat at their expense, some units of government have become obsolete, new hazards to life and limb have appeared, our patterns of leisure activity have radically altered. It is the task of education to induct young people into our culture as it is or as it is becoming, and yet in respect to automotive power our schools have failed unmistakably. Educators—churches, the press, and parents as well as the schools—did not discern the remarkable changes that were being wrought by our increasing use of automotive power, and consequently they did not modify their teaching to meet these changes. This lack of foresight has helped bring about the carnage on our highways, the unnecessary toll of life which we read about every day in our newspapers. It does not take much imagination to see that the airplane is to the automobile as the giant is to the pygmy so far as its potential ability to change our daily life is concerned. The main purpose of aviation education is to make students sensitive to the implications of air transport—to its great potentialities for good and evil—so that our society can adjust as rapidly and intelligently as possible to this enormous change in our conditions of existence.[18]

Our present subjects should be revised without causing other educational emphases to suffer so that the subjects can be accommodated to the educational needs of the air age. How this revamping can be done in five different areas of instruction has been detailed in a series of resource units prepared under the auspices of the Illinois Curriculum Program and distributed at cost by the Na-

[18] For a statement of the detailed objectives of aviation education see Charles W. Sanford, Harold C. Hand, and Willard B. Spalding, eds., *The Schools and National Security*, McGraw-Hill Book Company, New York, 1951, pp. 238-246.

tional Aviation Education Council, 1205 Connecticut Avenue, Washington 6, D. C.[19] The Council also prepares and distributes other excellent teaching aids. The Link Foundation, located in the Smithsonian Institution, is another organization which functions in all parts of the country and supports experiments in aviation education at all school levels; one of the many studies it has helped to finance is that relating to the Teachers' Flight Experience Course at the University of Illinois. Several major airlines, notably Eastern Air Lines, Pan-American World Airways, Trans-World Airlines, and United Air Lines, have also been helping schools to undertake aviation education programs for many years. The Air Transport Association of America, an organization to which all our major scheduled airlines belong, is now co-ordinating and expanding this assistance to teachers. Furthermore, the Civil Air Patrol has for many years been giving its assistance to secondary schools in the establishment of aviation education programs. It also sponsors workshops for teachers; a particularly outstanding one, attended by more than one thousand teachers, was held during the summer of 1957 at Miami University, Oxford, Ohio.

Education for critical thinking. We mentioned in Chapter 4 a very significant project in curriculum development which teachers of English, mathematics, social studies, and science are conducting in pilot schools in the Chicago metropolitan area. The project is still uncompleted as this book is being written. Known popularly on the campus as the Thinking Project, the program was led by Kenneth B. Henderson and B. Othanel Smith of the University of Illinois. In essence, the project is an experiment to devise and test practical techniques for helping high school students develop their powers of critical thought in terms of their regular school subjects. The techniques consist chiefly of the use of ingenious exercises which draw heavily upon resources of logic and semantics.[20] Hap-

[19] Virginia Casey, *English Teaching Aids for a Stronger America,* 1955.
Emery G. Fritsch, *Science Teaching Aids for a Stronger America,* 1955.
Harry D. Lovelass, *Guidance Aids for a Stronger America,* 1955.
Jack C. Merwin, *Mathematics Teaching Aids for a Stronger America,* 1955.
Annette Sheel, *Social Studies Teaching Aids for a Stronger America,* 1955.
[20] Mary Jane Aschner, "Teaching the Anatomy of Criticism," *School Review,* Vol. 34, October, 1954, pp. 317-22.
Kenneth B. Henderson, B. Othanel Smith, and others, *Guide to Clear Thinking,* Illinois Curriculum Program, Office of Superintendent of Public Instruction, Springfield, 1954.

pily, logic and semantics are also playing an increasing role in the preparation of future teachers.[21]

Special education for atypical children. Our concern for adapting our public schools to the needs and capabilities of all educable adolescents suggests another project for curriculum improvement—one which affects all the subjects offered by the high school and all its other services as well. How can the school reach constructively into the minds of *all* our children? This is the question that more and more teachers in our good schools are asking themselves, and little by little we come closer to the answer. One important step toward the answer—according to the teachers and principals in the pilot schools where it was tested—is an instrument published by the Illinois Curriculum Program.[22] The device consists of two things: first, an inventory by means of which the school can locate precisely those students who are (a) gifted, (b) slow learners, (c) hard of hearing, (d) visually handicapped, (e) impeded in speech, (f) crippled, (g) emotionally maladjusted, (h) environmentally handicapped, or (i) malachievers; second, a balanced variety of workable suggestions for adapting the curriculum to each of these special types. We can illustrate the kind of suggestions which are included by quoting here the section which applies to gifted students:

> *The gifted*
> The suggestions for work with gifted children fall into four main categories—enrichment, special grouping, acceleration, and counseling. You may want to try two or more of these at the same time. No one can say which of these is best for your situation. Experience and research show that almost any special effort for the gifted produces worthwhile results if given an honest trial. This would seem to indicate also that most gifted children need something in addition to what they receive in the regular classroom.
> In developing any of the four types of program you will want to consider:
>
> —using conferences, institutes, and workshops to create more awareness of gifted children, of materials available, and of methods to reach them.

[21] Kenneth B. Henderson, "Training in Linguistic Analysis in Teacher-Education Curricula," *American Association of College Teachers of Education Yearbook,* 1956, Ann Arbor, pp. 64-74.

[22] Illinois Curriculum Program, *How to Study Your School Population,* Office of Superintendent of Public Instruction, Springfield, 1957.

—developing a central library of materials on teaching methods with the gifted.

—developing a central library of books to be read by gifted children on a variety of subjects at advanced reading levels, but adapted to the interests of children of their age.

—developing lists of community resources.

(1) *Enrichment* means challenging the student to a deeper and broader study of the usual subject matter. It calls for individualized instruction and out-of-classroom activities and materials, but not for administrative reorganization. It is done by the regular teacher in his own room, but it does require that classes be relatively small. Enrichment is simply what the best teachers do every day, and includes among other things:

—directing pupils to additional materials for individual projects which are of special interest to them and which can be reported or demonstrated to the class.

—using people in the community to stimulate and help children to engage in these projects or to come to class to talk about their special interests.

—enabling teachers from different levels (grade, high school, college) to work out special courses for the gifted at each level.

(2) *Special grouping* involves separating children by levels of ability or areas of interest into different groups for special instruction. Special grouping happens every day in adult life in clubs, churches, friendship groups, business and industry, etc. It also happens in most schools; common examples are special groupings for the musically talented (band, orchestra, chorus), for the athletically talented (varsity sports), and for the talented in writing (school papers and yearbooks). Grouping can be done in many ways:

—Grouping within classes (reading groups, etc.) is used by most primary grade teachers, but it can be just as useful at the upper-elementary or junior or senior high school levels.

—Special activities or clubs can be planned to meet regularly after school hours, such as science clubs, art and dramatic groups, music and dance groups. They can be sponsored by the school in school buildings, and teachers can be paid for their extra time; or they can be sponsored by community groups (YM, YW, Scouts, Little Theatre, etc.) with their own space and leadership. This requires relatively little cost or organization.

—In high school some grouping occurs naturally through the student's choice of courses; however, special classes at advanced levels can be added that would appeal to the more able students (conversational foreign languages, atomic science, college math and physics, etc.). Individual project seminars to develop independent thinking, research methods, and discussion skills are especially helpful at the junior and senior high school level.

—Advanced standing for college level courses can be arranged with some colleges, thereby increasing the interest and motivation of some students.

(3) *Acceleration* is accomplished by moving a student through school at a more rapid rate than usual. Any acceleration should be done only after careful consideration of the student's social, academic, and physical development. However, research seems to show that most gifted students can profit from some acceleration. For instance:

—After the primary grades, credit can be given for some courses if the student can pass an examination without taking the course; then he can move into other more advanced courses.

—At the eleventh and twelfth grade levels some students are able to take courses at the college level along with their high school courses. This can sometimes be arranged with a nearby college, or by correspondence courses.

(4) *Counseling* with both gifted children and their parents is frequently important in helping them recognize the potentialities of the child and see the possibilities of the future. Also, gifted children probably have no greater emotional problems than average children; but they, too, need counseling help with personal problems. Furthermore, these children and their parents should be made aware of the many scholarships available for advanced education.

These recommendations for work with gifted children reflect practices which have already been adopted successfully in a number of high schools throughout the country. For instance, a recent report by the New York City Board of Education includes the following descriptions: [23]

The special progress classes in the junior high schools of New York City are so named because pupils in such classes complete three years of schooling in two years' time. Graduates of these classes enter the 10th grade of the senior high school. Many junior high schools also organize classes for artistically gifted pupils in the fields of music, art and dancing. Classes are or-

[23] *Curriculum Report,* Board of Education, Bureau of Curriculum Research, New York, December 15, 1955, p. 6.

ganized also for children who show outstanding ability and interest in English or science.

On the high school level the usual patterns or variations of acceleration, enrichment or ability grouping have been widely used. New York City has specialized high schools in operation (Stuyvesant High School, Brooklyn Technical High School, Bronx High School of Science, Music and Art High School, and The School of Performing Arts), and all schools, both academic and vocational, have made local curriculum adaptations for the superior, gifted or talented student.

In describing secondary school practices designed to serve gifted students, Paul F. Brandwein[24] has called attention to advanced courses which offer material at a college level, special courses in which original work is done, special groups which meet in after-school hours to do advanced work, advanced schools within the high school structure which offer carefully selected students courses of study designed to carry them through the first year of college, and special high schools for gifted students. Outstanding examples of special high schools are the Bronx High School of Science and the High School of Music and Art of New York City.

Resource units.   We have discussed in this subsection a number of different kinds of projects for curriculum improvement. In pursuing any of them teachers are often asked to construct their own resource units. A resource unit is not a teaching unit or a lesson plan. It is a reservoir upon which the teacher can draw in preparing teaching units or lesson plans. It is a body of materials related to a given problem or area of knowledge which is to be dealt with in the instructional program of the school. It contains suggestions for three kinds of activities in which pupils engage—initiatory, developmental, and evaluative. From a good resource unit, therefore, a teacher can select one or more initiatory activities to arouse the interest of his students in the given area of knowledge. He can then select from the developmental activities those which best fit his students' interests and capabilities and his own capacities—things for his students to read, write, view, listen to, discuss, debate, dramatize, construct, demonstrate, or experiment with—all processes by which the students can attain mastery of the facts, skills, and understand-

---

[24] Paul F. Brandwein, as quoted in "Secondary School Programs," by Lloyd S. Michael, in *The Education of Gifted Children*, 57th Yearbook, Part II, National Society for the Study of Education, Chicago (distributed by U. of Chicago Press), 1958, pp. 3-7.

ings related to the problem or topic. Finally, the suggested evaluative activities offer the teacher a choice of techniques to enable him and his students to appraise what they have accomplished.

This brief sketch of a good resource unit shows that such materials can be valuable in the work of any teacher, and that those who construct such units must be skilled in assessing what will interest students, as well as what and how students ought to learn, and in devising ways to measure what has been learned.

Teachers are encouraged to help select
instructional materials

Work of this kind often accompanies work on the development of curriculum improvement projects and resource units. Whether it does or not, however, the job of selecting textbooks, reference works, films, and other instructional materials is one of the most crucial aspects of the school's responsibility, since the choice of instructional materials very closely affects what the students will learn. A good school will always try to improve its curriculum by involving all of its teachers in making these selections.

Teachers are encouraged to help shape
the achievement testing program in their school

This, too, often accompanies the planning of curriculum improvement projects and the constructing of resource units. In good schools teachers and principals alike realize that in many respects their true objectives are revealed by the achievement tests which they approve and use in their work. They know that these tests reveal to everyone—teachers, pupils, and parents—what the school believes to be important. Achievement tests should include all the things and only the things which are in accord with the proper objectives of public education in this country. To bring any school's achievement testing program into agreement with this requirement is to improve the school's instructional program, for the generality of teachers will teach whatever is required on the tests.

Teachers are encouraged to engage in action research

By this we mean that teachers are encouraged to search for new ways of proceeding which will improve the curriculum; to make arrangements in advance for securing evidence which will evaluate it; to put it into effect; to gather the evaluative evidence and use this evidence to decide whether to continue the proceeding. All improvements require that changes be made, but not all changes in school practices result in improvement in the school program. The teacher should find out which changes improve the program and which do not, and this is the major purpose of action research. The day is dawning, the author believes, when teachers will be encouraged not only to conduct such research but to publish their findings for the benefit of others in the profession.[25] Several workshops have already been held in which classroom teachers have been trained by an ingenious procedure to conduct action research respecting the practical problems which they confront in their daily work.[26]

Summary

This chapter has been concerned with the question of improving the curriculum of the public secondary school. The term "curriculum" connotes the total experience which the student is encouraged to have while he is under the control of the school. Consequently, the improvement of the curriculum means the improvement of any aspect of the student's school experience.

Chapters 4 through 10, then, have dealt directly with the work of improving the school's curriculum. The basic principles presented in Chapter 4 either designate the objectives which all curriculum improvements should be designed to achieve, or specify the conditions which must be met if these objectives are to be realized. Chapters 5 through 10 describe what the high school must do to meet these conditions as they relate to the school's holding power, its public relations, its discipline, its guidance and extra-class programs, and its appraising and reporting system. Teachers are helping to improve the curriculum of their school whenever they assist in better orienting their school to its proper purposes, in providing more of the conditions necessary for effective learning, and in im-

---

25 For an excellent example see Paul F. Brandwein, *The Gifted Student as Future Scientist*, Harcourt, Brace and Co., New York, 1955.

26 Fred P. Barnes, *Practical Research Processes: A Guidebook in Research Methods for Practitioners in Education*, Office of Superintendent of Public Instruction, Springfield, Illinois, 1957.

proving its holding power, public relations, discipline, guidance program, extra-class activities, or appraising and reporting system.

Certain principal things are done, especially in our better schools, to involve teachers in the work of improving the curriculum. The climate in our better schools encourages continuous self-appraisal, thus stimulating teachers to search for better ways to honor the basic principles. Teachers are encouraged to do a number of other things in order to improve the curriculum: to use their vacations for significant work and travel, to join professional organizations and work actively in them, to keep up their professional reading and other kinds of study, to make professional visits, to use supervisory assistance, to participate in the Parent-Teacher Association and other community organizations, to use community agencies which serve young people, to make case studies of representative pupils, to help their schools conduct many kinds of evaluative studies, to help execute projects for improving particular aspects of the curriculum, to help create and use resource units, to help select instructional materials, to assist in designing the achievement-testing program, and to engage in action research to evaluate their efforts to improve their courses and extra-class activities.

In sum, every professional activity in which the secondary school teacher engages finds its justification in the contribution it makes to the improvement of the curriculum.

chapter 12

THE TEACHER'S ROLE

IN ADMINISTERING THE SCHOOL

Everyone benefits when the high school is well administered. The pupils and the community at large are served more efficiently, the morale of teachers is raised by better teaching conditions and community relations, and the principal has the satisfaction of knowing that his responsibility, which he cannot delegate or evade and which encompasses everything that happens in the school, has been discharged capably. No public school teacher should ever forget that the principal is strictly accountable to the superintendent of schools, who in turn is accountable to the board of education for everything that happens in the schools of his district.

Teachers must perform many essentially administrative duties if their school is to run well. Too many beginning teachers—the author was once one himself—enter their first jobs without knowing what these duties are. High school principals ought to be able to assume that young men and women with teaching certificates have been taught what these administrative duties are, but many have not. Hence most principals remedy this deficiency as quickly, pleasantly, and effectively as possible by entrusting the orientation of new teachers to experienced members of the faculty. Here, then, is one administrative duty which the teacher is likely to be asked to perform: if he shows during his first years of teaching that he can instruct other teachers in their administrative roles, he will probably be asked to do so.

Most students of education want to learn as much as they can ahead of time about what they will be expected to contribute to the operation of the schools in which they will begin their teaching careers. Consequently, in this chapter we shall describe the chief administrative duties of the teacher. These duties are concerned with the opening of the school year, with the routines of the school's normal operation, or with the closing of the school year.

Administrative duties that teachers help perform at the opening of the school year

Principals and teachers in our best secondary schools aspire "to have the new term open as though school were merely being resumed after a week-end recess." [1] This ideal, of course, is seldom realized. But schools where teachers discharge their administrative duties well can approach it.

Preregistering students

The preregistration of all students except those in the graduating class is usually accomplished during the closing weeks of the spring semester. The usual procedure is to allow time during homeroom periods, division meetings, or core-course classes for teachers to help the students to select their courses and their extra-class activities for the following year. In good high schools, descriptions of each subject and each extra-class activity are prepared and kept up to date by committees of teachers and students working under the direction of guidance counselors. These descriptions should always be part of the study materials given to students to help them plan their programs. Sometimes teachers who are helping students choose their courses will invite other teachers to present verbal descriptions of their courses and extra-class activities. Anything which helps the student make an intelligent choice is welcomed by conscientious teachers.

These homeroom, division, or core teachers, with some assistance from guidance counselors, help the students define their interests, evaluate their capabilities, and then make suitable educational and vocational plans. The students' selections of subjects and extra-class activities are entered on preregistration forms, which are then for-

[1] Paul B. Jacobson, William C. Reavis, and James D. Logsdon, *The Effective School Principal,* Prentice-Hall, Inc., New York, 1954, p. 51.

warded by the teacher to the central office where each student's program for the following year is prepared.

Each student then receives his program card before the opening of the fall term so that on the opening day of school he knows not only what subjects and extra-class activities he is enrolled in but where and when he should report for each of them.

Building the high school calendar

The well-designed school calendar gives the opening and closing dates of each term, the days and dates of all school holidays, and the times and places of all school events in which most of the students, teachers, and people of the community are interested. Beyond this, the school should design its calendar to avoid conflicts between the dates of school and community events, thus freeing its schedule from competition for the attention of pupils, parents, and townspeople. Ideally, the calendar is completed no later than the week before the opening of school so that copies can be made available to all students, teachers, and patrons at the beginning of the academic year.

Teachers should contribute to the calendar because they sponsor or supervise most of the special events which it chronicles, and they know best when and where these events should be scheduled. In addition, teachers in the aggregate belong to a wide variety of community organizations whose schedules must be considered in planning school events if the school is to maintain good public relations.

Reporting for duty early
in order to prepare for the opening of school

More and more schools hold a week-long preschool conference attended by the school faculty and principal. In these conferences, usually held just before the opening of the fall term, curriculum-improvement projects are planned or continued from the previous year, books and other instructional materials are requisitioned, and the teachers are given lists of the students enrolled in their courses so that they may consult these students' cumulative records. Consultations with supervisors are held, and departmental groups meet to discuss important problems. Teachers are usually given time to prepare their desks and classrooms, laboratories, shops, gymnasiums, and so on, for the opening day. The final preparation of the school calendar may also be postponed until the early days of the preschool conference.

Certain tasks, whether accomplished through a conference or not, must be accomplished before the opening day of the fall term. If they are put off until after the school year is under way, they will be done inefficiently with much confusion or not done at all.

Classifying, registering, and scheduling students
who come to the school for the first time on opening day

In most well-administered high schools, a week or two during the latter part of the summer is set aside for the registration of new students who have not preregistered in the spring. The business of classifying, registering, and scheduling these students is conducted by members of the central staff, and the registration period is well advertised so that all new students and their parents should know about it. In spite of these precautions, however, there will almost always be newcomers who will appear for the first time on the opening day of the fall term. Consequently, a few teachers must be available for an hour or so before school opens and during their free periods to help these new arrivals fit themselves into the school program. Usually the teachers do this work because the guidance counselors have their hands full with more difficult cases, especially during the first days of school. If the school is located in a community whose population is largely transient, probably all the teachers on the faculty will be detailed to registration duty on the opening day.

In addition, a student who has attended school during the summer in order to correct a deficiency in his academic record or to enrich his program may have to be reclassified. This reclassification is an opening-day job for teachers acquainted with the subjects the students took and possibly with the student himself.

Issuing or authorizing the issuance of
instructional materials

In large schools textbooks and other instructional supplies are often issued by a central bookstore, but in a great many schools the classroom teacher issues them on the first day of school. Even when textbooks are given out by a bookstore, teachers must usually authenticate the requisitions before they can be honored. When teachers issue the materials themselves, they should, of course, keep accurate records of all the books and supplies they give out.

When textbooks and other supplies are rented to students, teachers should not be required to collect payments of any kind from their students. If such collections must be made at all—and this is a practice which should be avoided wherever possible (see Chapter 5)—the collections should be made only by some properly trained and bonded employee of the central office who has the clerical help necessary for keeping accurate and up-to-the-minute records of all transactions. Books should be issued only to students who present a receipted "book order." Unfortunately, schools which are unable to provide a central bookstore are usually also unable to employ a central cashier. The consequence is that teachers must handle both the books and other materials, and the students' money. A teacher can be virtually ruined by even the suspicion of financial irregularity, especially in his dealings with students; very often teachers are not properly trained to conduct financial operations involving many different accounts. A teacher who is required to conduct financial transactions with students should be extremely careful to issue a duplicated, signed, and dated receipt for all monies received, and he should insist that the student initial the teacher's copy of the receipt as an attest of its accuracy.

Issuing locker keys or padlocks

This is another duty with which teachers ought not to be burdened, though they often are. Locker keys and padlocks should be issued solely by someone in the central office who is equipped to maintain scrupulously accurate records. If a teacher must issue keys and padlocks and receive deposits against their safe return, he should safeguard his own reputation and the peace of the school by following the receipting procedure described in the preceding paragraph.

Making new students feel quickly at home

It is not uncommon for new students to be assigned to upperclassmen—they are frequently called Big Brothers or Big Sisters—during the first term of school, or sometimes for the whole first year. This is a good system, but these upperclassmen must be supervised by wise and sympathetic teachers. Usually the students who are to guide the newcomers have been recruited and instructed during the preceding spring semester, but they should always meet again with their faculty sponsor in order to renew their sense of responsibility and refresh their knowledge of what they must do; preferably these meetings should occur just before the opening of the fall term or early in the first day of school. The sponsor should meet again with his student guides before the end of the first week of school to discuss any unanticipated problems that have arisen and any improvements which the upperclassmen can suggest for this part of the orientation program.

Orientation is, of course, a function of guidance, not properly of administration. But this part of the orientation program is an administrative function of the teacher and is exceedingly important to the efficiency of the school's operations during the opening weeks of the school year.

Reporting the enrollments in each class at the end of the first day of school

The capable school principal insists on knowing whether or not his school's affairs are proceeding according to plan, and if they aren't, he wants to know why not. For example, he must see that the enrollments among the different class sections of each subject are balanced. If all students were registered during the preregistration period and if all have followed their program cards faithfully, the classes will be as well balanced as the principal can make them. But new students enter, and others, as the principal knows, will misplace or ignore their program cards and will attend class sections to which they have not been assigned. Therefore, the principal asks each teacher to report not only the number but the names of the students who appear in his classes on opening day. If each teacher has been supplied, as he should have been, with alphabetical lists of all students assigned to his classes, he should report only the absentees and students who are present but not included in the class lists.

Administrative duties that teachers help perform throughout the school year

The principal is held accountable for providing the best possible educational program for the students in his school. His chief purpose is to see that his school's program continuously improves. Everything that the good high school principal does, including the sharing of administrative duties with teachers, he does to accomplish this purpose.

We shall note the year-round administrative duties of teachers under two rubrics: first, those which are designed to improve the school's curriculum (see Chapter 10), and next those which are designed to preserve past improvements. But first let us consider briefly the nature of democratic school administration.

The establishment of a democratic milieu is necessarily one of the primary responsibilities of the public secondary school (see Chapter 4). The democratic ethos does not permit one to do whatever one pleases, whenever or however one pleases to do it. The democratic American dedicates himself to the traditional American principles; he follows them in his everyday actions. Of all the ways of life, the democratic one is both the most difficult to learn and the most civilized that man has yet been able to devise.

Principals, teachers, and pupils also may not do what they please, when they please, or as they please. To fulfill its proper function, the public school must be administered democratically; i.e., each person in the school must be treated as of supreme and equal moral worth (see Chapter 4); all educable youths must be equally well served by the school; all these youths must be helped to make themselves as competent as possible to think and communicate effectively in respect to all of the basic social processes and to carry on these processes democratically, healthfully, and vigorously.

The purposes and methodology of democratic school administration are not determined by any person or group within the school. They are derived from the purposes and methodology of the democratic society whose agent the public secondary school is. The principal and teachers can properly only decide how to apply this enjoined methodology to these enjoined purposes.

The wise principal recognizes that the proper application of the method of intelligence requires shared thinking and planning within the school to determine how it shall accomplish the purposes defined by society. He recognizes that the more people there are involved—representative parents, other laymen, and pupils as well as teachers and the principal—the more capable the planning will probably be. All whose cooperation is necessary to, and all who are likely to feel directly affected by, a contemplated action should help decide how this action is to be accomplished. After the decision has been made, the principal delegates the authority to carry out the action to one or more members of the faculty or of the student body. If the latter, some staff member is assigned to supervise the student or students.

The discussion of the many routine administrative duties of teachers which follows is based on this conception of the democratic school administration.

Serving on the principal's administrative council

The existence of such a council or "cabinet" is one of the marks of a good high school. The membership of the council ought to include department heads, representative teachers, the head of the school's P.T.A., and the elected head of the student body. The council's purpose is to establish direct channels of intercommunication among all the elements in the school population. Except in cases of emergency, when the principal must take immediate action, the council should discuss all major and most minor administrative policies. The council should consider the desirability and workability of all proposals, whether they originate with the principal, with the faculty, with students, or with outsiders.

Proposing school improvements and evaluating proposals submitted by others

The good principal invites all teachers to come forward with their proposals for improving the school's program or its administrative efficiency. Such suggestions are seldom acted upon unilaterally by the principal. The principal generally seeks the counsel of his faculty and, if it is appropriate, the counsel of students and parents as well, before he decides to accept or reject a proposed change. The wise principal knows that the more people there are who consent to a plan, the more there will be who feel a sense of psychological ownership and, therefore, the more successful the plan will be.

In many of our better schools, students are invited to consider the school's problems. Discussion of these problems is usually carried on in homerooms or in courses, such as core courses or social studies, whose subject matter is closely related to school improvement. Here, by serving as an agent of democratic school administration, the teacher is helping his pupils to practice good school citizenship.

*Planning and conducting
the school's in-service faculty education program*

The faculty members of a superior school will be capable leaders and people who keep abreast of the ever-changing educational needs of its community and of its students, the ever-expanding world of scholarship, and the ever-growing body of knowledge about pedagogy. Ideally the teacher's education never ends. Good principals entrust the planning and administration of the in-service program to the teachers, and they encourage the teachers to use the opportunities provided by the program. A superior school will also have adequate public support, both financial and psychological, and an enthusiastic student body. The efforts of well-trained teachers who continue to improve themselves do not go unnoticed or unrewarded by either the patrons or the pupils of the school. Teachers who are enthusiastic generate enthusiasm among others, and this enthusiasm is expressed, in part, in adequate financial support for the school and in the pride of the students and townspeople in their educational system.

The author—and perhaps those readers acquainted with a wide range of secondary schools—has been struck by an arresting fact: in good schools—that is, in schools with able leaders and well-trained teachers who continue to improve themselves—one encounters a great awareness of unresolved problems of curriculum development and a great sensitivity to the ways in which the schools fail to serve the needs of the community, even though those schools may be better than nine-tenths of the rest of our schools in these respects. Poor schools are usually poor because their principals and teachers are either largely unaware of or complacent about their problems and failures.

Supervising instruction

At one time supervision in our schools was considered chiefly a process of inspection in which a supposedly all-knowing principal visited a classroom and later told the teacher what he was doing wrong. Nowadays the concept of supervision has changed radically. The modern principal and teacher work together to solve an instructional problem which a teacher recognizes and wants to remedy; they share the responsibility for solving it. Such a system cannot work, of course, unless the teacher takes the initiative, either by going to the principal and telling him about his problem or by inviting the principal to visit the classroom to see for himself what the problem is. After the teacher has asked for help, the teacher and the principal together define the problem, discuss the alternative solutions, choose the most promising one, and plan the steps by which it can be carried out. If their first plan doesn't work, they try others until they find a satisfactory one. But the main point is that instructional supervision should consist of "assisted self-help," in which the teacher manifests his willingness to be helped.

If the beginning teacher will remember that the principal is accountable for everything that occurs in his school and hence that every teacher's success or failure is his success or failure, the relationship between the new teacher and the principal will be a rewarding one for both of them. The principal is eager for all his teachers to succeed, since their success means his own success, and he will go to great lengths to help any teacher, especially a beginning teacher, to overcome whatever difficulties he may be encountering. The principal knows that every new teacher, no matter how intelligent or well trained he may be, encounters unanticipated problems as he begins his new career. The principal will be pleased when teachers come to him with their problems; he will regard it as a sign of strength and determination to make good, not as an indication of weakness.

But this is not the only way in which teachers assist the principal in the supervision (improvement) of instruction. One good way to learn how to resolve a problem is to observe how other teachers are dealing with it successfully. When asked to do so either by the principal or by their troubled colleague, these other teachers usually will graciously permit their classes to be visited for this purpose and helpfully talk the matter over later with their visitor.

The modern supervision of instruction also takes many other forms; teachers are encouraged to visit business, industry, and labor in the community to increase their awareness of the educational needs which the school should fill; to visit other schools and confer with their opposite numbers there; to study the physiology, psychology, and sociology of adolescence in order that students may be better understood and hence better served by the school; to make case studies of pupils, for the same purpose. In their role as modern supervisors, high school principals also urge the faculty to make many other studies—of the holding power of the school, of the participation of its students in extra-class activities, of its hidden tuition costs, of its recent graduates' successes and failures, to name but four—whose findings indicate the strengths and weaknesses of their school's educational program. Teachers themselves can help plan visits and studies, thereby aiding the principal in the most important single administrative duty with which he is charged—that of improving the educational program of the school.

Planning and organizing
the school's instructional and service programs

Since there is a continuous program in any school except a brand-new one, what teachers generally do is assist in the replanning and reorganization of their school's educational program. It is a very rare high school which does not use the help of teachers when important changes are contemplated in the instructional, guidance, extra-class, or public relations programs, or in any of the services which are provided in the areas of health, safety, testing, libraries, and so on. Again, the better the school the greater will be the involvement of teachers in these aspects of its administration.

Administering the instructional program

Every good teacher is a capable administrator within the four walls of his classroom, laboratory, shop, studio, gymnasium—wherever he teaches. The administrative details which he must attend to in his routine work are many, varied, and exceedingly important to the success of the school. Good classroom management is simply another name for good administration on the classroom level. Principals contribute in many ways to the instructional program—by designing the class schedules; by classifying, registering, and programing students; by securing and assigning teachers; by procuring facilities, materials, and equipment; by providing custodial and other needed services—but it is essentially the administrative skill of the teacher within his own domain that determines whether or not the principal's efforts will succeed.

Administering the guidance program

A good guidance program includes seven important services (see Chapter 4), and teachers generally perform significant administrative tasks relating to all of them: they help organize the incoming students and recruit upperclassmen for orientation purposes, help select and give standardized tests, make arrangements for maintaining and using personnel records, make provisions whereby students can acquire educational and vocational information, see that students needing counseling are scheduled for it, and help organize or maintain the work of placement and follow-up.

Administering the health and safety program

The school should provide students with a safe and healthful environment in every classroom, laboratory, shop, studio, cafeteria, gymnasium, toilet, and corridor, and on every playing court, field, and school bus (see Chapter 4). Seeing to it that such an environment is provided is one of the most important of the principal's administrative duties, for the lives of pupils may be endangered if it is not performed capably. All teachers should share this duty. Teachers can direct their students to regulate the light, temperature, and ventilation properly; they can make their pupils responsible for preventing or removing hazards and for avoiding accidents; they can refer to the school nurse students who seem ill or have been injured, and to the school doctor those who seem to be deficient in hearing or vision; they can conduct fire or other prevention-of-disaster drills; they can report all unhygienic conditions and all hazards within or around the school to the proper official.

Administering the extra-class activities program

The teacher should so administer the activity which he is sponsoring that so far as possible the students engaged in it will learn to administer it by themselves, for these are voluntary undertakings on the students' part; the more the students plan, organize, and conduct them, the more they may learn from them. Teachers can chaperon school dances and parties, help plan and conduct school assemblies, supervise the lunchroom, assist in planning and supervising the students' noontime activities, oversee the students' conduct in the halls and on the grounds, serve as critics or judges at forensic events, supervise study halls in the (happily) decreasing number of schools that still have them, referee intramural events, or take tickets or help keep order at interscholastic contests.

Administering the public relations program

The primary requirements for good school-community relations are the unfailing adherence to the spirit of the Golden Rule on the part of all school personnel in dealing with students and with the laymen of the district, providing a good educational program, and involving the public in the school program (see Chapter 6). Teachers, as we have seen, are central in all that is done in these necessary respects. In addition, they often make arrangements with newspaper reporters or with radio or television program directors to publicize some important part of the work of the school. Even more frequently, teachers interpret their school's work to such lay groups as the P.T.A., mothers' groups, or fathers' clubs. Teachers can also help make arrangements for parents' visiting days, see that patrons feel welcome to visit at other times, or arrange for the visits of teachers to business, industry, and labor and arrange for return visits by representatives of business, of industry, and of labor to the school.

Planning and conducting faculty meetings

Some faculty meetings include all the teachers in the school, others only the members of a given department, and still others the staff members from different subject fields engaged in a project which involves two or more, but not all, subject fields. In the well-administered school virtually every faculty meeting is designed either to plan some improvement in the school, or to carry out or evaluate some project which teachers earlier helped plan. The plans for a meeting of the entire faculty usually originate in a committee of teachers of which the principal is a member. These tentative plans, based on problems which concern most of the teachers, are submitted to the faculty for modification and approval before they are carried out. The plans should call for the formation of voluntary work groups organized around problems felt by the teachers to be important. The nature of each problem determines the kind and number of faculty meetings which will be held later to discuss it. In sum, the faculty meetings of the well-administered school are in keeping with a climate of continuous self-appraisal; they are instruments for improving the program of the school.

Selecting instructional materials

Teachers teach better when they themselves select textbooks, reference works, films, and other instructional materials which help them carry out their own ideas and methods than when they are forced to tailor their classroom work to fit instructional materials selected by someone else. Teachers should accept the principal's invitation to solicit examination copies of books, maps, films, and other instructional materials, and to establish the criteria by which these materials are to be judged.

Preparing the budget

The administrative heads of better schools know that teachers are aware that the policies of the school are reflected in its budget. The more responsible the teachers of the school feel for these policies the more likely they will be to carry them out successfully. Good principals invite teachers, by departments usually, to submit their budget requests and later to review these requests so that a defensible balance can be reached and submitted to the board of education for approval.

Preparing the salary schedule

Teacher morale is greatly affected by the "pocketbook nerve." Principals in better schools invite representative teachers to help gather comparative data on salaries from similar schools and propose the criteria (such as level of training, successful experience, cost of living) for determining salaries. The finished plan is submitted to the board of education for consideration.

Formulating and applying a merit plan for salary raises

More and more lay citizens are finding it difficult to understand why the merit plan is not generally employed by the public schools. The difficulty of devising a workable plan viewed as just by most teachers is the principal objection to it. This difficulty is formidable, but not insurmountable. In Lansing, Michigan, a successful plan is in operation which the teachers have helped devise and operate. Like every aspect of the program in a superior school system, this plan is often reappraised by the teachers and the school administrators.

The author feels confident in predicting that the public will continue to urge the merit plan upon the schools for years to come. Lay leaders will soon realize, if they do not now, that the teaching profession must compete with the other professions for capable personnel, and that to compete, it must offer top salaries at least double the present average top salary (about $6,000). These lay leaders, and the majority of citizens, will not want to pay salaries of $12,000 and up per year to any but the most competent teachers. The author believes that citizens will either insist upon the use of a merit plan or refuse to raise teachers' salaries sufficiently above their present relative level. This merit plan will work only if teachers are actively involved in devising it and in carrying it out.

Keeping records, making out reports, and completing questionnaires

A school should maintain complete, accurate records of pupil attendance and achievement. Virtually all such records originate with teachers; thus teachers are obligated to report such information, usually in accordance with regulations prescribed by the state's school code or the accrediting association.

Reports to parents of their children's school attendance and accomplishments are also required of the teachers by every school board. In addition, many kinds of fruitful educational research necessitate soliciting, usually in questionnaire form, facts or opinions from high school teachers. Provided that he is competent to give the data requested, that he understands the purpose of the study and believes that the study will be valuable to the profession, and that the time and effort required are not excessive, the professional teacher will conscientiously comply with all such requests.

Planning the details of new school facilities

Rare indeed is the secondary school which will not need either an addition to its present building or buildings or an entirely new school plant in the years immediately ahead. A new addition or a new school should be so planned and constructed that the teachers who occupy it will be able to teach what should be taught the way it should be taught. To design it, then, the architect must know the kinds, sizes, and numbers of spaces and the items and equipment needed and how these should be related. He consults with the head of the school for this important information. The wise principal involves the entire faculty in order to secure it. He calls in consultants (specialists in the subject matter and in the teaching of the high school subjects) to meet with the teachers and to help them, first, to envisage a superior instructional program, then to specify the spaces and the equipment needed for this program. The care and the imagination which the teachers exercise in discharging this administrative duty will do much to determine the fruitfulness of their school's educational program in the years to come.

Advising the principal of all seniors
whose parents should be notified that their children may not graduate

Every conscientious teacher will enable his principal to prepare these reports, which in most instances should go out no later than the middle of the student's last semester. More than this, such a teacher will suggest to the principal any means of resolving a situation which is not clearly hopeless, and volunteer his help.

We have said that the possibility that a student will not graduate should be reported to his parents no later than midway through the last semester "in most instances." If possible it should be sent much earlier; it should reach his parents well before the student has arrived at the point of no return—i.e., well before it is too late to do whatever must be done if he is to graduate.

Teachers are often burdened with administrative details
which might better be discharged by others

Some such undesirable duties have already been pointed out in this chapter—the tasks of issuing books or locker keys or collecting funds, rental fees, and deposits. Other things which the teacher should not have to do, though in many schools he may be asked to do them, include reading aloud to the class routine notices (these should be published in daily or semi-weekly bulletins for all students, and students should be held responsible for reading the bulletins and complying with the instructions contained in them) and making solicitations of many kinds, which have no proper place in the public schools. If tickets and subscriptions to activities or publications must be sold, or if membership fees must be levied (we have seen in Chapter 5 why they should not), they should all be handled in out-of-class time.

Teachers should not be critical of the principal if, despite his efforts, the community has not supplied the necessary clerical help for issuing a bulletin, or if there are many hidden tuition costs in the school program. As in any other situation that needs improving, they should work with him toward a solution (see Chapter 5 for ways to eliminate hidden costs).

The administrative duties that teachers help perform at the closing of the school year

If school is to open in the fall as if it "were merely being resumed after a week-end recess," there are several administrative matters which must be settled by the closing day of the spring semester. There are also many others, concerned simply with the closing of the school, which must be performed. Two were noted earlier in this chapter (preregistering all returning students for the following fall term, and selecting and training students who are to serve as Big Brothers and Big Sisters to pupils in the next entering class).

We shall discuss first those administrative duties which relate to termination of the instructional program, and then those which concern the preparations for the fall semester.

Scheduling and conducting final examinations

Not all secondary schools conduct formal examinations at the end of the school year, but many do. Where such examinations are given, it is often the practice to assign a committee of teachers the work of scheduling the examinations, the aim being to make a schedule which will avoid conflicts and distribute the work of the students in a reasonable way. Class sections of each subject are usually combined for the final examination, and two or more teachers are usually asked to proctor it. Of course, in schools which have developed successful honor systems teachers are present at examinations only to distribute and receive test materials.

Turning in class lists indicating each pupil's attendance and achievement

These lists are, of course, alphabetized to facilitate posting to the permanent records of the school. Teachers should not be required to do this posting, but the lack of adequate clerical help often forces the high school principal to ask them to do so. Provided the faculty members in these less fortunate schools feel that they are not rushed and have time to talk things over a bit, this team posting by teachers does afford one advantage. The teacher gets a better picture of his students' accomplishments: in a good many instances the teachers will pause in their posting to "talk over" a student, to recite his virtues or to comment on his inadequacies. If the teacher has these pupils in his classes the following year, both the teacher and the youngsters may benefit from this increased knowledge.

Collecting school materials, returning deposits, and levying fines

At the end of the school year students surrender locker keys, locks, and rented textbooks, and teachers often are asked to collect these articles and either return deposits which have been held against their safekeeping or levy fines if students have lost or damaged them. Although these are things that teachers ought not to be asked to do, in many schools they are part of the teacher's year-end administrative duties, and he must perform them as well as he can. It is worth repeating that teachers who have to accept money from students should always issue dated duplicate receipts and have the students initial the teacher's copy.

Planning and supervising the events of graduation week

If the students are capable of it, they should plan and conduct their own graduation exercises and other commencement-week activities, for this can be a valuable learning experience. But some faculty involvement is always necessary, for these events exhibit the school to the community and the school's relations with the public can be damaged severely if the program goes badly. As always, the principal is responsible for all that happens, a fact of which he can never afford to be unaware. Consequently, he counts himself fortunate if there are at least a few teachers to whom he can safely entrust the guidance of students as they plan and conduct the activities associated with the commencement season—the prom, senior day, the honors assembly, the baccalaureate service, the commencement exercises, and whatever else the traditions of the school include.

Inventorying equipment and supplies,
reporting needed repairs, and estimating instructional needs
for the following school year

The superintendent is accountable to the board of education, and the principal to the superintendent, for an accurate accounting of the equipment and supplies on hand at the end of the school year. Ordinarily, the principal must rely upon his teachers to begin this inventory. Teachers should also report needed repairs and estimate their forthcoming requirements so the equipment can be repaired before school opens. Since stocks of books, films, equipment, and other supplies must be ordered well in advance of the opening of the fall term, teachers are usually asked to report their estimated needs in the spring.

Planning the fall preschool conference

On several occasions the author has been fortunate enough to be a consultant at preschool conferences planned and conducted entirely by representative committees of teachers. The atmosphere at these conferences—or workshops, as they are often called—is quite different from that which usually prevails at conferences planned entirely by a principal who has guessed at what the faculty needed, wanted, and would welcome discussing. If teachers plan and conduct these conferences, they are most likely to view and take part in them with enthusiasm.

Contributing to the principal's or superintendent's
annual report to the public

It is now quite usual for those in charge of our better school systems to issue reports at the end of each school year. They are usually attractively illustrated and made as simple but as instructive as possible. These reports tell the public what the school is accomplishing, and why and how, and what is contemplated for the future. (Two examples of such reports were discussed in Chapter 6.) School administrators depend upon teachers for most of the content of these reports. They solicit descriptions of student projects and accomplishments written by teachers, and they often ask them to collaborate in securing photographs of students at work or other illustrative materials.

Summary

In this chapter we have called attention to the chief administrative duties which teachers in the public secondary school are usually expected to help perform. We hope that the reader understands why these duties must be performed capably—that each is a necessary means to a necessary end. This necessary end is the central object of every dedicated teacher; it is that the public secondary school serve its proper purposes capably. As we have shown in this chapter, this end can best be achieved if public secondary school teachers regard themselves as partners of the principal in the administering of their school.

part

TO GAIN PERSPECTIVE

chapter 13

ACCOMPLISHMENTS AND PROSPECTS

OF THE PUBLIC SECONDARY SCHOOL

We shall trace the history of public secondary education in America in this chapter and evaluate it on the basis of our principles. We shall discuss this history in terms of each of our contributory principles (Principles 2-9). When we are finished, we should know how well the American public secondary school has fulfilled its basic task (Principle 1), and after that we shall see what the future years may hold.

We shall focus our attention in turn upon the growth of the public secondary school, its changing pattern of organization, the resurgence of lay involvement in shaping its purposes and program, and the increase in the number and variety of its services to the youths of this country.

The growth of the public secondary school [1]

The public secondary school must be designed to serve all educable youths if it is best to promote the general welfare (see Chapter 4). This goal is yet to be fulfilled (see Chapter 5)—one out of every five American youths of high school age is not enrolled in any secondary school, public or private. But great gains have been made, and all

---

[1] All statistics used in this section have been derived from *Statistical Summary of Education, 1951-52 Statistics of Public Secondary Day Schools, 1951-52,* or *Statistics of Special Education for Exceptional Children, 1952-53,* U.S. Office of Education bulletins.

recent trends indicate that gains will continue to be made in the future.

General enrollments, 1870-1952

The first general enrollment data published by the agency, established in 1867, which has since become the U.S. Office of Education covered the year 1870, and the latest complete figures available when this book was written covered the year 1952. In 1870 there were fewer than 2500 public high schools in this country, less than one for each of the 2600 counties into which the United States was divided at that time—to say nothing of the vast Western territories which had not yet become states. Less than a hundred years ago the opportunity to enroll in an American public high school was comparatively rare, so it is not surprising that less than 3 per cent of all American youths of high school age were attending public secondary schools in 1870. Approximately the same number were attending private secondary schools. The percentage of students who graduated was even smaller: in 1870 only about 2 per cent of all youths past school age were graduates of any secondary school, public or private. As recently as 1870, then, only a very small beginning had been made in the task of creating a system of universal public secondary education in this country.

Not only did relatively few young people attend public high schools in 1870, but those who did attend found themselves in schools so small that they could study virtually nothing but a few college preparatory subjects. The average public high school in 1870 had no more than three teachers and enrolled fewer than eighty pupils. Though there were a few outstanding exceptions, most of the private schools were no larger and no more abundantly staffed. Since about 2.0 per cent of the young people of the appropriate age were high school graduates, and since 1.68 per cent [2] of the young people of college age were enrolled in college, it is apparent that most of the students who graduated from high school went on to college. This means that in 1870 public and private sec-

[2] The figure 1.68 per cent includes all young people old enough to be enrolled as either freshmen, sophomores, juniors, or seniors in college. Since the freshman students far outnumbered those in any of the other classes, considerably more than 1.68 per cent (though, of course, less than 2.0 per cent) of the young people of freshman age were attending their first year of college.

ondary schools alike were designed to serve, not all the educable youth of the country, but only the very small minority of young people who were able to go to college. The statistics for 1952 tell a remarkably different story. There were then about 27,000 high schools in the United States. Approximately 24,000 were public schools; slightly more than 3000 were private. The average number of high schools in each of our 3000 counties was eight. Whereas in 1870 the number of public high school students was 80,000, in 1952 there were 6,596,000 students in our public secondary schools; the percentage of the adolescent population that was attending the public high school had risen from 3 per cent in 1870 to 65 per cent in 1952, and an additional 12 per cent were in private schools. And three out of every five (59 per cent) youths of the appropriate age, instead of one out of every fifty, were high school graduates. In the light of these figures there can be no disputing the great gains which we have made toward universalizing American public secondary education in the past eighty years.

The average enrollment in our public high schools has increased from the less than eighty pupils of 1870 to about 325 in 1952, more than a fourfold increase.[3] The average number of teachers in public high schools has increased even more—from three in 1870 to fourteen in 1952. Since 59 per cent of the youths of "graduation age" completed high school in 1952 while only 22 per cent of the young people of college age were enrolled in college in that year, it is obvious that today our public high schools are serving a vastly greater number of young people who leave high school to enter the vocational world than did the schools of 1870. This is strong presumptive evidence that great gains have been made by the public high school, not only in serving more nearly all of our educable youths, but also in serving them more nearly equally well.

Most private secondary schools are still small and concentrate on preparation for college.

Adolescent population and high school enrollments, 1890-1952

Let us break down the growth statistics further. The data supplied by the U.S. Office of Education are most complete for the period

[3] Although the *average* enrollment in all public secondary schools was about 325 pupils in 1951-1952, the *median* was only 175.

TABLE **8**

Increase in enrollments in grades nine through twelve in public secondary day schools, 1890-1952

YEAR	NUMBER OF PUPILS ENROLLED	NUMBER OF YOUTHS AGED 14–17, INCLUSIVE, IN THE U.S.	PER CENT OF YOUTHS AGED 14–17 ENROLLED
1890	202,963	5,354,633	3.8
1900	519,251	6,152,231	8.4
1910	915,061	7,220,298	12.7
1920	1,851,965	7,735,841	23.9
1930	4,135,171	9,341,221	44.3
1938	5,926,722	9,908,000	59.8
1946	5,417,122	8,897,000	60.9
1952	5,695,514	8,728,000	65.3
Percentage increase, 1952 over 1890	2,707	63	

from 1890 onward, so we shall confine ourselves to what has happened since that time (see Table 8).

The most striking aspect of the data in Table 8 is the sharp contrast between the increase in our adolescent population and the much greater increase in high school enrollments. The number of young people aged fourteen through seventeen years grew from 5,354,633 in 1890 to 8,728,000 in 1952, an increase of 63 per cent. Had public high school enrollments merely kept up with this increase—i.e., had the quantitative aspect of our seventh basic principle been no better satisfied in 1952 than it was in 1890—only 330,830 pupils would have been enrolled in our public high schools in 1952. Instead, high school enrollments in 1952 reached 5,695,514. More than twenty-eight times as many pupils were enrolled in our high schools in 1952 as in 1890.

Other aspects of this information reveal the increase just as dramatically. Notice, for instance, that the number of young people enrolled in public high schools about doubled every decade from

1890 to 1930, while the high school age population increased by only 75 per cent during the entire forty years. Notice, furthermore, that enrollments increased by 38 per cent from 1930 to 1952, during a time when the number of boys and girls of high school age actually decreased by about 7 per cent. This decline in the adolescent population was caused by the low birth rates of the 1930's; during and after World War II—from 1940 to 1955—the birth rate rose dramatically, by well over 60 per cent. As this book is being written, our elementary schools are bulging with pupils, and the high schools are already becoming overcrowded. Soon all previous enrollment records from kindergarten through the university will be shattered.

Enrollment of students
who need special education, 1938 and 1953

Next let us look at the enrollment figures for pupils who need special education because they differ so much from their fellows in one respect or another that the school must make special provisions for their schooling if it is to serve all educable youths equally well. An educational psychologist [4] estimates that from less than 1 per cent to about 6 per cent of the total population of high school age needs one of the kinds of special education signified by the different types of exceptional children enumerated in the first column of Table 9. (It will be noted that the population estimates are lower for 1953 than for 1938; this does not imply that there is a decreasing proportion of atypical children, but that there were fewer children in all, because the birth rate in the 1930's was lower than it was in the 1920's.)

Though it still falls far, far short of doing what it should for atypical youths, the public high school made enormous strides during these fifteen years. Exceptional children, whatever the reason for their divergence from the norm, are being given increasingly more attention in our public secondary schools. In 1938 slightly more than one out of every one hundred atypical youths in the total population was being furnished with the special schooling which his educational needs demanded; by 1953 this proportion had been increased more than seven times. The greatest gain was made in serv-

[4] R. Stewart Jones, University of Illinois, in a statement to the author.

TABLE **9**   *Enrollments in special classes and schools in public secondary day schools, 1938-1953*

All data given to nearest hundred or per cent

TYPE OF EXCEPTIONAL CHILD	ESTIMATED NUMBER IN TOTAL HIGH SCHOOL AGE GROUP (14–17)		NUMBER ENROLLED IN SPECIAL CLASSES AND SCHOOLS		PER CENT ENROLLED IN SPECIAL CLASSES AND SCHOOLS	
	1938	1953	1938	1953	1938	1953
Mentally gifted	123,900	114,500	700	19,200	—1	17
Mentally retarded	495,400	458,300	7,000	28,700	1	6
Speech defective	594,500	549,900	5,500	52,600	—1	10
Hearing defective	148,600	137,500	1,300	2,700	—1	2
Vision defective	24,800	22,900	1,200	1,700	5	7
Other debilitating conditions *	99,100	91,700	2,500	3,200	3	4
Total	1,486,300	1,374,800	18,200	108,100	1	8

* These include crippled youths, cardiac cases, epileptics, and pupils in delicate health.

ing mentally gifted children. The number of gifted children being served by special facilities was more than twenty-five times as great in 1953 as in 1938. In terms of percentages, special provisions for speech-defective children had increased more than ten times during the fifteen years, and special provisions for mentally retarded children had increased about six times. Each of the other three types of provisions for atypical pupils made similar if somewhat smaller gains.

Enrollment increases in terms of socioeconomic level

It is regrettable that neither the U.S. Office of Education nor any other agency supplies comparative data on the socioeconomic levels of the families of our high school population. The vastly increased holding power of the public high school is strong presumptive evidence, however, that the public secondary school has gradually improved its capacity for serving youths from families at all levels of the socioeconomic scale. In 1912 only about 18 per cent of the pupils who entered the ninth grade completed high school, and we can be confident that families of low socioeconomic status were rarely represented by the youths who graduated. By 1920 the holding power of the public high school had risen to 31 per cent, and by 1930 and 1946 this figure further increased to 41 and to 56 per cent, respectively. In 1952—the last year for which complete figures were available when this book was written—the public high school's holding power had increased to 60 per cent, and there is good reason to believe that this rise has continued in the years since then and will continue hereafter. It is almost certain that these increases in holding power represent increases in the number of youths from low socioeconomic backgrounds who remain in high school until graduation.

Summary

These comparative enrollment statistics show that truly enormous strides have been made by our public high schools toward the ideal of serving all our educable youths. Moreover, they yield strong presumptive evidence that the public high school has made great gains in serving all of these youths more nearly equally well. The seventh basic principle set forth in Chapter 4 is being honored more and more fully as the years pass.

Changes in the organization
of the public secondary school

At the beginning of this century the public high school was a four-year institution. It was preceded by the public elementary school, which in most parts of the United States offered an eight-year program. In several states, however, particularly the southeastern states, elementary schools included only grades one through seven. These are referred to as the 8-4 and the 7-4 plans of organization. In terms of organization, a "traditional" or "regular" high school denotes a four-year school which operates under either the 8-4 or the 7-4 plan of organization.[5]

The first reorganized secondary school in the United States came into being when the original junior high school was established in Berkeley, California, in 1909. This junior high school was a three-year institution embracing grades seven, eight, and nine. Here is the first example of the 6-3-3 plan—a public school system reorganized into a six-year elementary school, a three-year junior high school, and a three-year senior high school, all operated as separate institutions, but all under the same centralized administrative control. Somewhat later the 6-6 plan was introduced in some smaller cities; this embodied an elementary school of six years and a combined junior and senior high school of six years. "Reorganized" secondary schools are either the separately operated junior and senior high schools or the combined junior-senior high school.

Like so many other desirable innovations, the reorganization of public school systems proceeded slowly at first. In 1920 less than 7 per cent of our public secondary schools were reorganized, but they enrolled about 17 per cent of all public high school students (see Table 10). They were located chiefly in our larger cities. By 1952, nearly three-fifths (57 per cent) of the schools were reorganized, and three out of every four public secondary school pupils were enrolled in them. Table 10 shows that the combined junior-senior high school is the most popular type; in 1952 more than 63 per cent of the reorganized schools were of this kind. The combined junior-senior high school is most common in medium-sized and small cities where the number of pupils is too small to permit separate junior and senior high schools of a reasonable size.

[5] Since the 7-4 plan had by 1952 disappeared from all but two states, we shall make no further mention of it here.

TABLE **10**

Indices of growth of reorganized secondary day schools, 1920-1952

Data to the nearest per cent

		Schools				
YEAR	NUMBER ON WHICH PER CENT IS BASED	Junior	Senior	Junior-senior	Total	PER CENT REGULAR
			PER CENT REORGANIZED			
1920	14,326	−1	−1	6	6	94
1930	22,237	8	3	15	26	74
1938	25,057	10	4	25	38	62
1946	24,122	11	5	26	42	57
1952	23,746	14	7	36	57	43

		Pupils				
1920	1,999,106	2	−1	14	17	83
1930	5,212,179	20	10	19	49	51
1938	7,423,573	19	13	24	56	44
1946	6,840,799	19	17	26	62	39
1952	7,688,919	20	20	35	75	25

Now how does all this bear on the principles presented in Chapter 4? The business of reorganization bears directly upon two of these principles and is related to five others.

The 8-4 plan had been the subject of much justifiable criticism long before the reorganization movement got under way. The nub of this criticism was that certain of the conditions necessary for the most effective learning could best be provided only if there were a school for preadolescent children, another for pupils in early adolescence, and a third for youths in later adolescence, and that the 8-4 plan satisfied none of these conditions.

By the time he completes the eighth grade, the typical child is past his thirteenth birthday and is well into his early adolescence.

He cannot be treated as a child by his teachers. The elementary school which serves children only through grade six, i.e., until the average pupil is eleven or twelve years old, is much more nearly a school for preadolescent children. There are also important physiological differences between pupils in early adolescence and those who are at the threshold of young adulthood; they too cannot be treated alike by their teachers. A plan whereby one institution teaches grades seven, eight, and nine, and another teaches grades ten, eleven, and twelve, fits the secondary school to the facts of adolescence far better than the 7-4 or 8-4 plans do.

What a pupil is mentally and emotionally not ready to learn he cannot be taught effectively (see Chapter 4); the "teachable moment" is that at which he is ready in both ways—when it makes good sense to him to learn because of some need of which he is keenly aware. What little children, young adolescents, and youths on the threshold of adulthood are ready to learn is not at all the same, be it in the formal subjects of the school or in its extra-class activities program. Nor can they be supervised or controlled wholesomely in the same way, as everybody knows. Both what is to be learned and how it is to be taught must be suited to their maturation levels. The extra-class activity program must likewise be so suited if they are willingly—to say nothing of enthusiastically—to take part in and hence learn most through it. Chaos would result if the freedom which older adolescents should be able to handle were granted to little children, or if the restrictions necessary for the wholesome control of little children were imposed on boys and girls who were beginning to see themselves as young adults.

A reorganized secondary school, then, is better fitted to the facts of adolescence, and more fully honors the eighth basic principle of Chapter 4: that to promote the general welfare most fully the public secondary school must capitalize upon what is known about the learning process.

The reorganization of the secondary school also relates to another basic principle: all youths can be more nearly equally well served under the 6-3-3 plan of organization than under the 8-4 plan. The 6-6 plan is also better than the 8-4 plan, if the programs of the junior and senior divisions of the high school are appropriately differentiated.

Reorganization involves five other basic principles indirectly. When the conditions which facilitate learning are more fully provided, as they are when an education system is reorganized, the school can do a better job of orienting its pupils to the past and to the future, teaching them to think and to communicate, helping them to understand and appreciate the democratic way of life, acquainting them with the principles of safe and healthful living, and instructing them as they make a direct study of all of the other basic social processes.

The resurgence of lay participation

When public secondary education began in this country, its affairs were in the hands of the citizens who attended the New England town meeting, or of school committees which were named in these meetings. Citizens not only shaped the purposes of the Boston Latin Grammar School, established in 1636, and appraised its products, but also visited the school and passed judgment on the way it taught. These visitors were usually clergymen, the dominant group in early New England. There were no boards of education, superintendents of schools, or school principals as we know them today.

Schools continued to be lay-controlled for a considerable time after school boards were established. In the larger cities these school boards were enormous. Frequently they comprised a hundred or more members who represented the various geographical subdivisions of the city. The boards were usually divided into committees, each of which was assigned a particular aspect of school affairs for its supervision. In Chicago, for instance, during the latter part of the nineteenth century the board of education was divided into more than seventy committees. There was a committee for each subject then being taught in the public schools and a committee for each subject that was being considered for inclusion in the elementary or secondary curriculum. There were committees on attendance, equipment, finances, housing, supplies, tardiness, and teachers. Prior to the 1830's, the office of city superintendent of schools was unknown, and the technical operation of the public schools, as well as the determination of school policy and the evaluation of school performance, was directly determined by lay citizens.

This method of superintending the public schools was cumbersome; its inefficiencies became more and more apparent all the time (particularly as the schools grew); and the evils of patronage and political manipulation flourished. If one needs confirmation of the wisdom expressed in the second of the three stipulations of our ninth principle—that the technical operation of the school should be determined by competent professional personnel—it is abundantly at hand in the sorry record of public school administration during the first sixty or seventy years of the last century. Granted, there were a few giants among the early superintendents—particularly in Boston, Cleveland, New York, and St. Louis—but in general the public and school boards were not persuaded until well into the present century that technical matters should be entrusted to professionally trained personnel.

Unfortunately, however, when the change came it frequently went too far. Professional educators were given, or themselves preempted, not only the technical supervision of the schools but often the determination of educational policy as well. True, there were boards of education here and there whose members gave serious attention to school affairs, but most boards were preoccupied with the business of the school system—with salary schedules, budgets, purchasing, maintenance, site acquisitions, new construction, bus routes, and the like. Although the Parent-Teacher Association grew and was well represented by earnest citizens in a great many of our communities, even this splendid organization was often content to help the professional educators after they, the educators, had already decided what school policy would be. These facts reflect, however, not upon the school boards and Parent-Teacher Associations, but upon the professional educators, for both lay groups have shown a general willingness to help make the schools genuinely *public*, instead of *quasi-public*, institutions whenever the professionals have encouraged them to do so.

There are many hopeful signs, however, that the ninth basic principle is being followed more closely. Lay advisory councils are being formed in more and more communities; not long ago more than 450 of these councils were at work in a single Midwestern state. The leading authority [6] on these councils estimated that there were "thousands" of them in the United States in 1952, and many more have been organized since then. The formation of these councils has been traced back to 1911, and one has been in continuous operation

[6] Herbert M. Hamlin, *Citizens' Committees in the Public Schools*, Interstate Printing Company, Danville, Illinois, 1952, p. 10.

since 1919.[7] The questions of policy and evaluation with which these and all other lay groups interested in public education should concern themselves are so numerous and so important that Hamlin [8] required a book-length treatment to cover them. Ideally, lay advisory councils originate at the invitation of the local board of education, include citizens from all walks of life, and operate under a charter which specifies the functions of lay citizens working with professionals for school improvements.[9]

Citizens' school survey committees represent another very important kind of lay involvement in school affairs which accords well with our ninth basic principle. Such survey committees are groups of citizens, often several hundred people in large communities, who convene at the invitation of their board of education to study the educational needs of their community and its young people. They evaluate the present programs and facilities of the public schools, and they recommend improvements or expansions which they believe will enable the schools to meet these needs more effectively. Professional consultants are made available to the lay citizens on these survey committees, but it is the lay citizens whose recommendations are submitted to the board of education.[10] Time after time, these citizens' surveys have resulted in improved programs of instruction, guidance, extra-class activities, library services, health services, pupil transportation, etc., as well as in improved school facilities.

The National Citizens Commission for the Public Schools was formed in 1949, under the auspices of the Educational Policies Commission of the National Education Association,[11] and was succeeded in 1956 by the National Citizens Council for Better Schools. It involved millions of lay citizens and professional educators in a widespread collaboration for improving the public schools. The Commission assisted vigorously in the work of the White House Conference on Education called by President Eisenhower in 1955. The

---

[7] Hamlin, *Citizens' Committees,* p. 9.

[8] Herbert M. Hamlin, *The Public and Its Education,* Interstate Printing Company, Danville, Illinois, 1955.

[9] Herbert M. Hamlin, *A Charter for a System of School-Sponsored Citizens' Committees,* Office of Field Services, College of Education, University of Illinois, Urbana, Illinois, 1953.

[10] For an example see The Citizens School Survey Committee, *3,500 Citizens Looked At Our Schools,* Board of Education, Springfield, Illinois, 1954, p. 114.

[11] National Society for the Study of Education, *Citizen Co-operation for Better Public Schools,* 5835 Kimbark Avenue, Chicago, Illinois, 1954, p. 41.

National Citizens Council has carried on in the same spirit as the Commission, rallying citizens to the cause of public education.

The White House Conference on Education was preceded by similar but smaller conferences in each state. In most of the states still earlier conferences had been held at the local and county levels. The delegates to the county, state, and national meetings were predominantly lay citizens. At all levels—local, county, state, and national—the same six questions were considered:

1. What should our schools accomplish?
2. How can we organize our school systems more efficiently?
3. What are our school building needs?
4. How can we get enough good teachers—and keep them?
5. How can we finance our schools—build and operate them?
6. How can we obtain a continuing public interest in education?

The responses to these questions were eventually organized into about eighty detailed recommendations which were offered to President Eisenhower by the delegates to the national conference.[12] Scores of magazine articles and hundreds of newspaper editorials and news stories were devoted to these recommendations. Without a doubt they will provide impetus and direction to tens of thousands of public elementary and secondary schools in the years immediately ahead.

Unprecedented demands will shortly be made upon the public secondary school. It is fortunate that lay involvement in public school affairs seems to be becoming more widespread, more wholesome, and more effective than it has been; for only if the public secondary school is made and kept public in the best sense can it achieve its high purpose.

The increase in the public secondary school's services

A study of the evolution of the present-day secondary school from its earliest predecessor in seventeenth century New England may help us predict the school's future development. Let us trace the major elements in this evolutionary process.

[12] Committee for the White House Conference on Education, *A Report to the President*, U.S. Government Printing Office, Washington, 1956, p. 126.

The Latin grammar school

Our first public secondary school was the Boston Latin Grammar School, founded, as we said, in Boston in 1636. It was public in the sense that it was under public control and that it received some of its financial support from public funds. Much of the cost of the school, however, was met through fees paid by parents, although there were usually a few free places for promising boys.

The early Latin grammar school was designed to serve only some of the boys and none of the girls. It was imported from England where it was, among other things, a means for maintaining or achieving upper-class preferment. Whatever part of Europe they came from, most seventeenth-century colonists brought their ideas of social class with them. This usually meant that they believed in two kinds of schools, one kind for the sons of the upper classes (the Latin grammar school) and another kind for the children of the lower classes (the elementary school and various systems of apprenticeship training). This was the pattern throughout much of the colonial period. The elementary schools were crude and superficial. Children attended them in some cases for no more than a few weeks, seldom for more than three years. Little more was taught than the rudiments of reading, writing, and arithmetic. Those few who were to attend the Latin grammar school were expected to complete their elementary education by the age of seven or eight.

Two other motives besides the desire to perpetuate class distinctions led to the establishment of the Latin grammar school. One was the ancient belief that the best means to a liberal education was the study of classical languages and literature. The other was the belief that salvation was best assured for the laity if ministers read the scriptures in the original languages, and therefore that they had to be trained in the classics. During the early colonial period about 70 per cent of the graduates of Harvard and other colleges went into the ministry. But whether or not they were preparing for the ministry, young men who attended Harvard were required to read Latin and to use it in composition and speech. Addresses were made, notebooks were kept, and letters were written in Latin. An early rule of the college even required students to speak the Latin language on the campus. We do not know, of course, how successfully this or the other regulations just noted were enforced.

The early Latin grammar school taught Latin and Greek, and usually nothing else—and no wonder, for its chief, almost its only, function was to prepare boys for college, where knowledge of Latin and Greek was the only admission requirement. These boys generally entered the Latin grammar school at the age of seven or eight; at the beginning of the eighteenth century the course at the Boston Latin Grammar School lasted seven years, and this was probably the pattern in the better schools elsewhere. The school day generally lasted from seven or eight until eleven o'clock in the morning, and from one to four or five o'clock in the afternoon. School was frequently in session six days a week during all twelve months of the year. In addition, some boys had to attend a writing or reading school at other hours in order to learn to write or to read English. Sometimes, however, the Latin grammar school master tutored in these subjects or had an assistant who did so. The faculty seldom included more than these two persons; usually, there was but one teacher in the Latin grammar school.

Latin, Greek, sometimes a little Hebrew, and now and again some elementary instruction in the writing and reading of English was the typical educational bill of fare in the early Latin grammar school. Mathematics, science, modern foreign language, history or other social study, and physical education were almost never offered.

Historians tell us that the discipline was often severe, and that corporal punishment was often used. The school regulations often named the punishments which should be employed for cursing, fighting, lying, and playing cards or dice. This suggests that many of the concomitant learnings which Latin grammar school boys acquired were very undesirable.[13]

In 1647 the Massachusetts General Court passed an act requiring every town of one hundred or more families to establish a Latin grammar school; any town which did not comply was to be fined. All but one of the other colonies enacted similar laws. All later found it necessary to pass one or more additional laws increasing the amounts of the fines levied, in order to force reluctant communities to establish such a school. Since it was unsuited to the educational needs of all but a handful of boys, the Latin grammar school was viewed with skepticism or overt hostility by a great many colonists. It was destined to be supplanted by a protest institution (see below).

[13] R. Freeman Butts and Lawrence A. Cremin, *A History of Education in American Culture*, Henry Holt & Co., New York, 1953, pp. 121-24.

The private "English" school

If recognized educational needs are not being met, proprietary schools will be created to fill the educational vacuum. This was especially true in early New England. In addition to the need for a ministry trained in the classics, and the needs implied by the college-preparatory and class-preferment purposes of the classical education, a great many other educational needs—of girls as well as of boys—were recognized on the early American frontier, needs that the Latin grammar school left untouched. These were practical needs, and they were met in a practical way by practical courses offered by the proprietary schools that sprang up. The leading authority on early New England education, Robert F. Seybolt,[14] believed that private teachers appeared as early as 1630, thus antedating the Latin grammar school by five or six years. He has reported that the following subjects were taught to both boys and girls in one or the other of the small (one- or two-teacher institutions, for the most part) private secondary schools of the seventeenth and eighteenth centuries: reading, writing, spelling, arithmetic, algebra, geometry, trigonometry, slide rule, geography, surveying, navigation, astronomy, use of globes, calculation of eclipses, bookkeeping, merchant's accounts, shorthand, foreign exchange, natural philosophy, principles of Sir Isaac Newton, French, civil government, history, logic, letter writing, rhetoric, English grammar, composition, fortification and gunnery, fencing, back sword, small sword, singing, flute-playing, piano, violin-playing, dancing, drawing, spinning, hair-cutting, millinery, and many varieties of needlework. It was Professor Seybolt's judgment that "definite cultural and vocational needs which certainly existed in seventeenth century Boston" were reflected in the remarkably comprehensive programs of instruction which these early private schools, taken all together, provided. These have been called by Professors Butts and Cremin[15] the "English" private-venture schools, because English was the language of instruction which they employed.

The early Latin grammar school, then, prepared for college; the youths who wished to prepare directly for the everyday affairs of life were obliged to attend some private "English" school. Although

[14] Robert F. Seybolt, *The Private Schools of Colonial Boston*, Harvard University Press, Cambridge, 1935, pp. 3, 83-92.
[15] Butts and Cremin, *A History of Education*, p. 126.

the Latin grammar school was under public control and was in part publicly financed, it suffered from being resisted by a great many merchants, craftsmen, and farmers, most of whose sons it did not serve. The private "English" school suffered from two serious defects: each student had to pay his way in full, and in most instances neither its curriculum nor the quality of its instruction was adequately supervised by any responsible body representing the public interest. There was, then, real cause for dissatisfaction with both kinds of secondary schools. If the history of American secondary education teaches us anything, it is that when the American people become dissatisfied with their secondary schools they support a protest institution which promises to be more satisfactory. During the latter half of the eighteenth century both the Latin grammar school and the private "English" school were giving way to a protest institution—the academy, a new kind of secondary school, which attempted, under responsible auspices, to combine the values of the two kinds of schools it was supplanting.[16]

The academy

The proposal for the establishment of the academy, incorporated to assure the public that the institution would educate in the public service, seems to have originated with Benjamin Franklin. He proposed that the new institution be coeducational and that it have three departments, or schools—the English, the Classical, and the Mathematical—all equally respectable. He envisaged the English and mathematical departments as giving practical preparation for the affairs of civic and vocational life. The subjects in these two departments were to be English language, history, geography, political science, mathematics, natural science, and other subjects designed to produce a practical, well-balanced, and well-informed person. The modern foreign languages, French, German, and Spanish, were among these other subjects; so was drawing; so were practical experiences in

[16] On the academy as a protest institution see Butts and Cremin, *A History of Education*, pp. 99, 122, 126.

Ellwood P. Cubberley, *The History of Education*, Houghton Mifflin Co., Boston, 1920, pp. 696-99.

Paul Monroe, *Founding the American Public School System*, The Macmillan Company, New York, 1940, pp. 160-64.

Stuart G. Noble, *A History of American Education*, rev. ed., Rinehart & Company, Inc., New York, 1954, pp. 80-81.

agriculture and machinery; so was attention to physical education, manners, and morals.

In terms of the practices of that period, the proposal was essentially for a three-teacher school: one to teach mathematics and related subjects, a second to teach many of the other subjects which the proprietary schools were offering, and a third to teach the classical languages. Franklin's fondest hopes lay with the English and mathematical divisions; in fact, he probably included the classical division in his proposal to win support from influential partisans of the classics for the other parts of his plan. In 1751, two years after Franklin's proposal was made, the first academy was established in Philadelphia. His hopes for an English department as respectable as the classical department were vain, as it turned out. Thomas Woody [17] has told that Franklin complained in 1789 that the mathematical division had been included within the English school and that this school had been weakened in favor of what came to be known as the Latin division. Franklin said that the intention of the school's charter had been subverted, because the English master's teaching load had been doubled, though he received no more than half as much salary as the Latin master, who had far fewer duties to perform.

Franklin's educational ideas were ahead of educational theories of the day, but they accorded well with the educational needs of the times; the academy movement flourished, especially in the first half of the nineteenth century, and these new institutions taught most of the subjects that he advocated. In discussing the social conditions with which the academy was confronted, Monroe [18] described the need in the new country for men trained in practical subjects such as surveying, navigation, and accounting, all of which required a knowledge of mathematics. Lawyers had come to share the social prestige of ministers, and the training of a barrister demanded study in history, geography, and government. Further, Monroe observed that the new thought of the eighteenth century was largely expressed in French, so leaders needed proficiency in this tongue rather than in Latin. From his study of reports of the New York State Board of Regents, Monroe found that 149 different

[17] Thomas Woody, *Educational Views of Benjamin Franklin,* McGraw-Hill Book Co., New York, 1931, pp. 192-228.
[18] Monroe, *Founding the School System,* pp. 407-08.

subjects were taught in the academies during the period of 1787 to 1870; those reported for 1837, for instance, follow.

Mathematics

Algebra
Analytic Geometry
Arithmetic
Conic Sections

Logarithms
Plane Geometry
Trigonometry

Art

Architecture
Drawing
Embroidery

Painting
Perspective

English

Composition
Declamation
Elements of Criticism
Extemporaneous Speaking
Grammar
Mythology

Orthography
Penmanship
Pronunciation
Reading
Rhetoric

Social Science

Biblical Antiquities
Blackstone's *Commentaries*
Commercial Law
Constitution of New York
    State
Constitution of the United
    States
Constitutional Law
General History

Geography
Grecian Antiquities
History of New York State
History of the United States
Mercantile Law
Physical Geography
Political Economy
Roman Antiquities

Education

Principles of Teacher Training

Music

Instrumental Music

Vocal Music

Philosophy

Evidences of Christianity
Intellectual Philosophy
Logic

Moral Philosophy
Natural Philosophy
Natural Theology

Foreign Languages

French
German
Greek
Hebrew

Italian
Latin
Spanish

Business

Bookkeeping

Science and Technology

Astronomy	Natural History
Botany	Nautical Astronomy
Chemistry	Navigation
Civil Engineering	Physiology
Dialing (a method of	Statistics
surveying)	Surveying
Leveling	Technology
Mensuration	Topography
Mineralogy	

No single school offered all these subjects, of course.

Because of its curriculum, the academy became the college of the people—that is, of the people who could afford to attend it. It was generally open to both sexes. It filled many educational needs of its day and served young adults as well as adolescents. Although some subjects taught by the academy are now found in the elementary school curriculum, most were high-school-level subjects, and many were college-level. Virtually nothing was standardized—neither the number and variety of the courses offered, nor the length of attendance.

The academy was characteristically a boarding school and it served students who came from near and far. In terms of its financial support, it was quasi-public: many of the academies were aided in one degree or another by public subscriptions and state grants, but typically they were supported by tuition fees. The academy was an admixture of aristocratic and democratic elements: in its private control and heavy reliance upon fees it was aristocratic; in its attempt to meet the comprehensive educational needs of its day it was democratic.

The public high school

The functional character of what the academy taught was generally regarded favorably, but many were distressed by its private control and fee-charging practices. The idea of a free public elementary school system was well on its way to general acceptance while the nineteenth century was still young, and the argument that education was a public necessity rather than a private luxury seemed to many to apply to secondary as well as to elementary education. More and more people favored a tuition-free secondary school which would provide the functional training for which the academy was valued. In Boston the first public high school was established in

1821; it was known officially as the English High School from 1824 onward. In 1827 a Massachusetts law was passed requiring all towns above a certain size to maintain public high schools. These schools were gradually established in the other states as well.

After the Kalamazoo decision of 1874, which ruled that the high school was properly a part of the public school system and hence could be supported at public expense, the public high schools spread rapidly (see pp. 314-16).

Thus, at first gradually and then rapidly, the academy was supplanted by still another protest institution, the public high school, which became the dominant type of secondary school in this country. The few academies which remain today of the 6000 there once were are chiefly college-preparatory institutions.

In describing the program of studies of the first public high schools, Professors Butts and Cremin wrote,[19] "Inasmuch as the high school first emerged as an attempt to provide the academy's education at public expense to all who were qualified [rather than to those who could afford the academy's fees], one would expect the high school curriculum to resemble closely that of the average academy. This was clearly the situation."

It is interesting that the first public high school was not in any sense a college-preparatory institution; as Noble has pointed out,[20] "Pupils who desired to prepare themselves for college were directed to take the five-year classical course offered by the Boston Latin Grammar School." This first public high school taught no Latin or Greek. As Butts and Cremin have noted, it adopted the tradition of the English department of the academy. The business of this first public high school, then, was to prepare directly for life and not for college.

This state of affairs did not exist in the generality of the public high schools established later, however—or, if it did at first, it did not last. Noble[21] names Jacksonian democracy as the social force which required the new nonsectarian free day high schools, open alike to both sexes, to prepare *both* for college and for the immediate affairs of daily living. Since college entrance requirements throughout the eighteenth century called for little else besides a knowledge of Latin and Greek, and since these subjects continued to be required

[19] Butts and Cremin, *A History of Education*, pp. 278-79.
[20] Noble, *History of Education*, p. 209.
[21] Noble, *History of Education*, p. 211.

throughout the nineteenth century, the public high schools had to offer the classical as well as the practical subjects. This set the stage for difficulties which have persisted to the present day.

The private "English" schools and the early academies from which the public high school received part of its tradition seem to have had little difficulty in bringing themselves to offer the practical subjects which the noncollege-bound youths of the community needed, or to teach these subjects as their purposes seemed to suggest. But this does not seem to have been the case when the public high school was made to include both the practical and the time-honored classical subjects. "When, during the early national period, the newer subjects entered into active competition with the classics," Noble has written,[22] "conservative scholars decried them as too simple and too poorly organized to meet the requirements of mental discipline. Scholars looked askance at the newer offerings and for many years the new studies were to wage an uphill fight for recognition."

This was long before Thorndike's studies raised serious doubts about the easy, long-standing assumptions regarding mental discipline; nearly everybody accepted the conservative scholars' premise. So, as Noble chronicled it, the instructors in all the practical fields of study tried to make their subjects respectable—and their way of doing it was to make them difficult and even abstruse through organization, and to render them methodological rather than informational. Mathematics was the first upstart subject to be accepted. Teachers of English, in order to make their subject respectably difficult, considered the possibility of conducting their instruction in Anglo-Saxon. It was difficult to persuade conservative educators that a more informational subject such as history was as respectable as those older subjects which were definitely methodological. Further, Noble [23] wrote that Americans became involved in the battle between leading British scientists and the British public school classicists who declared that "the sciences were shallow, informational subjects, lacking in organization, unsuited for discipline, and altogether unworthy of the effort of a high-minded scholar." Noble has noted that attempts were made to formalize each of the practical subjects which new social conditions demanded. In addition to English, history, mathematics, and science, the subjects affected were

[22] Noble, *History of Education*, p. 339.
[23] Noble, *History of Education*, p. 342.

foreign languages, manual training, business education, agriculture, home economics, and physical education. In each case, this formalization tended to divorce the subject from the practical purpose for which it had been introduced. According to Noble,[24] much the same fate was suffered by art and music. Attempts to make them respectable merely made them sterile and formalistic.

Especially in English, mathematics, modern foreign languages, science, and the social studies, the effort to attain respectability had by the last quarter of the nineteenth century separated most of the instructional program from the everyday experiences and concerns of youth. The resulting educational problems were vastly compounded by the sudden growth of the high school population after 1870, for, in the words of the Harvard Committee, this progressively brought into the high school "masses of students of every conceivable shade of intelligence, background, means, interest, and expectation" instead of the predominantly college-preparatory group who had attended high school prior to about 1870. Compulsory education laws which followed, requiring all youths to attend school to various stipulated ages, did not help the situation. (The legal school-leaving age in most states today is sixteen, unless the twelfth grade has already been completed.)

The Harvard Committee exposed the heart of the problem in these words: [25] "We are stating the simple fact that in an industrial age, no alternative exists to the widespread unemployment of minors[26] except some concept of schooling which meets the vast actual differences among students. . . . Unlike the old high school in which no one was compelled to stay if he could not or did not wish to do the work, the modern high school must find place for every kind of student whatever his hopes and talents. It cannot justly fail to adapt itself, within reason, to any."

Entering ninth-grade pupils range in chronological age—and, presumably, in social and physiological development as well—from eleven to fifteen years, a spread of five years. Entering pupils vary more than eleven years in both academic aptitude and academic achievement. If the public secondary school is to serve all of these widely different adolescents equally well, it must adapt its program

[24] Noble, *History of Education*, pp. 339-61.
[25] Harvard Committee, *General Education in a Free Society*, Cambridge, Harvard University Press, 1945, p. 9.
[26] "And consequent juvenile delinquency," the author would add.

to the widely different requirements which they present. How can the school do this? "It cannot do so," the Harvard Committee asserted, "simply by offering the conventional academic subjects to all students indiscriminately. . . . Something closer to their experience is needed which, by meeting them halfway, will lead them out and beyond themselves." The Committee went on: [27] "Manual training, business training, work in mechanics and agriculture, courses in health and home economics—these and a thousand more functional adaptations of older disciplines, such as general mathematics instead of algebra and geometry, discussion courses instead of composition and literature, study of work and government in the United States instead of formal history—all reflect in part at least the search for the right means of influencing the great mass of students who, through bent or background or both, learn little from the conventional studies. This search will continue and will almost certainly produce a yet greater diversity."

Statistics supplied by the U.S. Office of Education demonstrate how the public high school program has been diversified since 1890.[28] No enrollments in English are reported by the U.S. Office of Education for that year, and history is the only social study recorded. The only sciences reported are chemistry and physics; the only mathematics, algebra and geometry; the only languages, French, German, and Latin. Finally, no courses in agriculture, art, business education, home economics, industrial education, music, or physical education are reported.[29]

Fewer than 4 per cent of all youths were attending the public high school in 1890, and a very sizable majority of these students later attended college. It is apparent that the public high school of 1890 was predominantly a college-preparatory institution with little

[27] Harvard Comm., *General Education,* pp. 10-11.

[28] All data are for grades nine through twelve of the public secondary day school and are reported in *Offerings and Enrollments in High School Subjects, 1948-49,* or in *Statistical Summary of Education, 1949-50;* in the latter work enrollment data are given for 1890 onward.

[29] The report of the U.S. Office of Education for 1890 apparently includes only those subjects which an appreciable number of high schools was offering. Studies of the pre-1890 offerings of a few city high schools have shown that rhetoric, grammar, and English literature; civil government and political economy; botany, geology, physiology, and zoology; arithmetic and trigonometry; and bookkeeping were available in several instances. Then as now, apparently, the high school program was more extensive in the cities than in the far more numerous towns and villages.

in its program for the student who did not intend to go to college.

By 1915, however, nearly one-fifth, rather than one-twenty-fifth, of the young people aged fourteen through seventeen were enrolled in the public secondary school. What was their educational bill of fare? All of the subjects taught in 1890 were still included in the school program, as they are, for that matter, today. But additions had appeared. In 1915 substantial enrollments were reported in English, and other new courses included agriculture, art, biology, book-keeping, civics, earth science, home economics, industrial education, music, physiology, psychology, Spanish, trigonometry, and zoology. In addition to strengthening its college-preparatory program, the public high school by 1915 had made a number of changes intended to serve young people whose education would terminate at the end of their secondary school training.

As compared to one-twenty-fifth in 1890 or one-fifth in 1915, about two-thirds of all youths of the appropriate age were attending the public high school in 1949, and the program of studies was much more diversified. Of the 1949 offerings (see below) nearly 60 per cent had not been reported in any previous (1922, 1928, 1934) survey.

English

English I-IV	English Literature
Advanced Composition	Grammar
American Literature	Journalism
Bible	Library Training
College-Preparatory	Penmanship
(English V)	Radio Speaking and
Creative Writing	Broadcasting
Current Literature	Remedial English
Debate	Speech and Public Speaking
Dramatic Art	Word Study
English for the Foreign-Born	World Literature

Social Studies

Advanced U.S. History	History of the Orient
American Geography	Industrial History and
American Government	Geography
Ancient History	International Relations
Community Civics	Latin-American History
Comparative Religion	Medieval History
Consumer Education	Modern European History
Economics	Negro History
English History	Occupations

Orientation
Problems of Democracy
Psychology
Sociology

State History
United States History
World Geography
World History

Science
Advanced Biology
Advanced (college level)
   Chemistry
Advanced General Science
Advanced (college level)
   Physics
Aeronautics
Applied Biology (including
   Eugenics, Genetics, Prenatal
   Development)
Applied Chemistry
Applied Physics
Biology
Botany
Chemistry

Conservation
Earth Science
Fundamentals of Electricity
Fundamentals of Machines
General Science
Laboratory Techniques
Metallurgy
Nature Study
Physical Science
Physics
Physiology
Radio (including Electronics)
Related Science
Zoology

Mathematics
Advanced (college level)
   Algebra
Advanced General Mathe-
   matics
Analytics
Calculus
Elementary Algebra

General Mathematics
Intermediate Algebra
Mathematics Review
Plane Geometry
Solid Geometry
Trigonometry

Foreign Languages
Bohemian I, II
French I-IV and Conversa-
   tional
General Foreign Language
German I-IV and Conversa-
   tional
Greek I-IV
Hebrew I-IV
Italian I-IV

Latin I-IV
Norse I, II
Polish I-IV
Portuguese I, II
Russian
Spanish I-IV and Conversa-
   tional
Swedish I-IV

Nonvocational Industrial Arts
Automobile Mechanics
Aviation
Ceramics
Electrical Work
General Shop
Handicrafts

Home Mechanics
Industrial Arts I-IV
Mechanical Drawing
Metal Work
Millinery
Photography

Plastics
Printing
Textiles

Transportation Laboratory
Woodworking

Vocational Industrial Arts
Automobile Mechanics
Aviation (including Aircraft
  Engines, Aircraft Hydrau-
  lics, Aircraft Instruments,
  Aircraft Repair, and Air-
  craft Trades)
Barbering
Boatbuilding
Bookbinding
Cabinetmaking
Carpentry
Chef's Trade and Baking
Cleaning and Pressing
Coal Mining
Commercial Fisheries
Cosmetology
Dental Mechanics
Diversified Occupations
Electrical Work
Foundry and Forging
General Industrial Shop
Lapidary Work
Laundry
Leather Craft
Machine Shop

Masonry
Mechanical Drafting
Millinery
Modeling
Painting and Decorating
Pattern Making
Photography
Plastics
Plumbing
Power Sawing and Machine
  Operating
Printing
Radio
Refrigeration and Air Condi-
  tioning
Sheet Metal
Shoe Repair
Sign Painting
Surveying
Tailoring
Textiles
Upholstering
Watch and Jewelry Repair
Welding

Agriculture
Agriculture I-IV

Business
Advertising
Bookkeeping I-IV
Business Arithmetic
Business English
Business Law
Consumer Economics
Cooperative Office Training
Cooperative Story Training

Economic Geography
General Business
Office Practice
Retailing
Salesmanship
Shorthand I-IV
Typing I-IV

Home Economics
Child Development
Clothing I-IV
Consumer Buying
Family Relationships
Foods I-III

Health and Home Nursing
Home Furnishing and Deco-
  rating
Homemaking I-IV
Home Management

Art

Applied Art	Freehand Drawing
Art I-IV	General Art
Art Appreciation	School Services Art
Commercial Art	

Music

Band	Instrumental Music (several
Chorus	kinds)
General Music	Music Appreciation
Glee Club	Orchestra
Harmony	Theory and Practice of Music

Physical Education

Driver Education	Physical Education (four years
Health	including Dance, Games,
Hygiene	Recreational Leadership,
	Swimming, Tumbling)
	Safety Education

Core or unified study courses, group guidance courses, and special courses for gifted, mentally retarded, partially sighted, and hard-of-hearing pupils were also being given in 1949. And several small high schools were even offering a number of correspondence courses.

This list of the principal subjects reported in 1949 shows that the public high schools have greatly extended their course offerings since 1915 and 1890. The offerings of these latter-day schools are, in the aggregate, far better suited to the "masses of students of every conceivable shade of intelligence, background, means, interest, and expectation." The college preparatory subjects have been both extended in number and increased in scope; vocational subjects have likewise been extended and increased to make them better suited to the demands of the workaday world; instruction in health and safety has been expanded; a more extensive preparation for homemaking has been included in the program of studies; more skills and appreciations relating to the wholesome use of leisure have been provided for; and there is a greater range of courses relating to government, communication skills, and aesthetics.

More than ever before the public secondary school is now orienting its pupils to the future, and the increase in the number and variety of its courses in history suggests that high school students are scrutinizing the past more extensively.

In sum, our comparison of the program of studies for 1890, 1915, and 1949 shows that the public secondary school has increasingly fulfilled Principles 2 through 7 of Chapter 4.

The public secondary school is also adhering more and more to the eighth basic principle, which states that to promote the general welfare most fully, the school must make full use of what is known about the learning process. At the turn of the century much less was known about the learning process than is known today. During the nineties, much of what the public high school taught, as well as its methods of teaching, was based in large part on faculty psychology and the belief that transfer of training is more or less automatic. Neither of these beliefs is warranted, and the selection of what should be taught and the devising of effective teaching methods are matters which are by no means as easy to resolve as our pedagogical forebears seemed to think. As the Harvard Committee pointed out, the diversification of the present-day high school's program of studies is in large part based on a better understanding of what intelligence is. After noting that there has been "a very great enlargement of courses" offered by the secondary school and observing that it is important to see "why such an enlargement is a great gain," the Committee wrote: [30]

> The heart of the question is what is meant by difference of intelligence. For it is obviously for this reason that some students are at home in the traditional subjects, while others flounder and fail. . . . However finally rooted [it may be] in native endowment (the mere physical and nervous make-up of the brain), intelligence depends also on habit and outlook which in turn go back to earliest opportunity. . . . What passes for intelligence is certainly in part the same thing as opportunity, by which is meant the whole complex of surroundings which help to shape a child's view of the world and of his place in it. . . . Assuming that a young person's abilities to some extent reflect his surroundings and both together color his hopes of life and expectations of himself, then a truly democratic education must perforce try to equalize opportunity by counteracting impediments. But it cannot do so simply by offering the conventional academic subjects to all students indiscriminately. . . . Something closer to their experience is needed which, by meeting them halfway, will lead them out and beyond themselves.

The vast increase in the diversity of the subjects offered by the public secondary school results from attempts to "meet the students

[30] Harvard Comm., *General Education*, pp. 9-10.

halfway," to "lead them out and beyond themselves," and to provide the varied kinds of opportunities needed for the development of "what passes for intelligence."

The growth of the health service, mental hygiene, and guidance movements in the public high school is further evidence of the progressive fulfillment of our eighth basic principle. So are the provisions made for educational diagnosis and the advances which have been accomplished in providing special classes, and often special facilities, for educating the mentally gifted, the mentally retarded, the partially sighted, the hard-of-hearing, the crippled, and the pupils with speech deficiencies. Further evidence is afforded by the gradual growth of core and unified studies courses. Increased attention to problems of motivation and the growing employment of problem-centered instruction and of instruction organized around large and meaningful topics are additional evidences that the public secondary school is making more use of what is known about learning than it did earlier.

A summary and a look to the future

The increasing diversification of the public high school's program of studies represents an attempt to make the high school's teachings fill the divergent educational needs of the many different students who now attend it. This development is an extension of others which have characterized the history of secondary education in this country—the replacement of the Latin grammar school by the academy, which filled more educational needs of more youths, and the replacement of the academy by the public high school, which provided at public expense the education offered by the English departments of the fee-charging academy. From the beginning the public high school taught the classical as well as the practical subjects—prepared some youths for college and others directly for life. In 1890 it was little more than a college-preparatory institution, but since that time it has, through the vast diversification of its offerings, made itself much more serviceable to the pupils who do not go on to college as well as to those who do.

Early in the history of American secondary education the American people came to believe that not only the most likely future leaders, the bright youngsters, but *all* youths should attend high school. For a long time, the generality of Americans have recognized that all youths are going to be leaders or followers, husbands or wives, fathers or mothers, employers or employees, spenders of personal income, readers of newspapers and magazines, listeners to radio programs, television viewers (more recently), users of leisure time in many other ways, drivers of automobiles, shapers of public opinion, and voters. Even more today than in the past the average American wants all his children and all his neighbors' children educated to do these things as wisely as possible, and even more today than in the past he insists that the public high school help do the job. The average citizen expects the public high school to serve the dull as well as the bright, the physically handicapped as well as the robust, the dark-skinned as well as the white, and the poor as well as the rich.

It has not been easy for the public high school to bring about the present diversification in its program; and, for two principal reasons, it will be no less difficult to accomplish the still greater diversification which must be provided if *all* youths are to be served equally well.

First, there are many technical difficulties in the task of meeting the educational needs of an ever-increasing proportion of all educable children. Exclusive of veterans, the number of students who entered college in the fall of 1953 (607,570) was about half as great as the number of youths who graduated from all our public and private secondary schools the preceding spring (1,198,300).[31] High school graduates either do or do not go on to college; the requirements of the emerging future will make it necessary that both college-preparatory and terminal students be better served than ever before by the secondary school. To discharge their full obligations, secondary schools must continue to improve both their college-preparatory and their terminal programs. As we have implied if not made explicit throughout this book, this will be no easy task.

The second reason that the public secondary school will find it difficult to serve all educable youths well is that now as in the past the defenders of the old resist the new. New conditions give rise to the need for, and to the introduction of, modified or new secondary school subjects. These subjects are especially needed by the youths of lesser academic aptitude and those who for other reasons also

[31] *Statistics of Higher Education: Faculty, Students, and Degrees, 1953-1954,* Office of Education, U.S. Department of Health, Education, and Welfare, p. 58.

learn little from the conventional studies. As already noted in this chapter, a century or so ago the defenders of the old charged that the new offerings were shallow informational subjects "too simple and too poorly organized to meet the requirements of mental discipline" and "altogether unworthy of the efforts of a high-minded scholar." The new subjects became established in the curriculum nonetheless, for youths needed them. Now many of the vastly increased number of youths who attend the public secondary school need modifications in established subjects and entirely new subjects. In condemning today's new offerings, the latter-day defenders of the old use much stronger language than did their early counterparts. Some of the present-day critics speak darkly of "quackery in the public schools," of "anti-intellectualism," of "a retreat from learning," and of a vast "educational wasteland" when they view the efforts of the schoolmen to adapt the high school curriculum to the many different kinds of youths who constitute the student body today.

These latter-day accusations seem exaggerated when they are viewed in the light of such studies as those reported by Seyler and Bloom. Seyler [32] is the Recorder at the University of Illinois. He compared the scholastic records of the freshman class of 1949 (of whose 1,819 members only 83 were veterans) with those of the combined entering classes of 1935, 1936, and 1937 and found that, in every college in the university, the more recent high school graduates made higher grade-point averages. During this period the entrance requirements at the University of Illinois were not raised, but the scholastic standards within the university were.

Bloom [33] is the college examiner at the University of Chicago. He renormed the high school tests in the fields of English, mathematics, science, and social studies which are used by the United States Armed Forces Institute by giving them in 1955 to the twelfth-grade pupils in a representative 5 per cent sample of all the public high schools in this country, which is exactly the same thing that had been done with exactly the same tests in 1943. Bloom found that the 1955 seniors made higher average scores on each of these

[32] Earl Charles Seyler, "A Comparison of the Scholastic Records of the Freshman Class of 1949 with Those of the Combined Classes of 1935-36-37," *College and University*, Vol. 27, October, 1951, pp. 90-106.

[33] Benjamin Samuel Bloom, "1955 Normative Study of the Tests of General Educational Development," *School Review*, Vol. 64, March, 1956, pp. 110-24.

tests than the 1943 seniors had made, and that the superiority of the 1955 pupils was greatest in the field of mathematics.

Whether or not needed changes in the curriculum of the public high school are to be sanctioned by public opinion is at root the question to which most of the criticisms of the high school curriculum were related in years gone by, and it is no less the root question today. The American people have seen to it that these changes were made in the past by successively throwing their powerful weight behind protest institutions which promised to fill the educational needs of their child more adequately. Because the Latin grammar school had a classical curriculum which served only a few boys bound for college, the American people replaced it with the academy. Because the academy was privately controlled and charged fees, the American people replaced it with the public high school.

In the middle thirties the public high school was confronted by not one but three protest institutions—significantly, by protest institutions which were federally supported and controlled. Partly because of the vast increase in the size and in the diversity of its pupil population, and partly because of the paralyzing economic depression, the program and practices of the public high school were seriously unsuited to the capabilities and needs of a great many youths. The Civilian Conservation Corps (CCC), the National Youth Administration (NYA), and the Works Progress Administration (WPA) flourished. Of these emerging protest institutions the Dean of the Graduate School of Education at Harvard University wrote: [34]

> The CCC, the NYA, and the WPA are not historical freaks; they are not mere sports in the evolution of education in the United States. At least twice before in our educational history dissatisfaction with the established schools has expressed itself in the development of new educational institutions. After the close of the Revolutionary War, just such dissatisfaction led to the establishment of the Academy. . . . Following the Civil War, public dissatisfaction again brought about the establishment of a new institution—the public high school. . . .
> . . . The pattern for both these changes was the same. The new school provided kinds of teaching which the older schools declined to recognize as in their province. The new kind of

[34] Francis Trow Spaulding, "Challenge for Secondary Education," *National Association of Secondary School Principals Bulletin,* Vol. 25, March, 1941, pp. 13-16.

school was open to kinds of pupils whom the older schools thought . . . uneducable in any reputable sense. And the new school in both instances steadily and surely drove out the old. . . . The CCC, the NYA, and the WPA, growing up beside our established schools, are providing kinds of teaching which many school people seem to regard as appropriate enough for relief agencies, but outside the province of institutions that can properly be called schools. Perhaps that kind of teaching needs to be defined. It is teaching which has as its primary concern not the enforcement of academic disciplines, but the offering of immediate and practical help to the individual boy and girl. It is teaching which places a premium on man-sized work—but not necessarily skilled work—as an educational experience. It is teaching which accepts boys and girls as they are and proceeds from that point on, instead of pressing young people into the conventional mold of numbered grades and classified subjects.

And these same new institutions are accepting kinds of pupils who have been rejected by the public schools—or who, finding the schools wanting, have themselves rejected the schools. . . . These pupils include . . . young people whom the schools have sent out armed with an academic diploma, and unarmed in almost every other respect, to meet the thoroughly non-academic demands which are certain to be made on them.

Economic necessity, as much as anything else, drove youths into the CCC, the NYA, and the WPA. Then World War II, with its unparalleled premium on youth, killed off these organizations and gave the public secondary school a reprieve. But had there been no World War II more and more youths would have found their way into these protest organizations, and for its own protection if nothing else, society would have demanded that more and still more of an educational program be provided by them. Since the war much progress has been made in adapting the program of the public secondary school to the human materials with which it is called upon to deal, as the detailed listing of the subject titles for 1949 (see pp. 338-41) suggests. But much remains to be done. If the necessary adaptations are not made, a protest institution—probably federally controlled as well as federally supported—will come into existence. Some youths use the Air Force, the Army, the Marine Corps, and the Navy as protest institutions at the present time: in preference to completing high school they join these military organizations, at least in part, to secure the vocational training they provide.

The likelihood that a protest institution will arise if the public secondary school backs away from its great task of serving all youths equally well is suggested by the results of an anonymous poll conducted at the Illinois pre-White House Conference on Education held in Springfield in September, 1955. The delegates to this state meeting, about two-thirds of whom were laymen, had attended one or another of the several hundred community or county conferences held previously. In these preliminary conferences there had been considerable discussion of the proposal which some critics of the public secondary school support. This is that the public secondary school should make the traditional academic subjects the educational bill of fare for all pupils, and that it should be made a selective institution which should attempt to retain beyond the legal school-leaving age of sixteen only those youths who do well in these subjects. This was the essence of one of the two propositions which were included in the anonymous poll.

The second proposition accords with the position taken throughout this book: it asserted that the public secondary school should be a nonselective institution; that all youths, regardless of their capacity for achievement in the traditional academic subjects, should be provided with a high school education suited to their capacities and their life needs; that for many this would consist of college-preparatory work in the traditional academic subjects, but that for many others it would mean modified work in these subjects plus vocational and other useful courses; and that all educable youths should be encouraged to attend and to complete high school.

The vote in the poll was 95 per cent in favor of the second of these two propositions, which is about what would be predicted by anyone familiar with the temper of the American people regarding the education of their children.

If the more extreme academic critics of an earlier day had succeeded, our public secondary school pupils would have been deprived of the benefits of English, mathematics, modern foreign languages, science, history, and the other social studies. If the more extreme among the present-day academic critics succeed, these will be about the only subjects in the curriculum, and there will be no important modifications to suit these offerings to the full range of aptitude. It requires no great power of divination to prophesy that if this happens the public high school, like the Latin grammar school and the academy, will be supplanted by a protest institution which promises to accommodate itself to the full range of the capacities and educational needs of the youths of America. And, in all likelihood, this protest institution will be federally supported and controlled.

The public secondary school has made considerable progress since the close of World War II in better suiting its program to the educational needs of all of the youths of America. If this progress can be extended to make a high school education possible for and valuable to all youths, the public high school will have no publicly supported competitor. It is the hope—and the confident expectation—of the author that the men and women who read this book will help make the American public secondary school equal to its great task of providing an education which is suited to the requirements of a great nation and appropriate to the educational needs of *all* the educable adolescent children of *all* its people.

BIBLIOGRAPHY

A.A.U.W. Fact Sheet, Jan. 1953.

Adams, James Truslow, *The Epic of America*, Little, Brown & Co., Boston, 1931.

Allen, Charles M., *How to Conduct the Holding Power Study of the Illinois Curriculum Program*, rev. ed., Office of the Superintendent of Public Instruction, Springfield, Illinois, 1955.

American Association of School Administrators, *Conservation Education in American Schools*, 1201 Sixteenth Street N.W., Washington 6, D. C., 1951.

American Council on Education, *Evaluative Criteria of Secondary School Standards*, Washington, 1950.

American Federation of Labor, *Report of Executive Council*, Washington, 1951.

Association for Supervision and Curriculum Development, *Large Was Our Bounty*, 1201 Sixteenth Street N.W., Washington 6, D. C., 1948.

Ayers, Leonard P., *Laggards in Our Schools*, Charities Publishing Company, New York, 1909.

Beard, Charles A., *A Charter for the Social Sciences*, Charles Scribner's Sons, New York, 1932.

——, and Mary Beard, *The Rise of American Civilization*, The Macmillan Company, New York, 1933.

Bell, H. M., *Youth Tell Their Story*, American Council on Education, Washington, 1938.

Brewer, John M., *Education as Guidance*, The Macmillan Company, New York, 1932.

Briggs, Thomas H., *The Great Investment*, Harvard University Press, Cambridge, 1930.

Bryce, James, *The American Commonwealth*, rev. ed., The Macmillan Company, New York, 1941.

Cobb, M. V., "The Limits Set to Educational Achievement by Limited Intelligence," *Journal of Educational Psychology*, Vol. XIII, Nov. and Dec. 1922.

Commager, Henry Steele, "Our Schools Have Kept Us Free," *Life,* Oct. 16, 1950.

Commission on the Social Studies, American Historical Association, *Conclusions and Recommendations of the Commission,* Charles Scribner's Sons, New York, 1934.

Cook, Kermit A., "Effect of Two Patterns of High School Training on College Achievement," *School Review,* Vol. LIX, Mar. 1951.

Cooperative Study of Secondary School Standards, *Evaluative Criteria,* Washington, 1950.

Counts, George S., *The American Road to Culture,* John Day Company, New York, 1930.

———, *Education and American Civilization,* Bureau of Publications, Teachers College, Columbia University, New York, 1952.

———, *The Selective Character of American Secondary Education,* University of Chicago Press, Chicago, 1922.

Davidson, P. E., in Stanford Education Faculty, *The Challenge of Education,* McGraw-Hill Book Company, New York, 1937.

Dillon, Harold J., *Early School Leavers—A Major Educational Problem,* National Child Labor Committee, New York, 1949.

Eckert, R. E., and T. O. Marshall, *When Youth Leave School,* McGraw-Hill Book Company, New York, 1938.

Education Molds Our Future: Better Schools Build a Stronger America, Highlights Report of the National Citizens Commission for the Public Schools, New York, 1951.

Education Policies of the Chamber of Commerce of the United States, U.S. Government Printing Office, Washington, 1952.

Edwards, Newton, *Equal Educational Opportunity for Youth,* American Council on Education, Washington, 1939.

Encyclopedia of the Social Sciences, ed. by Edwin B. H. Seligman and Alvin Johnson, The Macmillan Company, New York, 1932.

Engler, Robert, "Collectivism—Domestic Variety," *New Republic,* Vol. XIII, No. 10, Mar. 5, 1956.

Fretwell, Elbert K., *Extra-Curricular Activities in Secondary Schools,* Houghton Mifflin Co., Boston, 1931.

Gabriel, Ralph H., *The Course of American Democratic Thought,* The Ronald Press Company, New York, 1940.

Gregg, Russell T., and Raymond E. Schultz, *Personal Expenditure for High-School Education,* School of Education, University of Wisconsin, Madison, 1951.

A Guide for the Study of the Holding Power in Minnesota Secondary Schools, Minnesota State Department of Education, Saint Paul, Minnesota, 1952.

Hamlin, Herbert M., *Citizen's Committees in the Public Schools,* The Interstate Printers and Publishers, Danville, Illinois, 1954.

Hand, Harold C., "Hidden Tuition Charges in Extra-Class Activities," *Educational Forum,* Vol. XIV, No. 1, Nov. 1949.

———, "Hidden Tuition Charges in High School Subjects," *Educational Forum,* Vol. XIII, No. 4, May 1949.

Hand, Harold C., *How to Conduct the Hidden Tuition Costs Study*, Office of the Superintendent of Public Instruction, Springfield, Illinois, 1949.

——, *How to Conduct the Participation in Extra-Class Activities Study*, Office of the Superintendent of Public Instruction, Springfield, Illinois, 1949.

——, *Principal Findings of the 1947-48 Basic Studies of the Illinois Secondary School Curriculum Program*, Office of the Superintendent of Public Instruction, Springfield, Illinois, 1949.

——, *What People Think about Their Schools*, World Book Company, Yonkers, New York, 1948.

——, and Eric H. Johnston, *How to Conduct the Local Area Consensus Studies of the Illinois Curriculum Program*, rev. ed., Office of the Superintendent of Public Instruction, Springfield, Illinois, 1956.

Handbook of National Association of Manufacturers Activities and Services for Education—Industry Cooperation, National Association of Manufacturers, New York, Oct. 1952.

Havighurst, Robert J., *Developmental Tasks and Education*, Longmans, Green & Co., Inc., New York, 1950.

Hecker, Stanley E., *Early School Leavers in Kentucky*, Bulletin of the Bureau of School Service, College of Education, University of Kentucky, Lexington, 1953.

Henderson, Kenneth B., *Principal Findings of the Follow-Up Study of the Illinois Secondary School Curriculum Program*, Office of the Superintendent of Public Instruction, Springfield, Illinois, 1951.

——, and John E. Goerwitz, *How to Conduct the Follow-Up Study*, Office of the Superintendent of Public Instruction, Springfield, Ill., 1950.

——, et al., *Guide to Clear Thinking*, Illinois Curriculum Program, Office of the Superintendent of Public Instruction, Springfield, Illinois, 1954.

——, et al., *Mathematical Needs of Prospective Students in the College of Engineering of the University of Illinois*, University of Illinois Bulletin, Vol. LXXXIX, No. 9, Sept. 1951.

Henry, Nelson B., ed., *Citizen Cooperation for Better Public Schools*, Fifty-third Yearbook of the National Society for the Study of Education, Part I, University of Chicago Press, Chicago, 1954.

Illinois Curriculum Program, *How to Conduct the Holding Power Study of the Illinois Curriculum Program*, rev. ed., Office of the Superintendent of Public Instruction, Springfield, Illinois, 1955.

——, *The Nature of the School Population in Illinois*, Office of Public Instruction, Springfield, Illinois, 1955.

"It Starts in the Classroom," National School Public Relations Association, 1201 Sixteenth Street N.W., Washington 6, D. C., 1951.

Johnson, E. S., and C. E. Legg, "Why Young People Leave School," *Bulletin of the National Association of Secondary School Principals*, Vol. XXXII, No. 157, Nov. 1948.

Johnston, Edgar G., and Roland C. Faunce, *Student Activities in Secondary Schools,* The Ronald Press Company, New York, 1952.

Joint Council on Economic Education, "A Brief Report on *JCEE's* Resource-Use Project, *The Classroom and the Joint Council,*" 2 West Forty-sixth Street, New York 36, N. Y., April, 1956.

Kalamazoo, Michigan, Board of Education, *How Much Did They Grow?* General Information Bulletin No. 164, Sept. 1952.

Kefauver, Grayson N., and Harold C. Hand, *Appraising Guidance in Secondary Schools,* The Macmillan Company, New York, 1941.

———, V. H. Noll, and E. C. Drake, *The Secondary School Population,* U.S. Government Printing Office, Washington, 1933.

Kennedy, Gail, *Education for Democracy,* D. C. Heath & Company, Boston, 1952.

Koos, Leonard V., and Grayson N. Kefauver, *Guidance in Secondary Schools,* The Macmillan Company, New York, 1932.

Kreps, Theodore, in Stanford Education Conference, *Social Education,* The Macmillan Company, New York, 1939.

Laski, Harold J., "Democracy," from *Encyclopedia of the Social Sciences,* Vol. V, The Macmillan Company, New York, 1932.

Lovejoy, G. W., *Paths to Maturity,* University of North Carolina, Chapel Hill, 1940.

Lovelass, Harry D., *How to Conduct the Study of the Guidance Services of the School,* Office of the Superintendent of Public Instruction, Springfield, Illinois, 1949.

Low, Camilla M., ed., *Guidance in the Curriculum,* Yearbook of the Association for Curriculum Development, National Education Association, 1955.

McElroy, Elizabeth J., *Participation in Extra-Curricular Activities as a Welfare Level Phenomenon,* unpublished master's thesis, Stanford University, Stanford, California, 1939.

Marsh, Daniel L., *The American Canon,* Abingdon Press, Nashville, Tennessee, 1939.

Meiklejohn, Alexander, *What Does America Mean?* W. W. Norton & Company, Inc., New York, 1935.

Merriam, Charles E., *Civic Education in the United States,* Charles Scribner's Sons, New York, 1934.

Monroe, Paul, *A Textbook in the History of Education,* The Macmillan Company, New York, 1930.

Monroe, Walter S., ed., *Encyclopedia of Educational Research,* The Macmillan Company, New York, 1950.

Myrdal, Gunnar, *An American Dilemma,* Harper & Brothers, New York, 1944.

National Americanism Commission of the American Legion, *Americanism Manual,* Indianapolis, 1952.

National Congress of Parents and Teachers, *Action Program,* Chicago, 1953.

National Education Association Research Division, "The 1956 Teacher Supply and Demand Report," *Journal of Teacher Education,* Vol. VII, No. 1, Mar. 1956.

Nystrom, P. H., *Economic Principles of Consumption*, The Ronald Press Company, New York, 1928.

Office of Education, U.S. Department of Health, Education, and Welfare, *Statistics of Public Secondary Day Schools, 1951-52*, U.S. Government Printing Office, Washington, 1954.

Our American Heritage: Education to Preserve, General Federation of Women's Clubs, Washington, 1952.

Palmer, E. G., *Pupils Who Leave School*, University of California, Berkeley, California, 1930.

Popper, Samuel H., ed., *Today's Challenge: Tomorrow's Citizen*, Office of Secondary and Vocational Education, Saint Paul Public Schools, Saint Paul, Minnesota, 1957.

Proctor, William M., *Educational and Vocational Guidance*, Houghton Mifflin Co., Boston, 1925.

Rapp, Oliver L., *Military Problems Facing High School Boys*, unpublished dissertation, College of Education, University of Illinois, Urbana, 1956.

Report of the Harvard Committee, *General Education in a Free Society*, Harvard University Press, Cambridge, 1945.

Report of the White House Conference on Education, Superintendent of Documents, U.S. Government Printing Office, Washington, 1956.

Robinson, Edgar Eugene, in Stanford Education Conference, *Social Education*, Stanford, California, 1939.

School Code, Board of Education, Saint Paul, Minnesota, 1954.

Schultz, Raymond E., "Can Parents Afford to Send Their Children to High School?" *School Review*, Vol. LX, Oct. 1952.

Scott, C. Winfield, and Clyde M. Hill, eds., *Public Education Under Criticism*, Prentice-Hall, Inc., Englewood Cliffs, New Jersey, 1954.

Smith, T. V., *The Promise of American Politics*, University of Chicago Press, Chicago, 1936.

Survey Committee, College of Education, University of Maryland, *A Program of Reorganization for the Public Secondary Schools of Prince George's County, Maryland*, University of Maryland, Baltimore, 1941.

Thorndike, E. L., *Elimination of Pupils from School*, U.S. Government Printing Office, Washington, 1907.

Tocqueville, Alexis de, *Democracy in America*, ed. by H. S. Commager, tr. by Henry Reeve, Oxford University Press, New York, 1947.

Warner, W. L., et al., *Who Shall Be Educated?* Harper & Brothers, New York, 1944.

Wells, George N., *We Grow*, Board of Education, Bloomington, Illinois, 1955.

Willis, Benjamin C., *We Build*, Board of Education, Chicago, 1956.

Wright, David, *Participation in Extra-Class Activities According to Economic Status*, unpublished master's thesis, Stanford University, Stanford, California, 1937.

Wrightstone, J. Wayne, *Appraisal of Newer Practices in Selected Public Schools,* Teachers College, Columbia University, New York, 1935.
———, and George Forlano, "Evaluation of the Experience Curriculum at Midwood High School," *High Points,* Vol. XXX, Dec. 1948.

INDEX

Numbers in italics refer to tables.